Designing Social Inquiry

Designing Social Inquiry

SCIENTIFIC INFERENCE IN QUALITATIVE RESEARCH

Gary King
Robert O. Keohane
Sidney Verba

PRINCETON UNIVERSITY PRESS

PRINCETON, NEW JERSEY

Library of Congress Cataloging-in-Publication Data

King, Gary.
Designing social inquiry : scientific inference in qualitiative
research / Gary King, Robert O. Keohane, Sidney Verba.
p. cm.
Includes bibliographical references and index
ISBN 0-691-03470-2 (cloth : alk. paper)
ISBN 0-691-03471-0 (pbk. : alk. paper)
1. Social sciences—Methodology.   2. Social sciences—
Research.   3. Inference
I. Keohane, Robert Owen.
II. Verba, Sidney.   III. Title.
H61.K5437   1994   93-39283
300'.72—dc20   CIP

This book has been composed in Adobe Palatino

Princeton University Press books are printed on
acid-free paper and meet the guidelines
for permanence and durability of the Committee
on Production Guidelines for Book Longevity
of the Council on Library Resources

Printed in the United States of America

20   19   18   17   16   15   14
ISBN-13: 978-0-691-03471-3 (pbk.)

ISBN-10: 0-691-03471-0 (pbk.)

Contents

Preface

IN THIS BOOK we develop a unified approach to valid descriptive and causal inference in qualitative research, where numerical measurement is either impossible or undesirable. We argue that the logic of good quantitative and good qualitative research designs do not fundamentally differ. Our approach applies equally to these apparently different forms of scholarship.

Our goal in writing this book is to encourage qualitative researchers to take scientific inference seriously and to incorporate it into their work. We hope that our unified logic of inference, and our attempt to demonstrate that this unified logic can be helpful to qualitative researchers, will help improve the work in our discipline and perhaps aid research in other social sciences as well. Thus, we hope that this book is read and critically considered by political scientists and other social scientists of all persuasions and career stages—from qualitative field researchers to statistical analysts, from advanced undergraduates and first-year graduate students to senior scholars. We use some mathematical notation because it is especially helpful in clarifying concepts in qualitative methods; however, we assume no prior knowledge of mathematics or statistics, and most of the notation can be skipped without loss of continuity.

University administrators often speak of the complementarity of teaching and research. Indeed, teaching and research are very nearly coincident, in that they both entail acquiring new knowledge and communicating it to others, albeit in slightly different forms. This book attests to the synchronous nature of these activities. Since 1989, we have been working on this book and jointly teaching the graduate seminar "Qualitative Methods in Social Science" in Harvard University's Department of Government. The seminar has been very lively, and it often has spilled into the halls and onto the pages of lengthy memos passed among ourselves and our students. Our intellectual battles have always been friendly, but our rules of engagement meant that "agreeing to disagree" and compromising were high crimes. If one of us was not truly convinced of a point, we took it as our obligation to continue the debate. In the end, we each learned a great deal about qualitative and quantitative research from one another and from our students and changed many of our initial positions. In addition to its primary purposes, this book is a statement of our hard-won unanimous position on scientific inference in qualitative research.

We completed the first version of this book in 1991 and have revised it extensively in the years since. Gary King first suggested that we write this book, drafted the first versions of most chapters, and took the lead through the long process of revision. However, the book has been rewritten so extensively by Robert Keohane and Sidney Verba, as well as Gary King, that it would be impossible for us to identify the authorship of many passages and sections reliably.

During this long process, we circulated drafts to colleagues around the United States and are indebted to them for the extraordinary generosity of their comments. We are also grateful to the graduate students who have been exposed to this manuscript both at Harvard and at other universities and whose reactions have been important to us in making revisions. Trying to list all the individuals who were helpful in a project such as this is notoriously hazardous (we estimate the probability of inadvertently omitting someone whose comments were important to us to be 0.92). We wish to acknowledge the following individuals: Christopher H. Achen, John Aldrich, Hayward Alker, Robert H. Bates, James Battista, Nathaniel Beck, Nancy Burns, Michael Cobb, David Collier, Gary Cox, Michael C. Desch, David Dessler, Jorge Domínguez, George Downs, Mitchell Duneier, Matthew Evangelista, John Ferejohn, Andrew Gelman, Alexander George, Joshua Goldstein, Andrew Green, David Green, Robin Hanna, Michael Hiscox, James E. Jones, Sr., Miles Kahler, Elizabeth King, Alexander Kozhemiakin, Stephen D. Krasner, Herbert Kritzer, James Kuklinski, Nathan Lane, Peter Lange, Tony Lavelle, Judy Layzer, Jack S. Levy, Daniel Little, Sean Lynn-Jones, Lisa L. Martin, Helen Milner, Gerardo L. Munck, Timothy P. Nokken, Joseph S. Nye, Charles Ragin, Swarna Rajagopalan, Shamara Shantu Riley, David Rocke, David Rohde, Frances Rosenbluth, David Schwieder, Collins G. Shackelford, Jr., Kenneth Shepsle, Daniel Walsh, Carolyn Warner, Steve Aviv Yetiv, Mary Zerbinos, and Michael Zürn. Our appreciation goes to Steve Voss for preparing the index, and to the crew at Princeton University Press, Walter Lippincott, Malcolm DeBevoise, Peter Dougherty, and Alessandra Bocco. Our thanks also go to the National Science Foundation for research grant SBR-9223637 to Gary King. Robert O. Keohane is grateful to the John Simon Guggenheim Memorial Foundation for a fellowship during the term of which work on this book was completed.

We (in various permutations and combinations) were also extremely fortunate to have had the opportunity to present earlier versions of this book in seminars and panels at the Midwest Political Science Association meetings (Chicago, 2–6 April 1990), the Political Methodology Group meetings (Duke University, 18–20 July 1990), the American

Political Science Association meetings (Washington, D.C., 29 August–1 September 1991), the Seminar in the Methodology and Philosophy of the Social Sciences (Harvard University, Center for International Affairs, 25 September 1992), the Colloquium Series of the Interdisciplinary Consortium for Statistical Applications (Indiana University, 4 December 1991), the Institute for Global Cooperation and Change seminar series (University of California, Berkeley, 15 January 1993), and the University of Illinois, Urbana-Champaign (18 March 1993).

Gary King
Robert O. Keohanne
Sidney Verba

Cambridge, Massachusetts

Designing Social Inquiry

CHAPTER 1

The *Science* in Social Science

1.1 INTRODUCTION

THIS BOOK is about research in the social sciences. Our goal is practical: designing research that will produce valid inferences about social and political life. We focus on political science, but our argument applies to other disciplines such as sociology, anthropology, history, economics, and psychology and to nondisciplinary areas of study such as legal evidence, education research, and clinical reasoning.

This is neither a work in the philosophy of the social sciences nor a guide to specific research tasks such as the design of surveys, conduct of field work, or analysis of statistical data. Rather, this is a book about research design: how to pose questions and fashion scholarly research to make valid descriptive and causal inferences. As such, it occupies a middle ground between abstract philosophical debates and the hands-on techniques of the researcher and focuses on the essential logic underlying all social scientific research.

1.1.1 *Two Styles of Research, One Logic of Inference*

Our main goal is to connect the traditions of what are conventionally denoted "quantitative" and "qualitative" research by applying a unified logic of inference to both. The two traditions appear quite different; indeed they sometimes seem to be at war. Our view is that these differences are mainly ones of style and specific technique. The same underlying logic provides the framework for each research approach. This logic tends to be explicated and formalized clearly in discussions of quantitative research methods. But the same logic of inference underlies the best qualitative research, and all qualitative and quantitative researchers would benefit by more explicit attention to this logic in the course of designing research.

The *styles* of quantitative and qualitative research are very different. Quantitative research uses numbers and statistical methods. It tends to be based on numerical measurements of specific aspects of phenomena; it abstracts from particular instances to seek general description or to test causal hypotheses; it seeks measurements and analyses that are easily replicable by other researchers.

Qualitative research, in contrast, covers a wide range of approaches, but by definition, none of these approaches relies on numerical measurements. Such work has tended to focus on one or a small number of cases, to use intensive interviews or depth analysis of historical materials, to be discursive in method, and to be concerned with a rounded or comprehensive account of some event or unit. Even though they have a small number of cases, qualitative researchers generally unearth enormous amounts of information from their studies. Sometimes this kind of work in the social sciences is linked with area or case studies where the focus is on a particular event, decision, institution, location, issue, or piece of legislation. As is also the case with quantitative research, the instance is often important in its own right: a major change in a nation, an election, a major decision, or a world crisis. Why did the East German regime collapse so suddenly in 1989? More generally, why did almost all the communist regimes of Eastern Europe collapse in 1989? Sometimes, but certainly not always, the event may be chosen as an exemplar of a particular type of event, such as a political revolution or the decision of a particular community to reject a waste disposal site. Sometimes this kind of work is linked to area studies where the focus is on the history and culture of a particular part of the world. The particular place or event is analyzed closely and in full detail.

For several decades, political scientists have debated the merits of case studies versus statistical studies, area studies versus comparative studies, and "scientific" studies of politics using quantitative methods versus "historical" investigations relying on rich textual and contextual understanding. Some quantitative researchers believe that systematic statistical analysis is the only road to truth in the social sciences. Advocates of qualitative research vehemently disagree. This difference of opinion leads to lively debate; but unfortunately, it also bifurcates the social sciences into a quantitative-systematic-generalizing branch and a qualitative-humanistic-discursive branch. As the former becomes more and more sophisticated in the analysis of statistical data (and their work becomes less comprehensible to those who have not studied the techniques), the latter becomes more and more convinced of the irrelevance of such analyses to the seemingly non-replicable and nongeneralizable events in which its practitioners are interested.

A major purpose of this book is to show that the differences between the quantitative and qualitative traditions are only stylistic and are methodologically and substantively unimportant. All good research can be understood—indeed, is best understood—to derive from the same underlying logic of inference. Both quantitative and qualitative research can be systematic and scientific. Historical research can be analytical, seeking to evaluate alternative explanations through a process of valid causal inference. History, or historical sociology, is not incompatible with social science (Skocpol 1984: 374–86).

Breaking down these barriers requires that we begin by questioning the very concept of "qualitative" research. We have used the term in our title to signal our subject matter, not to imply that "qualitative" research is fundamentally different from "quantitative" research, except in style.

Most research does not fit clearly into one category or the other. The best often combines features of each. In the same research project, some data may be collected that is amenable to statistical analysis, while other equally significant information is not. Patterns and trends in social, political, or economic behavior are more readily subjected to quantitative analysis than is the flow of ideas among people or the difference made by exceptional individual leadership. If we are to understand the rapidly changing social world, we will need to include information that cannot be easily quantified as well as that which can. Furthermore, all social science requires comparison, which entails judgments of which phenomena are "more" or "less" alike in degree (i.e., quantitative differences) or in kind (i.e., qualitative differences).

Two excellent recent studies exemplify this point. In *Coercive Cooperation* (1992), Lisa L. Martin sought to explain the degree of international cooperation on economic sanctions by quantitatively analyzing ninety-nine cases of attempted economic sanctions from the post–World War II era. Although this quantitative analysis yielded much valuable information, certain causal inferences suggested by the data were ambiguous; hence, Martin carried out six detailed case studies of sanctions episodes in an attempt to gather more evidence relevant to her causal inference. For *Making Democracy Work* (1993), Robert D. Putnam and his colleagues interviewed 112 Italian regional councillors in 1970, 194 in 1976, and 234 in 1981–1982, and 115 community leaders in 1976 and 118 in 1981–1982. They also sent a mail questionnaire to over 500 community leaders throughout the country in 1983. Four nationwide mass surveys were undertaken especially for this study. Nevertheless, between 1976 and 1989 Putnam and his colleagues conducted detailed case studies of the politics of six regions. Seeking to satisfy the "interocular traumatic test," the investigators "gained an intimate knowledge of the internal political maneuvering and personalities that have animated regional politics over the last two decades" (Putnam 1993:190).

The lessons of these efforts should be clear: neither quantitative nor qualitative research is superior to the other, regardless of the research problem being addressed. Since many subjects of interest to social scientists cannot be meaningfully formulated in ways that permit statistical testing of hypotheses with quantitative data, we do not wish to encourage the exclusive use of quantitative techniques. We are not trying to get all social scientists out of the library and into the computer center, or to replace idiosyncratic conversations with structured interviews. Rather, we argue that nonstatistical research will produce more reliable results if researchers pay attention to the rules of scientific inference—rules that are sometimes more clearly stated in the style of quantitative research. Precisely defined statistical methods that undergird quantitative research represent abstract formal models applicable to all kinds of research, even that for which variables cannot be measured quantitatively. The very abstract, and even unrealistic, nature of statistical models is what makes the rules of inference shine through so clearly.

The rules of inference that we discuss are not relevant to all issues that are of significance to social scientists. Many of the most important questions concerning political life—about such concepts as agency, obligation, legitimacy, citizenship, sovereignty, and the proper relationship between national societies and international politics—are philosophical rather than empirical. But the rules are relevant to all research where the goal is to learn facts about the real world. Indeed, the distinctive characteristic that sets social science apart from casual observation is that social science seeks to arrive at valid inferences by the systematic use of well-established procedures of inquiry. Our focus here on empirical research means that we sidestep many issues in the philosophy of social science as well as controversies about the role of postmodernism, the nature and existence of truth, relativism, and related subjects. We assume that it is possible to have some knowledge of the external world but that such knowledge is always uncertain.

Furthermore, nothing in our set of rules implies that we must run the perfect experiment (if such a thing existed) or collect all relevant data before we can make valid social scientific inferences. An important topic is worth studying even if very little information is available. The result of applying any research design in this situation will be relatively uncertain conclusions, but so long as we honestly report our uncertainty, this kind of study can be very useful. Limited information is often a necessary feature of social inquiry. Because the social world changes rapidly, analyses that help us understand those changes require that we describe them and seek to understand them contemporaneously, even when uncertainty about our conclusions is high. The urgency of a problem may be so great that data gathered by the most useful scientific methods might be obsolete before it can be accumulated. If a distraught person is running at us swinging an ax, administering a five-page questionnaire on psychopathy may not be the best strategy. Joseph Schumpeter once cited Albert Einstein, who said "as far as our propositions are certain, they do not say anything about reality, and as far as they do say anything about reality, they are not certain" (Schumpeter [1936] 1991:298–99). Yet even though certainty is unattainable, we can improve the reliability, validity, certainty, and honesty of our conclusions by paying attention to the rules of scientific inference. The social science we espouse seeks to make descriptive and causal inferences about the world. Those who do not share the assumptions of partial and imperfect knowability and the aspiration for descriptive and causal understanding will have to look elsewhere for inspiration or for paradigmatic battles in which to engage.

In sum, we do not provide recipes for scientific empirical research. We offer a number of precepts and rules, but these are meant to discipline thought, not stifle it. In both quantitative and qualitative research, we engage in the imperfect application of theoretical standards of inference to inherently imperfect research designs and empirical data. Any meaningful rules admit of exceptions, but we can ask that exceptions be justified explicitly, that their implications for the reliability of research be assessed, and that the uncertainty of conclusions be reported. We seek not dogma, but disciplined thought.

1.1.2 Defining Scientific Research in the Social Sciences

Our definition of "scientific research" is an ideal to which any actual quantitative or qualitative research, even the most careful, is only an approximation. Yet, we need a definition of good research, for which we use the word "scientific" as our descriptor.[1] This word comes with many connotations that are unwarranted or inappropriate or downright incendiary for some qualitative researchers. Hence, we provide an explicit definition here. As should be clear, we do not regard quantitative research to be any more scientific than qualitative research. Good research, that is, scientific research, can be quantitative or qualitative in style. In design, however, scientific research has the following four characteristics:

1. **The goal is inference.** Scientific research is designed to make descriptive or explanatory *inferences* on the basis of empirical information about the world. Careful descriptions of specific phenomena are often indispens-

[1] We reject the concept, or at least the word, "quasi-experiment." Either a research design involves investigator control over the observations and values of the key causal variables (in which case it is an experiment) or it does not (in which case it is nonexperimental research). Both experimental and nonexperimental research have their advantages and drawbacks; one is not better in all research situations than the other.

able to scientific research, but the accumulation of facts alone is not sufficient. Facts can be collected (by qualitative or quantitative researchers) more or less systematically, and the former is obviously better than the latter, but our particular definition of science requires the additional step of attempting to infer beyond the immediate data to something broader that is not directly observed. That something may involve *descriptive inference*—using observations from the world to learn about other unobserved facts. Or that something may involve *causal inference*—learning about causal effects from the data observed. The domain of inference can be restricted in space and time—voting behavior in American elections since 1960, social movements in Eastern Europe since 1989—or it can be extensive—human behavior since the invention of agriculture. In either case, the key distinguishing mark of scientific research is the goal of making inferences that go beyond the particular observations collected.

2. **The procedures are public.** Scientific research uses explicit, codified, and *public* methods to generate and analyze data whose reliability can therefore be assessed. Much social research in the qualitative style follows fewer precise rules of research procedure or of inference. As Robert K. Merton ([1949] 1968:71–72) put it, "The sociological analysis of qualitative data often resides in a private world of penetrating but unfathomable insights and ineffable understandings. . . . [However,] science . . . is public, not private." Merton's statement is not true of all qualitative researchers (and it is unfortunately still true of some quantitative analysts), but many proceed as if they had no method—sometimes as if the use of explicit methods would diminish their creativity. Nevertheless they cannot help but use some method. Somehow they observe phenomena, ask questions, infer information about the world from these observations, and make inferences about cause and effect. If the method and logic of a researcher's observations and inferences are left implicit, the scholarly community has no way of judging the validity of what was done. We cannot evaluate the principles of selection that were used to record observations, the ways in which observations were processed, and the logic by which conclusions were drawn. We cannot learn from their methods or replicate their results. Such research is not a *public* act. Whether or not it makes good reading, it is not a contribution to social science.

All methods—whether explicit or not—have limitations. The advantage of explicitness is that those limitations can be understood and, if possible, addressed. In addition, the methods can be taught and shared. This process allows research results to be compared across separate researchers and research projects studies to be replicated, and scholars to learn.

3. **The conclusions are uncertain.** By definition, inference is an imperfect process. Its goal is to use quantitative or qualitative data to learn about the world that produced them. Reaching perfectly certain conclusions

from uncertain data is obviously impossible. Indeed, uncertainty is a central aspect of all research and all knowledge about the world. Without a reasonable estimate of uncertainty, a description of the real world or an inference about a causal effect in the real world is uninterpretable. A researcher who fails to face the issue of uncertainty directly is either asserting that he or she knows everything perfectly or that he or she has no idea how certain or uncertain the results are. Either way, inferences without uncertainty estimates are not science as we define it.

4. **The content is the method.** Finally, scientific research adheres to a set of rules of inference on which its validity depends. Explicating the most important rules is a major task of this book.[2] The content of "science" is primarily the methods and rules, not the subject matter, since we can use these methods to study virtually anything. This point was recognized over a century ago when Karl Pearson (1892: 16) explained that "the field of science is unlimited; its material is endless; every group of natural phenomena, every phase of social life, every stage of past or present development is material for science. The unity of all science consists alone in its method, not in its material."

These four features of science have a further implication: science at its best is a *social enterprise*. Every researcher or team of researchers labors under limitations of knowledge and insight, and mistakes are unavoidable, yet such errors will likely be pointed out by others. Understanding the social character of science can be liberating since it means that our work need not to be beyond criticism to make an important contribution—whether to the description of a problem or its conceptualization, to theory or to the evaluation of theory. As long as our work explicitly addresses (or attempts to redirect) the concerns of the community of scholars and uses public methods to arrive at inferences that are consistent with rules of science and the information at our disposal, it is likely to make a contribution. And the contribution of even a minor article is greater than that of the "great work" that stays forever in a desk drawer or within the confines of a computer.

1.1.3 Science and Complexity

Social science constitutes an attempt to make sense of social situations that we perceive as more or less complex. We need to recognize, however, that what we perceive as complexity is not entirely inherent in phenomena; the world is not naturally divided into simple and com

[2] Although we do cover the vast majority of the important rules of scientific inference, they are not complete. Indeed, most philosophers agree that a complete, exhaustive inductive logic is impossible, even in principle.

plex sets of events. On the contrary, the perceived complexity of a situation depends in part on how well we can simplify reality, and our capacity to simplify depends on whether we can specify outcomes and explanatory variables in a coherent way. Having more observations may assist us in this process but is usually insufficient. Thus *"complexity" is partly conditional on the state of our theory.*

Scientific methods can be as valuable for intrinsically complex events as for simpler ones. Complexity is likely to make our inferences less certain but should *not* make them any less scientific. Uncertainty and limited data should not cause us to abandon scientific research. On the contrary: the biggest payoff for using the rules of scientific inference occurs precisely when data are limited, observation tools are flawed, measurements are unclear, and relationships are uncertain. With clear relationships and unambiguous data, method may be less important, since even partially flawed rules of inference may produce answers that are roughly correct.

Consider some complex, and in some sense unique, events with enormous ramifications. The collapse of the Roman Empire, the French Revolution, the American Civil War, World War I, the Holocaust, and the reunification of Germany in 1990 are all examples of such events. These events seem to be the result of complex interactions of many forces whose conjuncture appears crucial to the event having taken place. That is, independently caused sequences of events and forces converged at a given place and time, their interaction appearing to bring about the events being observed (Hirschman 1970). Furthermore, it is often difficult to believe that these events were inevitable products of large-scale historical forces: some seem to have depended, in part, on idiosyncracies of personalities, institutions, or social movements. Indeed, from the perspective of our theories, chance often seems to have played a role: factors outside the scope of the theory provided crucial links in the sequences of events.

One way to understand such events is by seeking generalizations: conceptualizing each case as a member of a *class of events* about which meaningful generalizations can be made. This method often works well for ordinary wars or revolutions, but some wars and revolutions, being much more extreme than others, are "outliers" in the statistical distribution. Furthermore, notable early wars or revolutions may exert such a strong impact on subsequent events of the same class—we think again of the French Revolution—that caution is necessary in comparing them with their successors, which may be to some extent the product of imitation. Expanding the class of events can be useful, but it is not always appropriate.

Another way of dealing scientifically with rare, large-scale events is to engage in counterfactual analysis: "the mental construction of a course of events which is altered through modifications in one or more 'conditions'" (Weber [1905] 1949:173). The application of this idea in a systematic, scientific way is illustrated in a particularly extreme example of a rare event from geology and evolutionary biology, both historically oriented natural sciences. Stephen J. Gould has suggested that one way to distinguish systematic features of evolution from stochastic, chance events may be to imagine what the world would be like if all conditions up to a specific point were fixed and then the rest of history were rerun. He contends that if it were possible to "replay the tape of life," to let evolution occur again from the beginning, the world's organisms today would be a completely different (Gould 1989a).

A unique event on which students of evolution have recently focused is the sudden extinction of the dinosaurs 65 million years ago. Gould (1989a:318) says, "we must assume that consciousness would not have evolved on our planet if a cosmic catastrophe had not claimed the dinosaurs as victims." If this statement is true, the extinction of the dinosaurs was as important as any historical event for human beings; however, dinosaur extinction does not fall neatly into a class of events that could be studied in a systematic, comparative fashion through the application of general laws in a straightforward way.

Nevertheless, dinosaur extinction can be studied scientifically: alternative hypotheses can be developed and tested with respect to their observable implications. One hypothesis to account for dinosaur extinction, developed by Luis Alvarez and collaborators at Berkeley in the late 1970s (W. Alvarez and Asaro, 1990), posits a cosmic collision: a meteorite crashed into the earth at about 72,000 kilometers an hour, creating a blast greater than that from a full-scale nuclear war. If this hypothesis is correct, it would have the observable implication that iridium (an element common in meteorites but rare on earth) should be found in the particular layer of the earth's crust that corresponds to sediment laid down sixty-five million years ago; indeed, the discovery of iridium at predicted layers in the earth has been taken as partial confirming evidence for the theory. Although this is an unambiguously unique event, there are many other observable implications. For one example, it should be possible to find the metorite's crater somewhere on Earth (and several candidates have already been found).[3]

The issue of the cause(s) of dinosaur extinction remains unresolved, although the controversy has generated much valuable research. For

[3] However, an alternative hypothesis, that extinction was caused by volcanic eruptions, is also consistent with the presence of iridium, and seems more consistent than the meteorite hypothesis with the finding that all the species extinctions did not occur simultaneously.

our purposes, the point of this example is that scientific generalizations are useful in studying even highly unusual events that do not fall into a large class of events. The Alvarez hypothesis cannot be tested with reference to a set of common events, but it does have observable implications for other phenomena that can be evaluated. We should note, however, that a hypothesis is not considered a reasonably certain explanation until it has been evaluated empirically and passed a number of demanding tests. At a minimum, its implications must be consistent with our knowledge of the external world; at best, it should predict what Imre Lakatos (1970) refers to as "new facts," that is, those formerly unobserved.

The point is that even apparently unique events such as dinosaur extinction can be studied scientifically if we pay attention to improving theory, data, and our use of the data. Improving our theory through conceptual clarification and specification of variables can generate more observable implications and even test causal theories of unique events such as dinosaur extinction. Improving our data allows us to observe more of these observable implications, and improving our use of data permits more of these implications to be extracted from existing data. That a set of events to be studied is highly complex does not render careful research design irrelevant. Whether we study many phenomena or few—or even one—the study will be improved if we collect data on as many observable implications of our theory as possible.

1.2 MAJOR COMPONENTS OF RESEARCH DESIGN

Social science research at its best is a creative process of insight and discovery taking place within a well-established structure of scientific inquiry. The first-rate social scientist does not regard a research design as a blueprint for a mechanical process of data-gathering and evaluation. To the contrary, the scholar must have the flexibility of mind to overturn old ways of looking at the world, to ask new questions, to revise research designs appropriately, and then to collect more data of a different type than originally intended. However, if the researcher's findings are to be valid and accepted by scholars in this field, all these revisions and reconsiderations must take place according to explicit procedures consistent with the rules of inference. A dynamic process of inquiry occurs within a stable structure of rules.

Social scientists often begin research with a considered design, collect some data, and draw conclusions. But this process is rarely a smooth one and is not always best done in this order: conclusions rarely follow easily from a research design and data collected in accordance with it. Once an investigator has collected data as provided by a research design, he or she will often find an imperfect fit among the main research questions, the theory and the data at hand. At this stage, researchers often become discouraged. They mistakenly believe that other social scientists find close, immediate fits between data and research. This perception is due to the fact that investigators often take down the scaffolding after putting up their intellectual buildings, leaving little trace of the agony and uncertainty of construction. Thus the process of inquiry seems more mechanical and cut-and-dried than it actually is.

Some of our advice is directed toward researchers who are trying to make connections between theory and data. At times, they can design more appropriate data-collection procedures in order to evaluate a theory better; at other times, they can use the data they have and recast a theoretical question (or even pose an entirely different question that was not originally foreseen) to produce a more important research project. The research, if it adheres to rules of inference, will still be scientific and produce reliable inferences about the world.

Wherever possible, researchers should also improve their research designs before conducting any field research. However, data has a way of disciplining thought. It is extremely common to find that the best research design falls apart when the very first observations are collected—It is not that the theory is wrong but that the data are not suited to answering the questions originally posed. Understanding from the outset what can and what cannot be done at this later stage can help the researcher anticipate at least some of the problems when first designing the research.

For analytical purposes, we divide all research designs into four components: the *research question*, the *theory*, the *data*, and the *use of the data*. These components are not usually developed separately and scholars do not attend to them in any preordained order. In fact, for qualitative researchers who begin their field work before choosing a precise research question, data comes first, followed by the others. However, this particular breakdown, which we explain in sections 1.2.1–1.2.4, is particularly useful for understanding the nature of research designs. In order to clarify precisely what *could* be done if resources were redirected, our advice in the remainder of this section assumes that researchers have unlimited time and resources. Of course, in any actual research situation, one must always make compromises. We believe that understanding the advice in the four categories that follow will help researchers make these compromises in such a way as to improve their research designs most, even when in fact their research is subject to external constraints.

1.2.1 *Improving Research Questions*

Throughout this book, we consider what to do once we identify the object of research. Given a research question, what are the ways to conduct that research so that we can obtain valid explanations of social and political phenomena? Our discussion begins with a research question and then proceeds to the stages of designing and conducting the research. But where do research questions originate? How does a scholar choose the topic for analysis? There is no simple answer to this question. Like others, Karl Popper (1968:32) has argued that "there is no such thing as a logical method of having new ideas. . . . Discovery contains 'an irrational element,' or a 'creative intuition.'" The rules of choice at the earliest stages of the research process are less formalized than are the rules for other research activities. There are texts on designing laboratory experiments on social choice, statistical criteria on drawing a sample for a survey of attitudes on public policy, and manuals on conducting participant observation of a bureaucratic office. But there is no rule for choosing which research project to conduct, nor if we should decide to conduct field work, are there rules governing where we should conduct it.

We can propose ways to select a sample of communities in order to study the impact of alternative educational policies, or ways to conceptualize ethnic conflict in a manner conducive to the formulation and testing of hypotheses as to its incidence. But there are no rules that tell us whether to study educational policy or ethnic conflict. In terms of social science methods, there are better and worse ways to study the collapse of the East German government in 1989 just as there are better and worse ways to study the relationship between a candidate's position on taxes and the likelihood of electoral success. But there is no way to determine whether it is better to study the collapse of the East German regime or the role of taxes in U.S. electoral politics.

The specific topic that a social scientist studies may have a personal and idiosyncratic origin. It is no accident that research on particular groups is likely to be pioneered by people of that group: women have often led the way in the history of women, blacks in the history of blacks, immigrants in the history of immigration. Topics may also be influenced by personal inclination and values. The student of third-world politics is likely to have a greater desire for travel and a greater tolerance for difficult living conditions than the student of congressional policy making; the analyst of international cooperation may have a particular distaste for violent conflict.

These personal experiences and values often provide the motivation to become a social scientist and, later, to choose a particular research question. As such, they may constitute the "real" reasons for engaging in a particular research project—and appropriately so. But, no matter how personal or idiosyncratic the reasons for choosing a topic, the methods of science and rules of inference discussed in this book will help scholars devise more powerful research designs. From the perspective of a potential contribution to social science, personal reasons are neither necessary nor sufficient justifications for the choice of a topic. In most cases, they should not appear in our scholarly writings. To put it most directly but quite indelicately, no one cares what we think—the scholarly community only cares what we can demonstrate.

Though precise rules for choosing a topic do not exist, there are ways—beyond individual preferences—of determining the likely value of a research enterprise to the scholarly community. Ideally, all research projects in the social sciences should satisfy two criteria. First, *a research project should pose a question that is "important" in the real world*. The topic should be consequential for political, social, or economic life, for understanding something that significantly affects many people's lives, or for understanding and predicting events that might be harmful or beneficial (see Shively 1990:15). Second, *a research project should make a specific contribution to an identifiable scholarly literature by increasing our collective ability to construct verified scientific explanations of some aspect of the world*. This latter criterion does not imply that all research that contributes to our stock of social science explanations in fact aims directly at making causal inferences. Sometimes the state of knowledge in a field is such that much fact-finding and description is needed before we can take on the challenge of explanation. Often the contribution of a single project will be descriptive inference. Sometimes the goal may not even be descriptive inference but rather will be the close observation of particular events or the summary of historical detail. These, however, meet our second criterion because they are prerequisites to explanation.

Our first criterion directs our attention to the real world of politics and social phenomena and to the current and historical record of the events and problems that shape people's lives. Whether a research question meets this criterion is essentially a societal judgment. The second criterion directs our attention to the scholarly literature of social science, to the intellectual puzzles not yet posed, to puzzles that remain to be solved, and to the scientific theories and methods available to solve them.

Political scientists have no difficulty finding subject matter that meets our first criterion. Ten major wars during the last four hundred years have killed almost thirty million people (Levy 1985:372); some "limited wars," such as those between the United States and North Vietnam and between Iran and Iraq, have each claimed over a million lives; and nuclear war, were it to occur, could kill billions of human beings. Political mismanagement, both domestic and international, has led to economic privation on a global basis—as in the 1930s—as well as to regional and local depression, as evidenced by the tragic experiences of much of Africa and Latin America during the 1980s. In general, cross-national variation in political institutions is associated with great variation in the conditions of ordinary human life, which are reflected in differences in life expectancy and infant mortality between countries with similar levels of economic development (Russett 1978:913–28). Within the United States, programs designed to alleviate poverty or social disorganization seem to have varied greatly in their efficacy. It cannot be doubted that research which contributes even marginally to an understanding of these issues is important.

While social scientists have an abundance of significant questions that can be investigated, the tools for understanding them are scarce and rather crude. Much has been written about war or social misery that adds little to the understanding of these issues because it fails either to describe these phenomena systematically or to make valid causal or descriptive inferences. Brilliant insights can contribute to understanding by yielding interesting new hypotheses, but brilliance is not a method of empirical research. All hypotheses need to be evaluated empirically before they can make a contribution to knowledge. This book offers no advice on becoming brilliant. What it can do, however, is to emphasize the importance of conducting research so that it constitutes a contribution to knowledge.

Our second criterion for choosing a research question, "making a contribution," means explicitly locating a research design within the framework of the existing social scientific literature. This ensures that the investigator understand the "state of the art" and minimizes the chance of duplicating what has already been done. It also guarantees that the work done will be important to others, thus improving the success of the community of scholars taken as a whole. Making an explicit contribution to the literature can be done in many different ways. We list a few of the possibilities here:

1. Choose a hypothesis seen as important by scholars in the literature but for which no one has completed a systematic study. If we find evidence in favor of or opposed to the favored hypothesis, we will be making a contribution.

2. Choose an accepted hypothesis in the literature that we suspect is false (or one we believe has not been adequately confirmed) and investigate whether it is indeed false or whether some other theory is correct.
3. Attempt to resolve or provide further evidence of one side of a controversy in the literature—perhaps demonstrate that the controversy was unfounded from the start.
4. Design research to illuminate or evaluate unquestioned assumptions in the literature.
5. Argue that an important topic has been overlooked in the literature and then proceed to contribute a systematic study to the area.
6. Show that theories or evidence designed for some purpose in one literature could be applied in another literature to solve an existing but apparently unrelated problem.

Focusing too much on making a contribution to a scholarly literature without some attention to topics that have real-world importance runs the risk of descending to politically insignificant questions. Conversely, attention to the current political agenda without regard to issues of the amenability of a subject to systematic study within the framework of a body of social science knowledge leads to careless work that adds little to our deeper understanding.

Our two criteria for choosing research questions are not necessarily in opposition to one another. In the long run, understanding real-world phenomena is enhanced by the generation and evaluation of explanatory hypotheses through the use of the scientific method. But in the short term, there may be a contradiction between practical usefulness and long-term scientific value. For instance, Mankiw (1990) points out that macroeconomic theory and applied macroeconomics diverged sharply during the 1970s and 1980s: models that had been shown to be theoretically incoherent were still used to forecast the direction of the U.S. economy, while the new theoretical models designed to correct these flaws remained speculative and were not sufficiently refined to make accurate predictions.

The criteria of practical applicability to the real world and contribution to scientific progress may seem opposed to one another when a researcher chooses a topic. Some researchers will begin with a real-world problem that is of great social significance: the threat of nuclear war, the income gap between men and women, the transition to democracy in Eastern Europe. Others may start with an intellectual problem generated by the social science literature: a contradiction between several experimental studies of decision-making under uncertainty or an inconsistency between theories of congressional voting and recent election outcomes. The distinction between the criteria is, of course, not hard and fast. Some research questions satisfy both criteria from the beginning, but in designing research, researchers often begin nearer one than the other.[4]

Wherever it begins, the process of designing research to answer a specific question should move toward the satisfaction of our two criteria. And obviously our direction of movement will depend on where we start. If we are motivated by a social scientific puzzle, we must ask how to make that research topic more relevant to real-world topics of significance—for instance, how might laboratory experiments better illuminate real-world strategic choices by political decision-makers or, what behavioral consequences might the theory have. If we begin with a real-world problem, we should ask how that problem can be studied with modern scientific methods so that it contributes to the stock of social science explanations. It may be that we will decide that moving too far from one criterion or the other is not the most fruitful approach. Laboratory experimenters may argue that the search for external referents is premature and that more progress will be made by refining theory and method in the more controlled environment of the laboratory. And in terms of a long-term research program, they may be right. Conversely, the scholar motivated by a real-world problem may argue that accurate description is needed before moving to explanation. And such a researcher may also be right. Accurate description is an important step in explanatory research programs.

In either case, a research program, and if possible a specific research project, should aim to satisfy our two criteria: it should deal with a significant real-world topic and be designed to contribute, directly or indirectly, to a specific scholarly literature. Since our main concern in this book is making qualitative research more scientific, we will primarily address the researcher who starts with the "real-world" perspective. But our analysis is relevant to both types of investigator.

If we begin with a significant real-world problem rather than with an established literature, it is essential to devise a workable plan for studying it. *A proposed topic that cannot be refined into a specific research project permitting valid descriptive or causal inference should be modified along the way or abandoned.* A proposed topic that will make no contri-

---

[4] The dilemma is not unlike that faced by natural scientists in deciding whether to conduct applied or basic research. For example, applied research in relation to a particular drug or disease may, in the short run, improve medical care without contributing as much to the general knowledge of the underlying biological mechanisms. Basic research may have the opposite consequence. Most researchers would argue, as we do for the social sciences, that the dichotomy is false and that basic research will ultimately lead to the powerful applied results. However, all agree that the best research design is one that somehow manages both to be directly relevant to solving real-world problems and to furthering the goals of a specific scientific literature.

bution to some scholarly literature should similarly be changed. Having tentatively chosen a topic, we enter a dialogue with the literature. What questions of interest to us have already been answered? How can we pose and refine our question so that it seems capable of being answered with the tools available? We may start with a burning issue, but we will have to come to grips both with the literature of social science and the problems of inference.

1.2.2 Improving Theory

A social science theory is a reasoned and precise speculation about the answer to a research question, including a statement about why the proposed answer is correct. Theories usually imply several more specific descriptive or causal hypotheses. A theory must be consistent with prior evidence about a research question. "A theory that ignores existing evidence is an oxymoron. If we had the equivalent of 'truth in advertising' legislation, such an oxymoron should not be called a theory" (Lieberson 1992:4; see also Woods and Walton 1982).

The development of a theory is often presented as the first step of research. It sometimes comes first in practice, but it need not. In fact, we cannot develop a theory without knowlege of prior work on the subject and the collection of some data, since even the research question would be unknown. Nevertheless, despite whatever amount of data has already been collected, there are some general ways to evaluate and improve the usefulness of a theory. We briefly introduce each of these here but save a more detailed discussion for later chapters.

First, choose theories that could be wrong. Indeed, vastly more is learned from theories that *are* wrong than from theories that are stated so broadly that they could not be wrong even in principle.[5] We need to be able to give a direct answer to the question: What evidence would convince us that we are wrong?[6] If there is no answer to this question, then we do not have a theory.

Second, to make sure a theory is falsifiable, choose one that is capable of generating as many *observable implications* as possible. This choice will allow more tests of the theory with more data and a greater variety of data, will put the theory at risk of being falsified more times, and will make it possible to collect data so as to build strong evidence for the theory.

[5] This is the principle of falsifiability (Popper 1968). It is an issue on which there are varied positions in the philosophy of science. However, very few of them disagree with the principle that theories should be stated clearly enough so that they could be wrong.

[6] This is probably the most commonly asked question at job interviews in our department and many others.

Third, in designing theories, be as concrete as possible. Vaguely stated theories and hypotheses serve no purpose but to obfuscate. Theories that are stated precisely and make specific predictions can be shown more easily to be wrong and are therefore better.

Some researchers recommend following the principle of "parsimony." Unfortunately, the word has been used in so many ways in casual conversation and scholarly writings that the principle has become obscured (see Sober [1988] for a complete discussion). The clearest definition of parsimony was given by Jeffreys (1961:47): "Simple theories have higher prior probabilities."[7] Parsimony is therefore a judgment, or even assumption, about the nature of the world: it is assumed to be simple. The principle of choosing theories that imply a simple world is a rule that clearly applies in situations where there is a high degree of certainty that the world is indeed simple. Scholars in physics seem to find parsimony appropriate, but those in biology often think of it as absurd. In the social sciences, some forcefully defend parsimony in their subfields (e.g., Zellner 1984), but we believe it is only occasionally appropriate. Given the precise definition of parsimony as an assumption about the world, we should never insist on parsimony as a general principle of designing theories, but it is useful in those situations where we have some knowledge of the simplicity of the world we are studying.

Our point is that we do not advise researchers to seek parsimony as an essential good, since there seems little reason to adopt it unless we already know a lot about a subject. We do not even need parsimony to avoid excessively complicated theories, since it is directly implied by the maxim that the theory should be just as complicated as all our evidence suggest. Situations with insufficient evidence relative to the complexity of the theory being investigated can lead to what we call "indeterminate research designs" (see section 4.1), but these are problems of research design and not assumptions about the world.

All our advice thus far applies if we have not yet collected our data and begun any analysis. However, if we have already gathered the data, we can certainly use these rules to modify our theory and gather new data, and thus generate new observable implications of the new theory. Of course, this process is expensive, time consuming, and probably wasteful of the data already collected. What then about the situation where our theory is in obvious need of improvement but we cannot afford to collect additional data? This situation—in which researchers often find themselves—demands great caution and self-

---

[7] This phrase has come to be known as the "Jeffreys-Wrinch Simplicity Postulate." The concept is similar to Occam's razor.

restraint. Any intelligent scholar can come up with a "plausible" theory for any set of data after the fact, yet to do so demonstrates nothing about the veracity of the theory. The theory will fit the data nicely and still may be wildly wrong—indeed, demonstrably wrong with most other data. Human beings are very good at recognizing patterns but not very good at recognizing nonpatterns. (Most of us even see patterns in random ink blots!) Ad hoc adjustments in a theory that does not fit existing data must be used rarely and with considerable discipline.[8]

There is still the problem of what to do when we have finished our data collection and analysis and wish to work on improving a theory. In this situation, we recommend following two rules: First, if our prediction is conditional on several variables and we are willing to drop one of the conditions, we may do so. For example, if we hypothesized originally that democratic countries with advanced social welfare systems do not fight each other, it would be permissible to extend that hypothesis to all modern democracies and thus evaluate our theory against more cases and increase its chances of being falsified. The general point is that after seeing the data, we may modify our theory in a way that makes it apply to a larger range of phenomena. Since such an alteration in our thesis exposes it more fully to falsification, modification in this direction should not lead to ad hoc explanations that merely appear to "save" an inadequate theory by restricting its range to phenomena that have already been observed to be in accord with it.

The opposite practice, however, is generally inappropriate. After observing the data, we should not just add a restrictive condition and then proceed as if our theory, with that qualification, has been shown to be correct. If our original theory was that modern democracies do not fight wars with one another due to their constitutional systems, it would be less permissible, having found exceptions to our "rule," to restrict the proposition to democracies with advanced social welfare systems *once it has been ascertained by inspection of the data that such a qualification would appear to make our proposition correct*. Or suppose that our original theory was that revolutions only occur under conditions of severe economic depression, but we find that this is not true in one of our case studies. In this situation it would not be reasonable merely to add general conditions such as, revolutions never occur during periods of prosperity except when the military is weak, the political leadership is repressive, the economy is based on a small number of prod-

---

[8] If we have chosen a topic of real-world importance and/or one which makes some contribution to a scholarly literature, the social nature of academia will correct this situation: someone will replicate our study with another set of data and demonstrate that we were wrong.

ucts, and the climate is warm. Such a formulation is merely a fancy (and misleading) way of saying "my theory is correct, except in country *x*." Since we have already discovered that our theory is incorrect for country *x*, it does not help to turn this falsification into a spurious generalization. Without efforts to collect new data, we will have no admissible evidence to support the new version of the theory.

So our basic rule with respect to altering our theory after observing the data is: *we can make the theory less restrictive (so that it covers a broader range of phenomena and is exposed to more opportunities for falsification), but we should not make it more restrictive without collecting new data to test the new version of the theory.* If we cannot collect additional data, then we are stuck; and we do not propose any magical way of getting unstuck. At some point, deciding that we are wrong is best; indeed, negative findings can be quite valuable for a scholarly literature. Who would not prefer one solid negative finding over any number of flimsy positive findings based on ad hoc theories?

Moreover, if we are wrong, we need not stop writing after admitting defeat. We may add a section to our article or a chapter to our book about future empirical research and current theoretical speculation. In this context, we have considerably more freedom. We may suggest additional conditions that might be plausibly attached to our theory, if we believe they might solve the problem, propose a modification of another existing theory or propose a range of entirely different theories. In this situation, we cannot conclude anything with a great deal of certainty (except perhaps that the theory we stated at the outset is wrong), but we do have the luxury of inventing new research designs or data-collection projects that could be used to decide whether our speculations are correct. These can be very valuable, especially in suggesting areas where future researchers can look.

Admittedly, as we discussed above, social science does not operate strictly according to rules: the need for creativity sometimes mandates that the textbook be discarded! And data can discipline thought. Hence researchers will sometimes, after confronting data, have inspirations about how they should have constructed the theory in the first place. Such a modification, even if restrictive, may be worthwhile if we can convince ourselves and others that modifying the theory in the way that we propose is something we could have done before we collected the data if we had thought of it. But until tested with *new* data, the status of such a theory will remain very uncertain, and it should be labeled as such.

One important consequence of these rules is that pilot projects are often very useful, especially in research where data must be gathered by interviewing or other particularly costly means. Preliminary data-gathering may lead us to alter the research questions or modify the theory. Then new data can be gathered to test the new theory, and the problem of using the same data to generate and test a theory can be avoided.

1.2.3 Improving Data Quality

"Data" are systematically collected elements of information about the world. They can be qualitative or quantitative in style. Sometimes data are collected to evaluate a very specific theory, but not so infrequently, scholars collect data before knowing precisely what they are interested in finding out. Moreover, even if data are collected to evaluate a specific hypothesis, researchers may ultimately be interested in questions that had not occurred to them previously.

In either case—when data are gathered for a specific purpose or when data are used for some purpose not clearly in mind when they were gathered—certain rules will improve the quality of those data. In principle, we can think about these rules for improving data separately from the rules in section 1.2.2 for improving theory. In practice any data collection effort requires some degree of theory, just as formulating any theory requires some data (see Coombs 1964).

Our first and most important guideline for improving data quality is: *record and report the process by which the data are generated*. Without this information we cannot determine whether using standard procedures in analyzing the data will produce biased inferences. Only by knowing the process by which the data were generated will we be able to produce valid descriptive or causal inferences. In a quantitative opinion poll, recording the data-generation process requires that we know the exact method by which the sample was drawn and the specific questions that were asked. In a qualitative comparative case study, reporting the precise rules by which we choose the small number of cases for analysis is critical. We give additional guidelines in chapter 6 for case selection in qualitative research, but even more important than choosing a good method is being careful to record and report whatever method was used and all the information necessary for someone else to apply it.[9]

In section 1.2.2 we argued for theories that are capable of generating

[9] We find that many graduate students are unnecessarily afraid of sharing data and the information necessary to replicate their results. They are afraid that someone will steal their hard work or even prove that they were wrong. These are all common fears, but they are almost always unwarranted. Publication (or at least sending copies of research papers to other scholars) and sharing data is the best way to guarantee credit for one's contributions. Moreover, sharing data will only help others follow along in the research you started. When their research is published, they will cite your effort and advance your visibility and reputation.

many observable implications. Our second guideline for improving data quality is *in order better to evaluate a theory, collect data on as many of its observable implications as possible*. This means collecting as much data in as many diverse contexts as possible. Each additional implication of our theory which we observe provides another context in which to evaluate its veracity. The more observable implications which are found to be consistent with the theory, the more powerful the explanation and the more certain the results.

When adding data on new observable implications of a theory, we can (a) collect more observations on the same dependent variable, or (b) record additional dependent variables. We can, for instance, disaggregate to shorter time periods or smaller geographic areas. We can also collect information on dependent variables of less direct interest; if the results are as the theory predicts, we will have more confidence in the theory.

For example, consider the rational deterrence theory: potential initiators of warfare calculate the costs and benefits of attacking other states, and these calculations can be influenced by credible threats of retaliation. The most direct test of this theory would be to assess whether, given threats of war, decisions to attack are associated with such factors as the balance of military forces between the potential attacker and the defender or the interests at stake for the defender (Huth 1988). However, even though using only cases in which threats are issued constitutes a set of observable implications of the theory, they are only part of the observations that could be gathered (and used alone may lead to selection bias), since situations in which threats themselves are deterred would be excluded from the data set. Hence it might be worthwhile also to collect data on an additional dependent variable (i.e., a different set of observable implications) based on a measurement of whether threats are made by states that have some incentives to do so.

Insofar as sufficient good data on deterrence in international politics is lacking, it could also be helpful to test a different theory, one with similar motivational assumptions, for a different dependent variable under different conditions but which is still an observable implication of the same theory. For instance, we could construct a laboratory experiment to see whether, under simulated conditions, "threats" are deterred rather than accentuated by military power and firm bargaining behavior. Or we could examine whether other actors in analogous situations, such as oligopolistic firms competing for market share or organized-crime families competing for turf, use deterrence strategies and how successful they are under varying conditions. Indeed, economists working in the field of industrial organization have used noncooperative game theory, on which deterrence theory also relies, to study such problems as entry into markets and pricing strategies (Fudenberg and Tirole 1989). Given the close similarity between the theories, empirical evidence supporting game theory's predictions about firm behavior would increase the plausibility of related hypotheses about state behavior in international politics. Uncertainty would remain about the applicability of conclusions from one domain to another, but the issue is important enough to warrant attempts to gain insight and evidence wherever they can be found.

Obviously, to collect data forever without doing any analysis would preclude rather than facilitate completion of useful research. In practice, limited time and resources will always constrain data-collection efforts. Although more information, additional cases, extra interviews, another variable, and other relevant forms of data collection will always improve the certainty of our inferences to some degree, promising, potential scholars can be ruined by too much information as easily as by too little. Insisting on reading yet another book or getting still one more data set without ever writing a word is a prescription for being unproductive.

Our third guideline is: *maximize the validity of our measurements*. Validity refers to measuring what we think we are measuring. The unemployment rate may be a good indicator of the state of the economy, but the two are not synonymous. In general, it is easiest to maximize validity by adhering to the data and not allowing unobserved or unmeasurable concepts get in the way. If an informant responds to our question by indicating ignorance, then we know he *said* that he was ignorant. Of that, we have a valid measurement. However, what he really *meant* is an altogether different concept—one that cannot be measured with a high degree of confidence. For example, in countries with repressive governments, expressing ignorance may be a way of making a critical political statement for some people; for others, it is a way of saying "I don't know."

Our fourth guideline is: *ensure that data-collection methods are reliable*. Reliability means that applying the same procedure in the same way will always produce the same measure. When a reliable procedure is applied at different times and nothing has happened in the meantime to change the "true" state of the object we are measuring, the same result will be observed.[10] Reliable measures also produce the same re-

---

[10] We can check reliability ourselves by measuring the same quantity twice and seeing whether the measures are the same. Sometimes this seems easy, such as literally asking the same question at different times during an interview. However, asking the question once may influence the respondent to respond in a consistent fashion the second time, so we need to be careful that the two measurements are indeed independent.

sults when applied by different researchers, and this outcome depends, of course, upon there being explicit procedures that can be followed.[11]

Our final guideline is: *all data and analyses should, insofar as possible, be replicable.* Replicability applies not only to data, so that we can see whether our measures are reliable, but to the entire reasoning process used in producing conclusions. On the basis of our research report, a new researcher should be able to duplicate our data and trace the logic by which we reached our conclusions. Replicability is important even if no one actually replicates our study. Only by reporting the study in sufficient detail so that it can be replicated is it possible to evaluate the procedures followed and methods used.

Replicability of data may be difficult or impossible in some kinds of research: interviewees may die or disappear, and direct observations of real-world events by witnesses or participants cannot be repeated. Replicability has also come to mean different things in different research traditions. In quantitative research, scholars focus on replicating the analysis after starting with the same data. As anyone who has ever tried to replicate the quantitative results of even prominent published works knows well, it is usually a lot harder than it should be and always more valuable than it seems at the outset (see Dewald et al. 1986 on replication in quantitative research).

The analogy in traditional qualitative research is provided by footnotes and bibliographic essays. Using these tools, succeeding scholars should be able to locate the sources used in published work and make their own evaluations of the inferences claimed from this information. For research based on direct observation, replication is more difficult. One scholar could borrow another's field notes or tape recorded interviews to see whether they support the conclusions made by the original investigator. Since so much of the data in field research involve conversations, impressions, and other unrecorded participatory information, this reanalysis of results using the same data is not often done. However, some important advances might be achieved if more scholars tried this type of replication, and it would probably also encourage others to keep more complete field notes. Occasionally, an entire research project, including data collection, has been replicated. Since we cannot go back in time, the replication cannot be perfect but can be quite valuable nonetheless. Perhaps the most extensive replication of

---

[11] An example is the use of more than one coder to extract systematic information from transcripts of in-depth interviews. If two people use the same coding rules, we can see how often they produce the same judgment. If they do not produce reliable measures, then we can make the coding rules more precise and try again. Eventually, a set of rules can often be generated so that the application of the same procedure by different coders will yield the same result.

a qualitative study is the sociological study of Middletown, Indiana, begun by Robert and Helen Lynd. Their first "Middletown" study was published in 1929 and was replicated in a book published in 1937. Over fifty years after the original study, a long series of books and articles are being published that replicate these original studies (see Caplow et al., 1983a, 1983b and the citations therein). All qualitative replication need not be this extensive, but this major research project should serve as an exemplar for what is possible.

All research should attempt to achieve as much replicability as possible: scholars should always record the exact methods, rules, and procedures used to gather information and draw inferences so that another researcher can do the same thing and draw (one hopes) the same conclusion. Replicability also means that scholars who use unpublished or private records should endeavor to ensure that future scholars will have access to the material on similar terms; taking advantage of privileged access without seeking access for others precludes replication and calls into question the scientific quality of the work. Usually our work will not be replicated, but we have the responsibility to act as if someone may wish to do so. Even if the work is not replicated, providing the materials for such replication will enable readers to understand and evaluate what we have done.

1.2.4 Improving the Use of Existing Data

Fixing data problems by collecting new and better data is almost always an improvement on trying to use existing, flawed data in better ways; however, the former approach is not always possible. Social scientists often find themselves with problematic data and little chance to acquire anything better; thus, they have to make the best of what they have.

Improving the use of previously collected data is the main topic taught in classes on statistical methods and is, indeed, the chief contribution of inferential statistics to the social sciences. The precepts on this topic that are so clear in the study of inferential statistics also apply to qualitative research. The remainder of this book deals with these precepts more fully. Here we provide merely a brief outline of the guidelines for improving the use of previously collected data.

First, whenever possible, we should use data to generate inferences that are "unbiased," that is, correct on average. To understand this very specific idea from statistical research, imagine applying the same methodology (in quantitative or qualitative research) for analyzing and drawing conclusions from data across many data sets. Because of small errors in the data or in the application of the procedure, a single application of this methodology would probably never be exactly correct. An "unbiased" procedure will be correct when taken as an average across many applications—even if no single application is correct. The procedure will not systematically tilt the outcome in one direction or another.

Achieving unbiased inferences depends, of course, both on the original collection of the data and its later use; and, as we pointed out before, it is always best to anticipate problems before data collection begins. However, we mention these issues briefly here because when using the data, we need to be particularly careful to analyze whether sources of bias were overlooked during data collection. One such source, which can lead to biased inferences, is that of selection bias: choosing observations in a manner that systematically distorts the population from which they were drawn. Although an obvious example is deliberately choosing only cases which support our theory, selection bias can occur in much more subtle ways. Another difficulty can result from omitted variable bias, which refers to the exclusion of some control variable that might influence a seeming causal connection between our explanatory variables and that which we want to explain. We discuss these and numerous other potential pitfalls in producing unbiased inferences in chapters 2–6.

The second guideline is based on the statistical concept of "efficiency": an efficient use of data involves maximizing the information used for descriptive or causal inference. Maximizing efficiency requires not only using all our data, but also using all the relevant information in the data to improve inferences. For example, if the data are disaggregated into small geographical units, we should use it that way, not just as a national aggregate. The smaller aggregates will have larger degrees of uncertainty associated with them, but if they are, at least in part, observable implications of the theory, they will contain some information which can be brought to bear on the inference problem.

1.3 THEMES OF THIS VOLUME

We conclude this overview chapter by highlighting the four important themes in developing research designs that we have discussed here and will elaborate throughout this book.

1.3.1 *Using Observable Implications to Connect Theory and Data*

In this chapter we have emphasized that every theory, to be worthwhile, must have implications about the observations we expect to find if the theory is correct. These *observable implications* of the theory must guide our data collection, and help distinguish relevant from irrelevant facts. In chapter 2.6 we discuss how theory affects data collection, as well as how data disciplines theoretical imagination. Here, we want to stress that theory and empirical research must be tightly connected. Any theory that does real work for us has implications for empirical investigation; no empirical investigation can be successful without theory to guide its choice of questions. Theory and data collection are both essential aspects of the process by which we seek to decide whether a theory should be provisionally viewed true or false, subject as it is in both cases to the uncertainty that characterizes all inference.

We should ask of any theory: What are its observable implications? We should ask about any empirical investigations: Are the observations relevant to the implications of our theory, and, if so, what do they enable us to infer about the correctness of the theory? In any social scientific study, the implications of the theory and the observation of facts need to mesh with one another: social science conclusions cannot be considered reliable if they are not based on theory and data in strong connection with one another and forged by formulating and examining the observable implications of a theory.

1.3.2 Maximizing Leverage

The scholar who searches for additional implications of a hypothesis is pursuing one of the most important achievements of all social science: *explaining as much as possible with as little as possible.* Good social science seeks to increase the significance of what is explained relative to the information used in the explanation. If we can accurately explain what at first appears to be a complicated effect with a single causal variable or a few variables, the *leverage* we have over a problem is very high. Conversely, if we can explain many effects on the basis of one or a few variables we also have high leverage. Leverage is low in the social sciences in general and even more so in particular subject areas. This may be because scholars do not yet know how to increase it or because nature happens not to be organized in a convenient fashion or for both of these reasons. Areas conventionally studied qualitatively are often those in which leverage is low. Explanation of anything seems to require a host of explanatory variables: we use a lot to explain a little. In such cases, our goal should be to design research with more leverage.

There are various ways in which we can increase our leverage over a research problem. The primary way is to increase the number of observable implications of our hypothesis and seek confirmation of those implications. As we have described above, this task can involve

(1) improving the theory so that it has more observable implications, (2) improving the data so more of these implications are indeed observed and used to evaluate the theory, and (3) improving the use of the data so that more of these implications are extracted from existing data. None of these, nor the general concept of maximizing leverage, are the same as the concept of parsimony, which, as we explained in section 1.2.2, is an assumption about the nature of the world rather than a rule for designing research.

Maximizing leverage is so important and so general that *we strongly recommend that researchers routinely list all possible observable implications of their hypothesis that might be observed in their data or in other data.* It may be possible to test some of these new implications in the original data set—as long as the implication does not "come out of" the data but is a hypothesis independently suggested by the theory or a different data set. But it is better still to turn to other data. Thus we should also consider implications that might appear in other data—such as data about other units, data about other aspects of the units under study, data from different levels of aggregation, and data from other time periods such as predictions about the near future—and evaluate the hypothesis in those settings. The more evidence we can find in varied contexts, the more powerful our explanation becomes, and the more confidence we and others should have in our conclusions.

At first thought, some researchers may object to the idea of collecting observable implications from any source or at any level of aggregation different from that for which the theory was designed. For example, Lieberson (1985) applies to qualitative research the statistical idea of "ecological fallacy"—incorrectly using aggregate data to make inferences about individuals—to warn against cross-level inference.[12] We certainly agree that we can use aggregate data to make incorrect inferences about individuals: if we are interested in individuals, then studying individuals is generally a better strategy if we can obtain these data. However, if the inference we seek to make is more than a very narrowly cast hypothesis, our theory may have implications at many levels of analysis, and we will often be able to use data from all these levels to provide some information about our theory. Thus, even if we are primarily interested in an aggregate level of analysis, we can

---

[12] The phrase "ecological fallacy" is confusing because the process of reasoning from aggregate- to individual-level processes is neither ecological nor a fallacy. "Ecological" is an unfortunate choice of word to describe the aggregate level of analysis. Although Robinson (1990) concluded in his original article about this topic that using aggregate analysis to reason about individuals is a fallacy, quantitative social scientists and statisticians now widely recognize that some information about individuals does exist at aggregate levels of analysis, and many methods of unbiased "ecological" inference have been developed.

often gain leverage about our theory's veracity by looking at the data from these other levels.

For example, if we develop a theory to explain revolutions, we should look for observable implications of that theory not only in overall outcomes but also such phenomena as the responses to in-depth interviews of revolutionaries, the reactions of people in small communities in minor parts of the country, and official statements by party leaders. We should be willing to take whatever information we can acquire so long as it helps us learn about the veracity of our theory. If we can test our theory by examining outcomes of revolutions, fine. But in most cases very little information exists at that level, perhaps just one or a few observations, and their values are rarely unambiguous or measured without error. Many different theories are consistent with the existence of a revolution. Only by delving deeper in the present case, or bringing in relevant information existing in other cases, is it possible to distinguish among previously indistinguishable theories.

The only issue in using information at other levels and from other sources to study a theory designed at an aggregate level is whether these new observations contain *some* information that is relevant to evaluating implications of our theory. If these new observations help to test our theory, they should be used even if they are not the implications of greatest interest. For example, we may not care at all about the views of revolutionaries, but if their answers to our questions are consistent with our theory of revolutions, then the theory itself will be more likely to be correct, and the collection of additional information will have been useful. In fact, an observation at the most aggregate level of data analysis—the occurrence of a predicted revolution, for example—is merely one observed implication of the theory, and because of the small amount of information in it, it should not be privileged over other observable implications. We need to collect information on as many observable implications of our theory as possible.

1.3.3 Reporting Uncertainty

All knowledge and all inference—in quantitative and in qualitative research—is uncertain. Qualitative measurement is error-prone, as is quantitative, but the sources of error may differ. The qualitative interviewer conducting a long, in-depth interview with a respondent whose background he has studied is less likely to mismeasure the subject's real political ideology than is a survey researcher conducting a structured interview with a randomly selected respondent about whom he knows nothing. (Although the opposite is also possible if, for instance, he relies too heavily on an informant who is not trustworthy.) However, the survey researcher is less likely to generalize inappropriately from the particular cases interviewed to the broader population than is the in-depth researcher. Neither is immune from the uncertainties of measurement or the underlying probabilistic nature of the social world.

All good social scientists—whether in the quantitative or qualitative traditions—report estimates of the uncertainty of their inferences. Perhaps the single most serious problem with qualitative research in political science is the pervasive failure to provide reasonable estimates of the uncertainty of the investigator's inferences (see King 1990). We can make a valid inference in almost any situation, no matter how limited the evidence, by following the rules in this book, but we should avoid forging sweeping conclusions from weak data. The point is not that reliable inferences are impossible in qualitative research, but rather that we should always report a reasonable estimate of the *degree of certainty* we have in each of our inferences. Neustadt and May (1986:274), dealing with areas in which precise quantitative estimates are difficult, propose a useful method of encouraging policymakers (who are often faced with the necessity of reaching conclusions about what policy to follow out of inadequate data) to judge the uncertainty of their conclusions. They ask "How much of your own money would you wager on it?" This makes sense as long as we also ask, "At what odds?"

1.3.4 Thinking like a Social Scientist: Skepticism and Rival Hypotheses

The uncertainty of causal inferences means that good social scientists do not easily accept them. When told A causes B, someone who "thinks like a social scientist" asks whether that connection is a true causal one. It is easy to ask such questions about the research of others, but it is more important to ask them about our own research. There are many reasons why we might be skeptical of a causal account, plausible though it may sound at first glance. We read in the newspaper that the Japanese eat less red meat and have fewer heart attacks than Americans. This observation alone is interesting. In addition, the explanation—too much steak leads to the high rate of heart disease in the United States—is plausible. The skeptical social scientist asks about the accuracy of the data (how do we know about eating habits? what sample was used? are heart attacks classified similarly in Japan and the United States so that we are comparing similar phenomena?). Assuming that the data are accurate, what else might explain the effects: Are there other variables (other dietary differences, genetic features, lifestyle characteristics) that might explain the result? Might we have inadvertently reversed cause and effect? It is hard to imagine how not having a heart attack might cause one to eat less red meat but it is possible. Perhaps people lose their appetite for hamburgers and steak late in life. If this were the case, those who did not have a heart attack (for whatever reason) would live longer and eat less meat. This fact would produce the same relationship that led the researchers to conclude that meat was the culprit in heart attacks.

It is not our purpose to call such medical studies into question. Rather we wish merely to illustrate how social scientists approach the issue of causal inference: with skepticism and a concern for alternative explanations that may have been overlooked. Causal inference thus becomes a *process* whereby each conclusion becomes the occasion for further research to refine and test it. Through successive approximations we try to come closer and closer to accurate causal inference.

CHAPTER 2

Descriptive Inference

SOCIAL SCIENCE RESEARCH, whether quantitative or qualitative, involves the dual goals of describing and explaining. Some scholars set out to describe the world; others to explain. Each is essential. We cannot construct meaningful causal explanations without good description; description, in turn, loses most of its interest unless linked to some causal relationships. Description often comes first; it is hard to develop explanations before we know something about the world and what needs to be explained on the basis of what characteristics. But the relationship between description and explanation is interactive. Sometimes our explanations lead us to look for descriptions of different parts of the world; conversely, our descriptions may lead to new causal explanations.

Description and explanation both depend upon rules of scientific inference. In this chapter we focus on description and descriptive inference. Description is far from mechanical or unproblematic since it involves selection from the infinite number of facts that could be recorded. There are several fundamental aspects of scientific description. One is that it involves inference: part of the descriptive task is to infer information about unobserved facts from the facts we have observed. Another aspect involves distinguishing between that which is systematic about the observed facts and that which is nonsystematic.

As should be clear, we disagree with those who denigrate "mere" description. Even if explanation—connecting causes and effects—is the ultimate goal, description has a central role in all explanation, and it is fundamentally important in and of itself. It is not description versus explanation that distinguishes scientific research from other research; it is whether systematic inference is conducted according to valid procedures. Inference, whether descriptive or causal, quantitative or qualitative, is the ultimate goal of all good social science. Systematically collecting facts is a very important endeavor without which science would not be possible but which does not by itself constitute science. Good archival work or well-done summaries of historical facts may make good descriptive history, but neither are sufficient to constitute social science.

In this chapter, we distinguish description—the collection of facts— from descriptive inference. In section 2.1 we discuss the relationship between the seemingly contradictory goals of scholarship: discovering general knowledge and learning about particular facts. We are then able to explain in more detail the concept of inference in section 2.2. Our approach in the remainder of the book is to present ideas both verbally and through very simple algebraic models of research. In section 2.3 we consider the nature of these models. We then discuss models for data collection, for summarizing historical detail, and for descriptive inference in sections 2.4, 2.5, and 2.6, respectively. Finally, we provide some specific criteria for judging descriptive inferences in section 2.7.

2.1 GENERAL KNOWLEDGE AND PARTICULAR FACTS

The world that social scientists study is made up of particulars: individual voters, particular government agencies, specific cities, tribes, groups, states, provinces, and nations. Good social science attempts to go beyond these particulars to more general knowledge. Generalization, however, does not eliminate the importance of the particular. In fact, the very purpose of moving from the particular to the general is to improve our understanding of both. The specific entities of the social world—or, more precisely, specific facts about these entities—provide the basis on which generalizations must rest. In addition, we almost always learn more about a specific case by studying more general conclusions. If we wish to know why the foreign minister of Brazil resigned, it will help to learn why other ministers resigned in Brazil, why foreign ministers in other countries have resigned, or why people in general resign from government or even nongovernmental jobs. Each of these will help us understand different types of general facts and principles of human behavior, but they are very important even if our one and only goal is to understand why the most recent Brazilian foreign minister resigned. For example, by studying other ministers, we might learn that all the ministers in Brazil resigned to protest the actions of the president, something we might not have realized by examining only the actions of the foreign minister.

Some social science research tries to say something about a class of events or units without saying anything in particular about a specific event or unit. Studies of voting behavior using mass surveys explain the voting decisions of people in general, not the vote of any particular individual. Studies of congressional finance explain the effect of money on electoral outcomes across all congressional districts. Most such studies would not mention the Seventh Congressional District in Pennsylvania or any other district except, perhaps, in passing or as exceptions to a general rule. These studies follow the injunction of

Przeworski and Teune (1982): eliminate proper names. However, though these studies may not seek to understand any particular district, they should not ignore—as sometimes is unfortunately done in this tradition—the requirement that the facts about the various districts that go into the general analysis must be accurate.

Other research tries to tell us something about a particular instance. It focuses on the French Revolution or some other "important" event and attempts to provide an explanation of how or why that event came about. Research in this tradition would be unthinkable—certainly uninteresting to most of the usual readers of such research—without proper names. A political scientist may write effectively about patterns of relationships across the set of congressional campaigns without looking at specific districts or specific candidates but imagine Robert Caro's discussion (1983) of the 1948 Senate race in Texas without Lyndon Johnson and Coke Stevenson.[1] Particular events such as the French Revolution or the Democratic Senate primary in Texas in 1948 may indeed be of intrinsic interest: they pique our curiosity, and if they were preconditions for subsequent events (such as the Napoleonic Wars or Johnson's presidency), we may need to know about them to understand those later events. Moreover, knowledge about revolution, rebellion, or civil war in general will provide invaluable information for any more focused study of the causes of the French Revolution in particular.

We will consider these issues by discussing "interpretation," a claimed alternative to scientific inference (section 2.1.1); the concepts of uniqueness and complexity of the subject of study (section 2.1.2); and the general area of comparative case studies (section 2.1.3).

2.1.1 "Interpretation" and Inference

In the human sciences, some historical and anthropological researchers claim to seek *only* specific knowledge through what they call "interpretation." Interpretivists seek accurate summaries of historical detail. They also seek to place the events they describe in an intelligible context within which the meaning of actions becomes explicable. As Ferejohn (in Goldstein and Keohane 1993:228) has written, "We want

---

[1] Nor can we dismiss Caro as someone in another business: a journalist/biographer whose goal differs from that of the social scientist. His work addresses some of the same issues that a political scientist would: What leads to success or failure in an election campaign? What is the role of money and campaign finance in electoral success? What motivates campaign contributors? The discussion focuses on a particular candidacy in a particular district, but the subject matter and the puzzles posed overlap with standard political science.

social science theories to provide causal explanations of events . . . [and] to give an account of the reasons for or meanings of social action. We want to know not only what caused the agent to perform some act but also the agent's reasons for taking the action." Geertz (1973:17) also writes that "it is not in our interest to bleach human behavior of the very properties that interest us before we begin to examine it."

Scholars who emphasize "interpretation" seek to illuminate the intentional aspects of human behavior by employing *Verstehen* ("empathy: understanding the meaning of actions and interactions from the members' own points of view" [Eckstein 1975:81]). Interpretivists seek to explain the reasons for intentional action in relation to the whole set of concepts and practices in which it is embedded. They also employ standards of evaluation: "The most obvious standards are coherence and scope: an interpretative account should provide maximal coherence or intelligibility to a set of social practices, and an interpretative account of a particular set of practices should be consistent with other practices or traditions of the society" (Moon 1975: 173).

Perhaps the single most important operational recommendation of the interpretivists is that researchers should learn a great deal about a culture prior to formulating research questions. For only with a deep cultural immersion and understanding of a subject can a researcher ask the right questions and formulate useful hypotheses. For example, Duneier (1993) studied the collective life of working-class black and white men at one integrated cafeteria in Chicago. By immersing himself in this local culture for four years, he noticed several puzzles that had not previously occurred to him. For example, he observed that although these men were highly antagonistic to the Republican party, they articulated socially conservative positions on many issues.

Some scholars push the role of interpretation even further, going so far as to suggest that it is a wholly different paradigm of inquiry for the social sciences, "not an experimental science in search of law but an interpretive one in search of meaning" (Geertz 1973:5). In our view, however, science (as we have defined it in section 1.1.2) and interpretation are *not* fundamentally different endeavors aimed at divergent goals. Both rely on preparing careful descriptions, gaining deep understandings of the world, asking good questions, formulating falsifiable hypotheses on the basis of more general theories, and collecting the evidence needed to evaluate those hypotheses. The distinctive contribution of science is to present a set of procedures for discovering the *answers* to appropriately framed descriptive and causal questions.

Our emphasis on the methodology of inference is not intended to denigrate the significance of the process by which fruitful questions are formulated. On the contrary, we agree with the interpretivists that it is crucial to understand a culture deeply before formulating hypotheses or designing a systematic research project to find an answer. We only wish to add that evaluating the veracity of claims based on methods such as participant observation can only be accomplished through the logic of scientific inference, which we describe. Finding the right answers to the wrong questions is a futile activity. Interpretation based on *Verstehen* is often a rich source of insightful hypotheses. For instance, Richard Fenno's close observations of Congress (Fenno 1978), made through what he calls "soaking and poking," have made major contributions to the study of that institution, particularly by helping to frame better questions for research. "Soaking and poking," says Putnam in a study of Italian regions (1993:12), "requires the researcher to marinate herself in the minutiae of an institution—to experience its customs and practices, its successes and its failings, as those who live it every day do. This immersion sharpens our intuitions and provides innumerable clues about how the institution fits together and how it adapts to its environment." Any definition of science that does not include room for ideas regarding the generation of hypotheses is as foolish as an interpretive account that does not care about discovering truth.

Yet once hypotheses have been formulated, demonstrating their correctness (with an estimate of uncertainty) requires valid scientific inferences. The procedures for inference followed by interpretivist social scientists, furthermore, must incorporate the same standards as those followed by other qualitative and quantitative researchers. That is, while agreeing that good social science requires insightful interpretation or other methods of generating good hypotheses, we also insist that science is essential for accurate interpretation. If we could understand human behavior only through *Verstehen*, we would never be able to falsify our descriptive hypotheses or provide evidence for them beyond our experience. Our conclusions would never go beyond the status of untested hypotheses, and our interpretations would remain personal rather than scientific.

One of the best and most famous examples in the interpretative tradition is Clifford Geertz's analysis of Gilbert Ryle's discussion of the difference between a twitch and a wink. Geertz (1973:6) writes

> Consider . . . two boys rapidly contracting the eyelids of their right eyes. In one, this is an involuntary twitch; in the other, a conspiratorial signal to a friend. The two movements are, as movements, identical; from an I-am-a-camera, "phenomenalistic" observation of them alone, one could not tell which was twitch and which was wink, or indeed whether both or either was twitch or wink. Yet the difference, however unphotographable, be-

tween a twitch and a wink is vast; as anyone unfortunate enough to have had the first taken for the second knows. The winker is communicating, and indeed communicating in a precise and special way: (1) deliberately, (2) to someone in particular, (3) to impart a particular message, (4) according to a socially established code, and (5) without cognizance of the rest of the company. As Ryle points out, the winker has done two things, contracted his eyelids and winked, while the twitcher has done only one, contracted his eyelids. Contracting your eyelids on purpose when there exists a public code in which doing so counts as a conspiratorial signal *is* winking.

Geertz is making an important conceptual point. Without the concept of "winking," given meaning by a theory of communication, the most precise quantitative study of "eyelid contracting by human beings" would be meaningless for students of social relations. In this example, the theory, which emerged from months of "soaking and poking" and detailed cultural study, is essential to the proper question of whether eyelid contraction even could be "twitches" or "winks." The magnificent importance of interpretation suggested by this example is clear: it provides new ways of looking at the world—new concepts to be considered and hypotheses to be evaluated. Without deep immersion in a situation, we might not even think of the right theories to evaluate. In the present example, if we did not think of the difference between twitches and winks, everything would be lost. If interpretation—or anything else—helps us arrive at new concepts or hypotheses, then it is unquestionably useful, and interpretation, and similar forms of detailed cultural understanding, have been proven again and again.

Having made a relevant theoretical distinction, such as that between a wink and a twitch, the researcher then needs to *evaluate* the hypothesis that winking is taking place. It is in such evaluation that the logic of scientific inference is unsurpassed. That is, the best way of determining the meaning of eyelid contractions is through the systematic methods described in this book. If distinguishing a twitch from wink were pivotal, we could easily design a research procedure to do so. If, for instance, we believe that particular eyelid contractions are winks imbued with political meaning, then other similar instances must also be observable, since a sophisticated signaling device such as this (a "public code"), once developed, is likely to be used again. Given this likelihood, we might record every instance in which this actor's eyelid contracts, observe whether the other key actor is looking at the right time, and whether he responds. We could even design a series of experiments to see if individuals in this culture are accustomed to communicating in this fashion. Understanding the culture, carefully describing the event, and having a deep familiarity with similar situations will all help us ask the right questions and even give us additional confidence in our conclusions. But only with the methods of scientific inference will we be able to evaluate the hypothesis and see whether it is correct.

Geertz's wink interpretation is best expressed as a causal hypothesis (which we define precisely in section 3.1): the hypothetical causal effect of the wink on the other political actor is the other actor's response given the eyelid contraction minus his response if there were no movement (and no other changes). If the eyelid contraction were a wink, the causal effect would be positive; if it were only a twitch, the causal effect would be zero. If we decided to estimate this causal effect (and thus find out whether it was a wink or a twitch), all the problems of inference discussed at length in the rest of this book would need to be understood if we were to arrive at the best inference with respect to the interpretation of the observed behavior.

If what we interpret as winks were actually involuntary twitches, our attempts to derive causal inferences about eyelid contraction on the basis of a theory of voluntary social interaction would be routinely unsuccessful: we would not be able to generalize and we would know it.[2]

Designing research to distinguish winks and twitches is not likely to be a major part of most political science research, but the same methodological issue arises in much of the subject area in which political scientists work. We are often called on to interpret the meaning of an act. Foreign policy decision makers send messages to each other. Is a particular message a threat, a negotiating point, a statement aimed at appealing to a domestic audience? Knowledge of cultural norms, of conventions in international communications, and of the history of particular actors, as well as close observation of ancillary features of the communication, will all help us make such an interpretation. Or consider the following puzzle in quantitative research: Voters in the United States seem to be sending a message by not turning out at the polls. But what does the low turnout mean? Does it reflect alienation with the political system? A calculation of the costs and benefits of voting with the costs being greater? Disappointment with recent candidates or recent campaigns? Could it be a consequence of a change in the minimum age of voting? Or a sign that nothing is sufficiently up-

---

[2] For the sake of completeness, it is worth noting that we could imagine an altogether different theory in which an eyelid contraction was not a wink but still had a causal effect on other actors. For example, the twitch could have been misinterpreted. If we were also interested in whether the person with the eyelid contraction *intended* to wink, we would need to look for other observable consequences of this same theory.

setting to get them to the polls? The decision of a citizen not to vote, like a wink or a diplomatic message, can mean many things. The sophisticated researcher should always work hard to ask the right questions and then carefully design scientific research to find out what the ambiguous act did in fact mean.

We would also like to briefly address the extreme claims of a few proponents of interpretation who argue that the goal of some research ought to be feelings and meanings with no observable consequences. This is hardly a fair characterization of all but a small minority of researchers in this tradition, but the claims are made sufficiently forcefully that they seem worth addressing explicitly. Like the over-enthusiastic claims of early positivists, who took the untenable position that unobservable concepts had no place in scientific research, these arguments turn out to be inappropriate for empirical research. For example, Psathas (1968:510) argues that

> any behavior by focusing only on that part which is overt and manifested in concrete, directly observable acts is naive, to say the least. The challenge to the social scientist who seeks to understand social reality, then, is to understand the meaning that the actor's act has for him.

Psathas may be correct that social scientists who focus on only overt, *observable*, behaviors are missing a lot, but how are we to know if we cannot see? For example, if two theories of self-conception have identical observable manifestations, then *no* observer will have sufficient information to distinguish the two. This is true no matter how clever or culturally sensitive the observer is, how skilled she is at interpretation, how well she "brackets" her own presuppositions, or how hard she tries. Interpretation, feeling, thick description, participant observation, nonparticipant observation, depth interviewing, empathy, quantification and statistical analysis, and all other procedures and methods are inadequate to the task of distinguishing two theories without differing observable consequences. On the other hand, if the two theories have some observable manifestations that differ, then the methods we describe in this book provide ways to distinguish between them.

In practice, ethnographers (and all other good social scientists) *do* look for observable behavior in order to distinguish among their theories. They may immerse themselves in the culture, but they all rely on various forms of *observation*. Any further "understanding" of the cultural context comes directly from these or other comparable observations. Identifying relevant observations is not always easy. On the contrary, finding the appropriate observations is perhaps the most difficult part of a research project, especially (and necessarily) for those areas of inquiry traditionally dominated by qualitative research.

2.1.2 "Uniqueness," Complexity, and Simplification

Some qualitatively oriented researchers would reject the position that general knowledge is either necessary or useful (perhaps even possible) as the basis for understanding a particular event. Their position is that the events or units they study are "unique." In one sense, they are right. There was only one French Revolution and there is only one Thailand. And no one who has read the biographical accounts or who lived through the 1960s can doubt the fact that there was only one Lyndon B. Johnson. But they go further. Explanation, according to their position, is limited to that unique event or unit: not why revolutions happen, but why the French Revolution happened; not why democratization sometimes seems to lag, but why it lags in Thailand; not why candidates win, but why LBJ won in 1948 or 1964. Researchers in this tradition believe that they would lose their ability to explain the specific if they attempted to deal with the general—with revolutions or democratization or senatorial primaries.

"Uniqueness," however, is a misleading term. The French Revolution and Thailand and LBJ are, indeed, unique. All phenomena, all events, are in some sense unique. The French Revolution certainly was; but so was the congressional election in the Seventh District of Pennsylvania in 1988 and so was the voting decision of every one of the millions of voters who voted in the presidential election that year. Viewed holistically, every aspect of social reality is infinitely complex and connected in some way to preceding natural and sociological events. Inherent uniqueness, therefore, is part of the human condition: it does not distinguish situations amenable to scientific generalizations from those about which generalizations are not possible. Indeed, as we showed in discussing theories of dinosaur extinction in chapter 1, even unique events can be studied scientifically by paying attention to the observable implications of theories developed to account for them.

The real question that the issue of uniqueness raises is the problem of complexity. The point is not whether events are inherently unique, but whether the key features of social reality that we want to understand can be abstracted from a mass of facts. One of the first and most difficult tasks of research in the social sciences is this act of *simplification*. It is a task that makes us vulnerable to the criticism of oversimplification and of omitting significant aspects of the situation. Nevertheless, such simplication is inevitable for all researchers. Simplification has been an integral part of every known scholarly work—quantitative and qualitative, anthropological and economic, in the social sciences and in the natural and physical sciences—and will probably always be. Even the most comprehensive description done by the best cultural interpreters with the most detailed contextual understanding will drastically simplify, reify, and reduce the reality that has been observed. Indeed, *the difference between the amount of complexity in the world and that in the thickest of descriptions is still vastly larger than the difference between this thickest of descriptions and the most abstract quantitative or formal analysis.* No description, no matter how thick, and no explanation, no matter how many explanatory factors go into it, comes close to capturing the full "blooming and buzzing" reality of the world. There is no choice but to simplify. Systematic simplification is a crucial step to useful knowledge. As an economic historian has put it, if emphasis on uniqueness "is carried to the extreme of ignoring all regularities, the very possibility of social science is denied and historians are reduced to the aimlesssness of balladeers" (Jones 1981:160).

Where possible, analysts should simplify their descriptions only after they attain an understanding of the richness of history and culture. Social scientists may use only a few parts of the history of some set of events in making inferences. Nevertheless, rich, unstructured knowledge of the historical and cultural context of the phenomena with which they want to deal in a simplified and scientific way is usually a requisite for avoiding simplications that are simply wrong. Few of us would trust the generalizations of a social scientist about revolutions or senatorial elections if that investigator knew little and cared less about the French Revolution or the 1948 Texas election.

In sum, we believe that, where possible, social science research should be both general and specific: it should tell us something about classes of events as well as about specific events at particular places. We want to be timeless and timebound at the same time. The emphasis on either goal may vary from research endeavor to research endeavor, but both are likely to be present. Furthermore, rather than the two goals being opposed to each other, they are mutually supportive. Indeed, *the best way to understand a particular event may be by using the methods of scientific inference also to study systematic patterns in similar parallel events.*

2.1.3 Comparative Case Studies

Much of what political scientists do is describe politically important events systematically. People care about the collapse of the Soviet Union, the reactions of the public in Arab countries to the UN-authorized war to drive Iraq from Kuwait, and the results of the latest congressional elections in the United States. And they rely on political scientists for descriptions that reflect a more comprehensive awareness of the relationship between these and other relevant events—contemporary and historical—than is found in journalistic accounts. Our descriptions of events should be as precise and systematic as possible. This means that when we are able to find valid quantitative measures of what we want to know, we should use them: What proportion of Soviet newspapers criticize government policy? What do public opinion polls in Jordan and Egypt reveal about Jordanian and Egyptian attitudes toward the Gulf war? What percentage of congressional incumbents were reelected?

If quantification produces precision, it does not necessarily encourage accuracy, since inventing quantitative indixes that do not relate closely to the concepts or events that we purport to measure can lead to serious measurement error and problems for causal inference (see section 5.1). Similarly, there are more and less precise ways to describe events that cannot be quantified. Disciplined qualitative researchers carefully try to analyze constitutions and laws rather than merely report what observers say about them. In doing case studies of government policy, researchers ask their informants trenchant, well-specified questions to which answers will be relatively unambiguous, and they systematically follow up on off-hand remarks made by an interviewee that suggest relevant hypotheses. Case studies are essential for description, and are, therefore, fundamental to social science. It is pointless to seek to explain what we have not described with a reasonable degree of precision.

To provide an insightful description of complex events is no trivial task. In fields such as comparative politics or international relations, descriptive work is particularly important because there is a great deal we still need to know, because our explanatory abilities are weak, and because good description depends in part on good explanation. Some of the sources of our need-to-know and explanatory weaknesses are the same: in world politics, for instance, patterns of power, alignments, and international interdependence have all been changing rapidly recently, both increasing the need for good description of new situations, and altering the systemic context within which observed interactions between states take place. Since states and other actors seek to anticipate and counter others' actions, causality is often difficult to establish, and expectations may play as important a part as observed actions in accounting for state behavior. A purported explanation of some aspect of world politics that assumes the absence of strategic interaction and anticipated reactions will be much less useful than a careful description that focuses on events that we have reason to believe are important and interconnected. Good description is better than bad explanation.

One of the often overlooked advantages of the in-depth case-study method is that the development of good causal hypotheses is *complementary* to good description rather than competitive with it. Framing a case study around an explanatory question may lead to more focused and relevant description, even if the study is ultimately thwarted in its attempt to provide even a single valid causal inference.

Comparative case studies can, we argue, yield valid causal inferences when the procedures described in the rest of this book are used, even though as currently practiced they often do not meet the standards for valid inference (which we explicate in chapter 3). Indeed, much of what is called "explanatory" work by historically-oriented or interpretative social scientists remains essentially descriptive because it does not meet these universally applicable standards. From this perspective, the advice of a number of scholars that comparative case studies must be more systematic for description or explanation is fundamental.

For example, Alexander George recommends a method of "structured, focused comparison" that emphasizes discipline in the way one collects data (George and McKeown 1985; see also Verba 1967). George and his collaborators stress the need for a systematic collection of the same information—the same variables—across carefully selected units. And they stress the need for theoretical guidance for asking carefully thought-out explanatory questions—in order to accomplish this systematic description, if causal inference is to be ultimately possible.[3]

The method of structured, focused comparison is a systematic way to employ what George and McKeown call the congruence procedure. Using this method, the investigator "defines and standardizes the data requirements of the case studies . . . by formulating theoretically relevant general questions to guide the examination of each case" (George and McKeown 1985:41). The point that George and McKeown (1985: 43) make is well-taken: "Controlled comparison of a small n should follow a procedure of systematic data compilation." Such "structured-focused comparison" requires collecting data on the same variables across units. Thus, it is not a different method from the one that we emphasize here so much as it is a way of systematizing the information in descriptive case studies in such a way that it could conceivably

---

[3] The literature on comparative case studies is vast. Some of the best additional works are Eckstein (1975), Lijphart (1971), and Collier (1991).

be used for descriptive or causal inference. Much valuable advice about doing comparative case studies, such as this, is rudimentary but often ignored.

2.2 INFERENCE: THE SCIENTIFIC PURPOSE OF DATA COLLECTION

Inference is the process of using the facts we know to learn about facts we do not know. The facts we do not know are the subjects of our research questions, theories, and hypotheses. The facts we do know form our (quantitative or qualitative) data or observations.

In seeking general knowledge, for its own sake or to understand particular facts better, we must somehow avoid being overwhelmed by the massive cacophony of potential and actual observations about the world. Fortunately, the solution to that problem lies precisely in the search for general knowledge. That is, the best scientific way to organize facts is as observable implications of some theory or hypothesis. Scientific simplification involves the productive choice of a theory (or hypothesis) to evaluate; the theory then guides us to the selection of those facts that are implications of theory. Organizing facts in terms of observable implications of a specific theory produces several important and beneficial results in designing and conducting research. First, with this criterion for the selection of facts, we can quickly recognize that more observations of the implications of a theory will only help in evaluating the theory in question. Since more information of this sort cannot hurt, such data are never discarded, and the process of research improves.

Second, we need not have a complete theory before collecting data nor must our theory remain fixed throughout. Theory and data interact. As with the chicken and the egg, some theory is always necessary before data collection and some data are required before any theorizing. Textbooks on research tell us that we use our data to test our theories. But learning from the data may be as important a goal as evaluating prior theories and hypotheses. Such learning involves reorganizing our data into observable implications of the new theory. This reorganizing is very common early in many research processes, usually after some preliminary data have been collected; after the reorganization, data collection then continues in order to evaluate the new theory. We should always try to continue to collect data even after the reorganization in order to test the new theory and thus avoid using the same data to evaluate the theory that we used to develop it.[4]

---

[4] For example, Coombs (1964) demonstrated that virtually every useful data-collection

Third, the emphasis on gathering facts as observable implications of a hypothesis makes the common ground between the quantitative and qualitative styles of research much clearer. In fact, once we get past thinking of cases or units or records in the usual very narrow or even naive sense, we realize that most qualitative studies potentially provide a very large number of observable implications for the theories being evaluated, yet many of these observations may be overlooked by the investigator. Organizing the data into a list of the specific observable implications of a theory thus helps reveal the essential scientific purpose of much qualitative research. In a sense, we are asking the scholar who is studying a particular event—a particular government decision, perhaps—to ask: "If my explanation is correct of why the decision came out the way it did, what else might I expect to observe in the real world?" These additional observable implications might be found in other decisions, but they might also be found in other aspects of the decision being studied: for instance, when it was made, how it was made, how it was justified. The crucial maxim to guide both theory creation and data gathering is: search for more observable implications of the theory.

Each time we develop a new theory or hypothesis, it is productive to list all implications of the theory that could, in principle, be observed. The list, which could then be limited to those items for which data have been or could easily be collected, then forms the basic operational guide for a research project. If collecting one additional datum will help provide one additional way to evaluate a theory, then (subject to the usual time, money, and effort constraints) it is worth doing. If an interview or other observation might be interesting but is not a potential observable implication of this (or some other relevant) theory, then it should be obvious that it will not help us evaluate our theory.

As part of the simplification process accomplished by organizing our data into observable implications of a theory, we need to systematize the data. We can think about converting the raw material of real-world phenomena into "classes" that are made up of "units" or "cases" which are, in turn, made up of "attributes" or "variables" or "parameters." The class might be "voters"; the units might be a sample of "voters" in several congressional districts; and the attributes or

---

task requires or implies some degree of theory, or "minitheory." However, much quantitative data and qualitative history is collected with the explicit purpose of encouraging future researchers to use them for purposes previously unforeseen. Fifteen minutes with the *Statistical Abstract of the United States* will convince most people of this point. Data-collection efforts also differ in the degree to which researchers rigidly follow prior beliefs.

variables might be income, party identification, or anything that is an observable implication of the theory being evaluated. Or the class might be a particular kind of collectivity such as communities or countries, the units might be a selection of these, and the attributes or variables might be their size, the type of government, their economic circumstances, their ethnic composition, or whatever else is measureable and of interest to the researcher. These concepts, as well as various other constructs such as typologies, frameworks, and all manner of classifications, are useful as temporary devices when we are collecting data but have no clear hypothesis to be evaluated. However, in general, we encourage researchers *not* to organize their data in this way. Instead, we need only the organizing concept inherent in our theory. That is, our observations are either implications of our theory or irrelevant. If they are irrelevant or not observable, we should ignore them. If they are relevant, then we should use them. Our data need not all be at the same level of analysis. Disaggregated data, or observations from a different time period, or even from a different part of the world, may provide additional observable implications of a theory. We may not be interested at all in these subsidiary implications, but if they are consistent with the theory, as predicted, they will help us build confidence in the power and applicability of the theory. Our data also need not be "symmetric": we can have a detailed study of one province, a comparative study of two countries, personal interviews with government leaders from only one policy sector, and even a quantitative component—just so long as each is an observable consequence of our theory. In this process, we go beyond the particular to the general, since the characterization of particular units on the basis of common characteristics is a generalizing process. As a result, we learn a lot more about both general theories and particular facts.

In general, we wish to bring as much information to bear on our hypothesis as possible. This may mean doing additional case studies, but that is often too difficult, time consuming, or expensive. We obviously should not bring in irrelevant information. For example, treating the number of conservative-held seats in the British House of Commons as a monthly variable instead of one which changes at each national election, would increase the number of observations substantially but would make no sense since little new information would be added. On the other hand, disaggregating U.S. presidential election results to the state or even county level increases both the number of cases and the amount of information brought to bear on the problem.

Such disaggregated information may seem irrelevant since the goal is to learn about the causes of a particular candidate's victory in a race for the presidency—a fundamentally aggregate-level question. However, most explanations of the outcome of the presidential election have different observable implications for the disaggregated units. If, for instance, we predict the outcome of the presidential election on the basis of economic variables such as the unemployment rate, the use of the unemployment rates on a state-by-state basis provides many more observations of the implications of our theory than does the aggregate rate for the nation as a whole. By verifying that the theory holds in these other situations—even if these other situations are not of direct interest—we increase the confidence that the theory is correct and that it correctly explains the one observable consequence of the theory that is of interest.

2.3 FORMAL MODELS OF QUALITATIVE RESEARCH

A *model* is a simplification of, and approximation to, some aspect of the world. Models are never literally "true" or "false," although good models abstract only the "right" features of the reality they represent.

For example, consider a six-inch toy model of an airplane made of plastic and glue. This model is a small fraction of the size of the real airplane, has no moving parts, cannot fly, and has no contents. None of us would confuse this model with the real thing; asking whether any aspect of the model is true is like asking whether the model who sat for Leonardo DaVinci's *Mona Lisa* really had such a beguiling smile. Even if she did, we would not expect Leonardo's picture to be an exact representation of anyone, whether the actual model or the Virgin Mary, any more than we would expect an airplane model fully to reflect all features of an aircraft. However, we *would* like to know whether this model abstracts the correct features of an airplane for a particular problem. If we wish to communicate to a child what a real airplane is like, this model might be adequate. If built to scale, the model might also be useful to airplane designers for wind tunnel tests. The key feature of a real airplane that this model abstracts is its shape. For some purposes, this is certainly one of the right features. Of course, this model misses myriad details about an airplane, including size, color, the feeling of being on the plane, strength of its various parts, number of seats on board, power of its engines, fabric of the seat cushions, and electrical, air, plumbing, and numerous other critical systems. If we wished to understand these aspects of the plane, we would need an entirely different set of models.

Can we evaluate a model without knowing which features of the subject we wish to study? Clearly not. For example, we might think that a model that featured the amount of dirt on an airplane would not be of much use. Indeed, for the purposes of teaching children or wind tunnel tests, it would be largely irrelevant. However, since even carpet dust can cause a plane to weigh more and thus use more expensive fuel, models of this sort are important to the airline industry and have been built (and saved millions of dollars).

All models range between restrictive and unrestrictive versions. Restrictive models are clearer, more parsimonious, and more abstract, but they are also less realistic (unless the world really is parsimonious). Models which are unrestrictive are detailed, contextual, and more realistic, but they are also less clear and harder to estimate with precision (see King 1989: section 2.5). Where on this continuum we choose to construct a model depends on the purpose for which it is to be put and on the complexity of the problem we are studying.

Whereas some models are physical, others are pictorial, verbal, or algebraic. For example, the qualitative description of European judicial systems in a book about that subject is a model of that event. No matter how thick the description or talented the author, the book's account will always be an abstraction or simplification compared to the actual judicial system. Since understanding requires some abstraction, the sign of a good book is as much what is left out as what is included.

While qualitative researchers often use verbal models, we will use algebraic models in our discussion below to study and improve these verbal models. Just as with models of toy airplanes and book-long studies of the French Revolution, our algebraic models of qualitative research should not be confused with qualitative research itself. They are only meant to provide especially clear statements of problems to avoid and opportunities to exploit. In addition, we often find that they help us to discover ideas that we would not have thought of otherwise.

We assume that readers have had no previous experience with algebraic models, although those with exposure to statistical models will find some of the models that follow familiar. But the logic of inference in these models applies to both quantitative and qualitative research. Just because quantitative researchers are probably more familiar with our terminology does not mean that they are any better at applying the logic of scientific inference. Moreover, these models do *not* apply more closely to quantitative than to qualitative research; in both cases, the models are useful abstractions of the research to which they are applied. To ease their introduction, we introduce all algebraic models with verbal descriptions, followed by a box where we use standard algebraic notation. Although we discourage it, the boxes may be skipped without loss of continuity.

2.4 A FORMAL MODEL OF DATA COLLECTION

Before formalizing our presentation of descriptive and causal inference—the two primary goals of social science research—we will develop a model for the data to be collected and for summarizing these
data. This model is quite simple, but it is a powerful tool for analyzing
problems of inference. Our algebraic model will not be as formal as
that in statistics but nevertheless makes our ideas clearer and easier to
convey. By *data collection*, we refer to a wide range of methods, including observation, participant observation, intensive interviews, large-
scale sample surveys, history recorded from secondary sources, randomized experiments, ethnography, content analyses, and any other
method of collecting reliable evidence. *The most important rule for all
data collection is to report how the data were created and how we came to
possess them.* Every piece of information that we gather should contribute to specifying observable implications of our theory. It may help us
develop a new research question, but it will be of no use in answering
the present question if it is not an observable implication of the question we seek to answer.

We model data with *variables, units,* and *observations.* One simple example is the annual income of each of four people. The data might be
represented simply by four numbers: $9,000, $22,000, $21,000, and
$54,292. In the more general case, we could label the income of four
people (numbered 1, 2, 3, and 4) as $y_1, y_2, y_3,$ and $y_4.$ One variable
coded for two unstructured interviews might take on the values "participatory," "cooperative," or "intransigent," and might be labeled y_1
and $y_2.$ In these examples, the *variable* is y; the *units* are the individual
people; and the *observations* are the values of the variables for each unit
(income for dollars or degree of cooperation). The symbol y is called a
variable because its values vary over the units, and in general, a variable can represent anything whose values change over a set of units.
Since we can collect information over time or across sectional areas,
units may be people, countries, organizations, years, elections, or decades, and often, some combination of these or other units. Observations can be numerical, verbal, visual, or any other type of empirical
data.

For example, suppose we are interested in international organizations since 1945. Before we collect our data, we need to decide what
outcomes we want to explain. We could seek to understand the size
distribution of international organizational activity (by issue area or
by organization) in 1990; changes in the aggregate size of international
organizational activity since 1945; or changes in the size distribution of

international organizational activity since 1945. Variables measuring organizational activity could include the number of countries belonging to international organizations at a given time, the number of tasks performed by international organizations, or the sizes of budgets and staffs. In these examples, the units of analysis would include international organizations, issue areas, country memberships, and time periods such as years, five-year periods, or decades. At the data-collection stage, no formal rules apply as to what variables to collect, how many units there should be, whether the units must outnumber the variables, or how well variables should be measured. The only rule is our judgment as to what will prove to be important. When we have a clearer idea of how the data will be used, the rule becomes finding as many observable implications of a theory as possible. As we emphasized in chapter 1, empirical research can be used both to evaluate a priori hypotheses or to suggest hypotheses not previously considered; but if the latter approach is followed, new data must be collected to evaluate these hypotheses.

It should be very clear from our discussion that most works labeled "case studies" have numerous variables measured over many different types of units. Although case-study research rarely uses more than a handful of cases, the total number of observations is generally immense. It is therefore essential to distinguish between the number of cases and the number of observations. The former may be of some interest for some purposes, but only the latter is of importance in judging the amount of information a study brings to bear on a theoretical question. We therefore reserve the commonly used n to refer only to the number of observations and not to the number of cases. Only occasionally, such as when individual observations are partly dependent, will we distinguish between information and the number of observations. The terminology of the number of observations comes from survey sampling where n is the number of persons to be interviewed, but we apply it much more generally. Indeed, our definition of an "observation" coincides exactly with Harry Eckstein's (1975:85) definition of what he calls a "case." As Eckstein argues, "A study of six general elections in Britain may be, but need not be, an $n = 1$ study. It might also be an $n = 6$ study. It can also be an $n = 120,000,000$ study. It depends on whether the subject of study is electoral systems, elections, or voters." The "ambiguity about what constitutes an 'individual' (hence 'case') can only be dispelled by not looking at concrete entities but at the measures made of them. On this basis, a 'case' can be defined technically as a phenomenon for which we report and interpret only a single measure on any pertinent variable." The only difference in our usage is that since Eckstein's article, scholars have continued to use the word "case" to refer to a full case study, which still has a fairly imprecise definition. Therefore, wherever possible we use the word "case" as most writers do and reserve the word "observation" to refer to measures of one or more variables on exactly one unit.

We attempt in the rest of this chapter to show how concepts like variables and units can increase the clarity of our thinking about research design even when it may be inappropriate to rely on quantitative measures to summarize the information at our disposal. The question we pose is: How can we make descriptive inferences about "history as it really was" without getting lost in a sea of irrelevant detail? In other words, how can we sort out the essential from the ephemeral?

2.5 SUMMARIZING HISTORICAL DETAIL

After data are collected, the first step in any analysis is to provide summaries of the data. Summaries describe what may be a large amount of data, but they are not directly related to inference. Since we are ultimately interested in generalization and explanation, a summary of the facts to be explained is usually a good place to start but is not a sufficient goal of social science scholarship.

Summarization is necessary. We can never tell "all we know" about any set of events; it would be meaningless to try to do so. Good historians understand which events were crucial, and therefore construct accounts that emphasize essentials rather than digressions. To understand European history during the first fifteen years of the nineteenth century, we may well need to understand the principles of military strategy as Napoleon understood them, or even to know what his army ate if it "traveled on its stomach," but it may be irrelevant to know the color of Napoleon's hair or whether he preferred fried to boiled eggs. Good historical writing includes, although it may not be limited to, a compressed verbal summary of a welter of historical detail.

Our model of the process of summarizing historical detail is a *statistic*. A statistic is an expression of data in abbreviated form. Its purpose is to display the appropriate characteristics of the data in a convenient format.[5] For example, one statistic is the *sample mean*, or average:

$$\bar{y} = \frac{1}{n}(y_1 + y_2 + \ldots + y_n) = \frac{1}{n}\sum_{i=1}^{n} y_i$$

[5] Formally, for a set of n units on which a variable y is measured ($y_1, \ldots, y_n$), a statistic h is a real-valued function defined as follows: $h = h(y) = h(y_1, \ldots, y_n)$.

where $\sum_{i=1}^{n} y_i$ is a convenient way of writing $y_1 + y_2 + y_3 + \ldots + y_n$. Another statistic is the *sample maximum*, labeled y_{max}:

$$y_{max} = \text{Maximum}(y_1, y_2, \ldots, y_n) \tag{2.1}$$

The sample mean of the four incomes from the example in section 2.4 ($9,000, $22,000, $21,000, and $54,292) is $26,573. The sample maximum is $54,292. We can summarize the original data containing four numbers with these two numbers representing the sample mean and maximum. We can also calculate other sample characteristics, such as the minimum, median, mode, or variance.

Each summary in this model reduces all the data (four numbers in this simple example, or our knowledge of some aspect of European history in the other) to a single number. Communicating with summaries is often easier and more meaningful to a reader than using all the original data. Of course, if we had only four numbers in a data set, then it would make little sense to use five different summaries; presenting the four original numbers would be simpler. Interpreting a statistic is generally easier than understanding the entire data set, but we necessarily lose information by describing a large set of numbers with only a few.

What rules govern the summary of historical detail? The first rule is that *summaries should focus on the outcomes that we wish to describe or explain.* If we were interested in the growth of the average international organization, we would not be wise to focus on the United Nations; but if we were concerned about the size distribution of international organizations, from big to small, the United Nations would surely be one of the units on which we ought to concentrate. The United Nations is not a representative organization, but it is an important one. In statistical terms, to investigate the typical international organization, we would examine mean values (of budgets, tasks, memberships, etc.), but to understand the range of activity, we would want to examine the variance. A second, equally obvious precept is that *a summary must simplify the information at our disposal.* In quantitative terms, this rule means that we should always use fewer summary statistics than units in the original data, otherwise, we could as easily present all the original data without any summary at all.[6] Our summary should also be sufficiently simple that it can be understood by our audience. No phenomenon can be summarized perfectly, so standards of adequacy must depend on our purposes and on the audience. For ex-

---

[6] This point is closely related to the concept of indeterminant research designs, which we discuss in section 4.1.

ample, a scientific paper on wars and alliances might include data involving 10,000 observations. In such a paper, summaries of the data using fifty numbers might be justified; however, even for an expert, fifty separate indicators might be incomprehensible without some further summary. For a lecture on the subject to an undergraduate class, three charts might be superior.

2.6 DESCRIPTIVE INFERENCE

Descriptive inference is the process of understanding an unobserved phenomenon on the basis of a set of observations. For example, we may be interested in understanding variations in the district vote for the Conservative, Labour, and Social Democratic parties in Britain in 1979. We presumably have some hypotheses to evaluate; however, what we actually observe is 650 district elections to the House of Commons in that year.

Naively, we might think that we were directly observing the electoral strength of the Conservatives by recording their share of the vote by district and their overall share of seats. But a certain degree of randomness or unpredictability is inherent in politics, as in all of social life and all of scientific inquiry.[7] Suppose that in a sudden fit of absent-mindedness (or in deference to social science) the British Parliament had agreed to elections every week during 1979 and suppose (counter-factually) that these elections were independent of one another. Even if the underlying support for the Conservatives remained constant, each weekly replication would not produce the same number of votes for each party in each district. The weather might change, epidemics might break out, vacations might be taken—all these occurrences would affect voter turnout and electoral results. Additionally, fortuitous events might happen in the international environment, or scandals might reach the mass media; even if these had no long-term significance, they could affect the weekly results. Thus, numerous, transitory events could effect slightly different sets of election returns. Our observation of any one election would not be a perfect measure of Conservative strength after all.

As another example, suppose we are interested in the degree of conflict between Israelis (police and residents) and Palestinians in communities on the Israeli-occupied West Bank of the Jordan River. Official reports by both sides seem suspect or are censored, so we decide to conduct our own study. Perhaps we can ascertain the general level of conflict in different communities by intensive interviews or participa-

[7] See Popper (1982) for a book-length defense of indeterminism.

tion in family or group events. If we do this for a week in each community, our conclusions about the level of conflict in each one will be a function in part of whatever chance events occur the week we happen to visit. Even if we conduct the study over a year, we still will not perfectly know the true level of conflict, even though our uncertainty about it will drop.

In these examples, the variance in the Conservative vote across districts or the variance in conflict between West Bank communities can be conceptualized as arising from two separate factors: *systematic* and *nonsystematic* differences. Systematic differences in our voter example include fundamental and predictable characteristics of the districts, such as differences in ideology, in income, in campaign organization, or in traditional support for each of the parties. In hypothetical weekly replications of the same elections, systematic differences would persist, but the nonsytematic differences such as turnout variations due to the weather, would vary. In our West Bank example, systematic differences would include the deep cultural differences between Israelis and Palestinians, mutual knowledge of each other, and geographic patterns of residential housing segregation. If we could start our observation week a dozen different times, these systematic differences between communities would continue to affect the observed level of conflict. However, nonsystematic differences, such as terrorist incidents or instances of Israeli police brutality, would not be predictable and would only affect the week in which they happened to occur. With appropriate inferential techniques, we can usually learn about the nature of systematic differences even with the ambiguity that occurs in one set of real data due to nonsystematic, or random, differences.

Thus, *one of the fundamental goals of inference is to distinguish the systematic component from the nonsystematic component of the phenomena we study*. The systematic component is not more important than the nonsystematic component, and our attention should not be focused on one to the exclusion of the other. However, distinguishing between the two is an essential task of social science. One way to think about inference is to regard the data set we compile as only one of many possible data sets—just as the actual 1979 British election returns constitute only one of many possible sets of results for different hypothetical days on which elections could have been held, or just as our one week of observation in one small community is one of many possible weeks.

In descriptive inference, we seek to understand the degree to which our observations reflect either typical phenomena or outliers. Had the 1979 British elections occurred during a flu epidemic that swept through working-class houses but tended to spare the rich, our observations might be rather poor measures of underlying Conservative strength, precisely because the nonsystematic, chance element in the data would tend to overwhelm or distort the systematic element. If our observation week had occurred immediately after the Israeli invasion of Southern Lebanon, we would similarly not expect results that are indicative of what usually happens on the West Bank.

The political world is theoretically capable of producing multiple data sets for every problem but does not always follow the needs of social scientists. We are usually only fortunate enough to observe one set of data. For purposes of a model, we will let this one set of data be represented by one variable y (say, the vote for Labor) measured over all $n = 650$ units (districts): $y_1, y_2, \ldots, y_n$ (for example, y_1 might be 23,562 people voting for Labor in district 1). The set of *observations* which we label y is a *realized variable*. Its values vary over the n units. In addition, we define Y as a *random variable* because it varies randomly across hypothetical replications of the same election. Thus, y_5 is the number of people voting for Labor in district 5, and Y_5 is the random variable representing the vote across many hypothetical elections that could have been held in district 5 under essentially the same conditions. The observed votes for the Labor party in the one sample we observe, $y_1, y_2, \ldots, y_n$, differ across constituencies because of systematic and random factors. That is, to distinguish the two forms of "variables," we often use the term *realized variable* to refer to y and *random variable* to refer to Y.

The same arrangement applies to our qualitative example. We would have no hope or desire of quantifying the level of tension between Israelis and Palestinians, in part because "conflict" is a complicated issue that involves the feelings of numerous individuals, organizational oppositions, ideological conflicts, and many other features. In this situation, y_5 is a realized variable which stands for the total conflict observed during our week in the fifth community, say El-Bireh.[8] The random variable Y_5 represents both what we observe in El-Bireh and what we could have observed; the randomness comes from the variation in chance events over the possible weeks we could have chosen to observe.[9]

One goal of inference is to learn about *systematic features* of the random variables $Y_1, \ldots, Y_n$. (Note the contradictory, but standard, terminology: although in general we wish to distinguish systematic from nonsystematic components in our data, in a specific case we wish to

---

[8] Obviously the same applies to all the other communities we might study.

[9] Note that the randomness is not exactly over different actual weeks, since both chance events and systematic differences might account for observed differences. We therefore create the more ideal situation in which we imagine running the world again with systematic features held constant and chance factors allowed to vary.

take a random variable and extract its systematic features.) For example, we might wish to know the expected value of the Labor vote in district 5 (the average Labor vote Y_5 across a large number of hypothetical elections in this district). Since this is a systematic feature of the underlying electoral system, the expected value is of considerable interest to social scientists. In contrast, the Labor vote in one observed election, y_5, is of considerably less long-term interest since it is a function of systematic features *and* random error.[10]

The expected value (one feature of the systematic component) in the fifth West Bank community, El-Bireh, is expressed formally as follows:

$$E(Y_5) = \mu_5$$

where $E(\cdot)$ is the expected value operation, producing the average across an infinite number of hypothetical replications of the week we observe in community 5, El-Bireh. The parameter μ_5 (the Greek letter mu with a subscript 5) represents the answer to the expected value calculation (a level of conflict between Palestinians and Israelis) for community 5. This parameter is part of our model for a systematic feature of the random variable Y_5. One might use the observed level of conflict, y_5, as an estimate of μ_5, but because y_5 contains many chance elements along with information about this systematic feature, better estimators usually exist (see section 2.7).

Another systematic feature of these random variables which we might wish to know is the level of conflict in the *average* West Bank community:

$$\frac{1}{n}\sum_{i=1}^{n} E(Y_i) = \frac{1}{n}\sum_{i=1}^{n}\mu_i = \mu \qquad (2.2)$$

One estimator of μ might be the average of the observed levels of conflict across all the communities studied, $\bar{y}$, but other estimators for this systematic feature exist, too. (Note that the same summary of data in our discussion of summarizing historical detail from section 2.5 is used for the purpose of estimating a descriptive inference.) Other systematic features of the random variables include the variance and a variety of causal parameters introduced in section 3.1.

Still another systematic feature of these random variables that might be of interest is the variation in the level of conflict within a commu-

---

[10] Of course, y_5 may be of tremendous interest to the people in district 5 for that year, and thus both the random and systematic components of this event might be worth studying. Nevertheless, we should always try to distinguish the random from the systematic.

nity even when the systematic features do not change: the extent to which observations over different weeks (different hypothetical realizations of the same random variable) produce divergent results. This is, in other words, the size of the nonsystematic component. Formally, this is calculated for a single community by using the variance (instead of the expectation):

$$V(Y_i) = \sigma_i^2 \tag{2.3}$$

where σ^2 (the Greek letter sigma) denotes the result of applying the variance operator to the random variable Y_i. Living in a West Bank community with a high level of conflict between Israelis and Palestinians would not be pleasant, but living in a community with a high variance, and thus unpredictability, might be worse. In any event, both may be of considerable interest for scholarly researchers.

To understand these issues better, we distinguish two fundamental views of random variation.[11] These two perspectives are extremes on a continuum. Although significant numbers of scholars can be found who are comfortable with each extreme, most political scientists have views somewhere between the two.

Perspective 1: A Probabilistic World. Random variation exists in nature and the social and political worlds and can never be eliminated. Even if we measured all variables without error, collected a census (rather than only a sample) of data, and included every conceivable explanatory variable, our analyses would still never generate perfect predictions. A researcher can divide the world into apparently systematic and apparently nonsystematic components and often improve on predictions, but nothing a researcher does to analyze data can have any effect on reducing the fundamental amount of nonsystematic variation existing in various parts of the empirical world.

Perspective 2: A Deterministic World. Random variation is only that portion of the world for which we have no explanation. The division between systematic and stochastic variation is *imposed* by the analyst and depends on what explanatory variables are available and included in the analysis. Given the right explanatory variables, the world is entirely predictable.

These differing perspectives produce various ambiguities in the inferences in different fields of inquiry.[12] However, for most purposes

---

[11] See King (1991b) for an elaboration of this distinction.

[12] Economists tend to be closer to Perspective 1, whereas statisticians are closer to Perspective 2. Perspective 1 is also especially common in the field of engineering called "quality control." Physicists have even debated this distinction in the field of quantum mechanics. Early proponents of Perspective 2 subscribed to the "hidden variable theory"

these *two perspectives can be regarded as observationally equivalent*. This is especially true if we assume, under Perspective 2, that at least some explanatory variables remain unknown. Thus, observational equivalence occurs when these unknown explanatory variables in Perspective 2 become the interpretation for the random variation in Perspective 1. Because of the lack of any observable implications with which to distinguish between them, a choice between the two perspectives depends on faith or belief rather than on empirical verification.

As another example, with both perspectives, distinguishing whether a particular political or social event is the result of a systematic or nonsystematic process depends upon the choices of the researcher. From the point of view of Perspective 1, we may tentatively classify an effect as systematic or nonsystematic. But unless we can find another set of data (or even just another case) to check for the persistence of an effect or pattern, it is very difficult to make the right judgment.

From the extreme version of Perspective 2, we can do no more than describe the data—"incorrectly" judging an event as stochastic or systematic is impossible or irrelevant. A more realistic version of this perspective admits to Perspective 1's correct or incorrect attribution of a pattern as random or systematic, but it allows us some latitude in deciding what will be subject to examination in any particular study and what will remain unexplained. In this way, we begin any analysis with all observations being the result of "nonsystematic" forces. Our job is then to provide evidence that particular events or processes are the result of systematic forces. Whether an unexplained event or process is a truly random occurrence or just the result of as yet unidentified explanatory variables is left as a subject for future research.

This argument applies with equal force to qualitative and quantitative researchers. Qualitative research is often historical, but it is of most use as social science when it is also explicitly inferential. To conceptualize the random variables from which observations are generated and to attempt to estimate their systematic features—rather than merely summarizing the historical detail—does *not* require large-scale data collections. Indeed, one mark of a good historian is the ability to distinguish systematic aspects of the situation being described from idiosyncratic ones. This argument for descriptive inference, therefore, is certainly not a criticism of case studies or historical work. Instead,

---

of quantum mechanics. However, more modern work seems to provide a fundamental verification of Perspective 1: the physical world seems intrinsically probabilistic. We all await the resolution of the numerous remaining contradictions of this important theory and its implications for the nature of the physical world. However, this dispute in physics, although used to justify much of the philosophy of social science, is unlikely to affect the logic of inference or practice of research in the social sciences.

any kind of social science research should satisfy the basic principles of inference discussed in this book. Finding evidence of systematic features will be more difficult with some kinds of evidence, but it is no less important.

As an example of problems of descriptive inference in historical research, suppose that we are interested in the outcomes of U.S.–Soviet summit meetings between 1955 and 1990. Our ultimate purpose is to answer a causal question: under what conditions and to what extent did the summits lead to increased cooperation? Answering that question requires resolving a number of difficult issues of causal analysis, particularly those involving the direction of causality among a set of systematically related variables.[13] In this section, however, we restrict ourselves to problems of descriptive inference.

Let us suppose that we have devised a way of assessing—through historical analysis, surveying experts, counting "cooperative" and "conflictual" events or a combination of these measurement techniques—the extent to which summits were followed by increased superpower cooperation. And we have some hypotheses about the conditions for increased cooperation—conditions that concern shifts in power, electoral cycles in the United States, economic conditions in each country, and the extent to which previous expectations on both sides have been fulfilled. Suppose also that we hope to explain the underlying level of cooperation in each year, and to associate it somehow with the presence or absence of a summit meeting in the previous period, as well as with our other explanatory factors.

What we observe (even if our indices of cooperation are perfect) is only the degree of cooperation *actually* occurring in each year. If we observe high levels of cooperation in years following summit meetings, we do not know without further study whether the summits and subsequent cooperation are systematically related to one another. With a small number of observations, it could be that the association between summits and cooperation reflects randomness due to fundamental uncertainty (good or bad luck under Perspective 1) or to as yet unidentified explanatory variables (under Perspective 2). Examples of such unidentified explanatory variables include weather fluctuations leading to crop failures in the Soviet Union, shifts in the military balance, or leadership changes, all of which could account for changes in the extent of cooperation. If identified, these variables are alternative explanations—omitted variables that could be collected or examined

---

[13] In our language, as we will discuss in section 3.5 below, the issue is that of *endogeneity*. Anticipated cooperation could lead to the convening of summit meetings, in which case, instead of summit meetings explaining cooperation, anticipated cooperation would explain actual cooperation—hardly a startling finding if actors are rational!

to assess their influence on the summit outcome. If unidentified, these variables may be treated as nonsystematic events that could account for the observed high degree of superpower cooperation. To provide evidence against the possibility that random events (unidentified explanatory variables) account for the observed cooperation, we might look at many other years. Since random events and processes are by definition not persistent, they will be extremely unlikely to produce differential cooperation in years with and without superpower summits. Once again, we are led to the conclusion that only repeated tests in different contexts (years, in this case) enable us to decide whether to define a pattern as systematic or just due to the transient consequences of random processes.

Distinguishing systematic from nonsystematic processes is often difficult. From the perspective of social science, a flu epidemic that strikes working-class voters more heavily than middle-class ones is an unpredictable (nonsystematic) event that in one hypothetical replication of the 1979 election would decrease the Labor vote. But a persistent pattern of class differences in the incidence of a disabling illness would be a systematic effect lowering the average level of Labor voting across many replications.

The victory of one candidate over another in a U.S. election on the basis of the victor's personality or an accidental slip of the tongue during a televised debate might be a random factor that could have affected the likelihood of cooperation between the USSR and the United States during the Cold War. But if the most effective campaign appeal to voters had been the promise of reduced tensions with the USSR, consistent victories of conciliatory candidates would have constituted a systematic factor explaining the likelihood of cooperation.

Systematic factors are persistent and have consistent consequences when the factors take a particular value. Nonsystematic factors are transitory: we cannot predict their impact. But this does not mean that systematic factors represent constants. Campaign appeals may be a systematic factor in explaining voting behavior, but that fact does not mean that campaign appeals themselves do not change. It is the *effect* of campaign appeals on an election outcome that is constant—or, if it is variable, it is changing in a predictable way. When Soviet-American relations were good, promises of conciliatory policies may have won votes in U.S. elections; when relations were bad, the reverse may have been true. Similarly, the weather can be a random factor (if intermittent and unpredictable shocks have unpredictable consequences) or a systematic feature (if bad weather always leads to fewer votes for candidates favoring conciliatory policies).

In short, summarizing historical detail is an important intermediate step in the process of using our data, but we must also make descriptive inferences distinguishing between random and systematic phenomena. Knowing what happened on a given occasion is not sufficient by itself. *If we make no effort to extract the systematic features of a subject, the lessons of history will be lost, and we will learn nothing about what aspects of our subject are likely to persist or to be relevant to future events or studies.*

2.7 CRITERIA FOR JUDGING DESCRIPTIVE INFERENCES

In this final section, we introduce three explicit criteria that are commonly used in statistics for judging methods of making inferences—unbiasedness, efficiency, and consistency. Each relies on the random-variable framework introduced in section 2.6 but has direct and powerful implications for evaluating and improving qualitative research. To clarify these concepts, we provide only the simplest possible examples in this section, all from descriptive inference. A simple version of inference involves estimating parameters, including the expected value or variance of a random variable (μ or σ^2) for a descriptive inference. We also use these same criteria for judging causal inferences in the next chapter (see section 3.4). We save for later chapters specific advice about doing qualitative research that is implied by these criteria and focus on the concepts alone for the remainder of this section.

2.7.1 Unbiased Inferences

If we apply a method of inference again and again, we will get estimates that are sometimes too large and sometimes too small. Across a large number of applications, do we get the right answer *on average*? If yes, then this method, or "estimator," is said to be unbiased. This property of an estimator says nothing about how far removed from the average any one application of the method might be, but being correct on average is desirable.

Unbiased estimates occur when the variation from one replication of a measure to the next is nonsystematic and moves the estimate sometimes one way, sometimes the other. Bias occurs when there is a systematic error in the measure that shifts the estimate more in one direction than another over a set of replications. If in our study of conflict in West Bank communities, leaders had created conflict in order to influence the study's results (perhaps to further their political goals), then the level of conflict we observe in every community would be biased toward greater conflict, on average. If the replications of our hypothetical 1979 elections were all done on a Sunday (when they could have been held on any day), there would be a bias in the estimates if that fact systematically helped one side and not the other (if, for instance, Conservatives were more reluctant to vote on Sunday for religious reasons). Or our replicated estimates might be based on reports from corrupt vote counters who favor one party over the other. If, however, the replicated elections were held on various days chosen in a manner unrelated to the variable we are interested in, any error in measurement would not produce biased results even though one day or another might favor one party. For example, if there were miscounts due to random sloppiness on the part of vote counters, the set of estimates would be unbiased.

If the British elections were always held by law on Sundays or if a vote-counting method that favored one party over another were built into the election system (through the use of a particular voting scheme or, perhaps, even persistent corruption), we would want an estimator that varied based on the mean vote that could be expected under the circumstances that included these systematic features. Thus, bias depends on the theory that is being investigated and does *not* just exist in the data alone. It makes little sense to say that a particular data set is biased, even though it may be filled with many individual errors.

In this example, we might wish to distinguish our definition of "statistical bias" in an *estimator* from "substantive bias" in an *electoral system*. An example of the latter are polling hours that make it harder for working people to vote—a not uncommon substantive bias of various electoral systems. As researchers, we may wish to estimate the mean vote of the actual electoral system (the one with the substantive bias), but we might also wish to estimate the mean of a hypothetical electoral system that doesn't have a substantive bias due to the hours the polls are open. This would enable us to estimate the amount of substantive bias in the system. Whichever mean we are estimating, we wish to have a statistically unbiased estimator.

Social science data are susceptible to one major source of bias of which we should be wary: people who provide the raw information that we use for descriptive inferences often have reasons for providing estimates that are systematically too high or low. Government officials may want to overestimate the effects of a new program in order to shore up their claims for more funding or underestimate the unemployment rate to demonstrate that they are doing a good job. We may need to dig deeply to find estimates that are less biased. A telling example is in Myron Weiner's qualitative study of education and child labor in India (1991). In trying to explain the low level of commitment to compulsory education in India compared to that in other countries, he had to first determine if the level of commitment was indeed low. In one state in India, he found official statistics that indicated that ninety-eight percent of school age children attend school. However, a closer look revealed that attendance was measured once, when children first entered school. They were then listed as attending for seven years, even if their only attendance was for one day! Closer scrutiny showed the actual attendance figure to be much lower.

A Formal Example of Unbiasedness. Suppose, for example, we wish to estimate μ in equation (2.2) and decide to use the average as an estimator, $\bar{y} = \frac{1}{n}\sum_{i=1}^{n} y_i$. In a single set of data, $\bar{y}$ is the proportion of Labor voters averaged over all $n = 650$ constituencies (or the average level of conflict across West Bank communities). But considered across an infinite number of hypothetical replications of the election in each constituency, the sample mean becomes a function of 650 random variables, $\bar{Y} = \frac{1}{n}\sum_{i=1}^{n} Y_i$. Thus, the sample mean becomes a random variable, too. For some hypothetical replications, $\bar{Y}$ will produce election returns that are close to μ and other times they will be farther away. The question is whether $\bar{Y}$ will be right, that is, equal to μ, on average across these hypothetical replications. To determine the answer, we use the expected value operation again, which allows us to determine the average across the infinite number of hypothetical elections. The rules of expectations enable us to make the following calculations:

$$E(\bar{Y}) = E\left(\frac{1}{n}\sum_{i=1}^{n} Y_i\right) \qquad (2.4)$$

$$= \frac{1}{n}\sum_{i=1}^{n} E(Y_i)$$

$$= \frac{1}{n} n\mu$$

$$= \mu$$

Thus, $\bar{Y}$ is an unbiased estimator of μ. (This is a slightly less formal example than appears in formal statistics texts, but the key features are the same.)

2.7.2 Efficiency

We usually do not have an opportunity to apply our estimator to a large number of essentially identical applications. Indeed, except for some clever experiments, we only apply it once. In this case, unbiasedness is of interest, but we would like more confidence that the *one* estimate we get is close to the right one. Efficiency provides a way of distinguishing among unbiased estimators. Indeed, the efficiency criterion can also help distinguish among alternative estimators with a small amount of bias. (An estimator with a large bias should generally be ruled out even without evaluating its efficiency.)

Efficiency is a relative concept that is measured by calculating the variance of the estimator across hypothetical replications. For unbiased estimators, the smaller the variance, the more efficient (the better) the estimator. A small variance is better because our one estimate will probably be closer to the true parameter value. We are not interested in efficiency for an estimator with a large bias because low variance in this situation will make it unlikely that the estimate will be near the true value (because most of the estimates would be closely clustered around the wrong value). As we describe below, we are interested in efficiency in the case of a small amount of bias, and we may often be willing to incur a small amount of bias in exchange for a large gain in efficiency.

Suppose again we are interested in estimating the average level of conflict between Palestinians and Israelis in the West Bank and are evaluating two methods: a single observation of one community, chosen to be typical, and similar observations of, for example, twenty-five communities. It should be obvious that twenty-five observations are better than a single observation—so long as the same effort goes into collecting each of the twenty-five as into the single observation. We will demonstrate here precisely why this is the case. This result explains why we should observe as many implications of our theory as possible, but it also demonstrates the more general concept of statistical efficiency, which is also relevant whenever we are deciding the best way to evaluate different ways of combining gathered observations into an inference.

Efficiency enables us to compare the single-observation case study ($n = 1$) estimator of μ with the large-n estimator ($n = 25$), that is the average level of conflict found from twenty-five separate week-long studies in different communities on the West Bank. If applied appropriately, both estimators are unbiased. If the same model applies, the single-observation estimator has a variance of $V(Y_{\text{typical}}) = \sigma^2$. That is, we would have chosen what we thought was a "typical" district, which would, however, be affected by random variables. The variance of the large-n estimator is $V(\bar{Y}) = \sigma^2/25$, that is, the variance of the sample mean. Thus, the single-observation estimator is twenty-five times more variable (i.e., less efficient) than the estimate when $n = 25$. Hence, we have the obvious result that more observations are better.

More interesting are the conditions under which a more detailed study of our one community would yield as good or better results as our large-n study. That is, although we should always prefer studies with more observations (given the resources necessary to collect them), there are situations where a single case study (as always, containing many observations) is better than a study based on more observations, each one of which is not as detailed or certain.

All conditions being equal, our analysis shows that the more observations, the better, because variability (and thus inefficiency) drops. In fact, the property of *consistency* is such that as the number of observations gets very large, the variability decreases to zero, and the estimate equals the parameter we are trying to estimate.[14]

But often, not all conditions are equal. Suppose, for example, that any single measurement of the phenomenon we are studying is subject to factors that make the measure likely to be far from the true value (i.e., the estimator has high variance). And suppose that we have some understanding—from other studies, perhaps—of what these factors might be. Suppose further that our ability to observe and correct for these factors decreases substantially with the increase in the number of communities studied (if, for no other reason, than that we lack the time and knowledge to make corrections for such factors across a large number of observations). We are then faced with a trade-off between a case study that has additional observations internal to the case and twenty-five cases in which each contains only one observation.

If our single case study is composed of only one observation, then it is obviously inferior to our 25-observation study. But case-study researchers have significant advantages, which are easier to understand if formalized. For example, we could first select our community very carefully in order to make sure that it is especially representative of the rest of the country or that we understand the relationship of this community to the others. We might ask a few residents or look at newspaper reports to see whether it was an average community or whether

---

[14] Note that an estimator can be unbiased but inconsistent. For example, Y_1 is an unbiased estimator of μ, but it is inconsistent because as the number of units increase, this estimator does not improve (or indeed change at all). An estimator can also be consistent but biased. For example, $\bar{Y} - 5/n$ is biased, but it is consistent because $5/n$ becomes zero as n approaches infinity.

some nonsystematic factor had caused the observation to be atypical, and then we might adjust the observed level of conflict to arrive at an estimate of the average level of West Bank conflict, μ. This would be the most difficult part of the case-study estimator, and we would need to be very careful that bias does not creep in. Once we are reasonably confident that bias is minimized, we could focus on increasing efficiency. To do this, we might spend many weeks in the community conducting numerous separate studies. We could interview community leaders, ordinary citizens, and school teachers. We could talk to children, read the newspapers, follow a family in the course of its everyday life, and use numerous other information-gathering techniques. Following these procedures, we could collect far more than twenty-five observations within this one community and generate a case study that is also not biased and *more* efficient than the twenty-five community study.

Consider another example. Suppose we are conducting a study of the international drug problem and want a measure of the percentage of agricultural land on which cocaine is being grown in a given region of the world. Suppose further that there is a choice of two methods: a case study of one country or a large-scale, statistical study of all the countries of the region. It would seem better to study the whole region. But let us say that to carry out such a study it is necessary (for practical reasons) to use data supplied to a UN agency from the region's governments. These numbers are known to have little relationship to actual patterns of cropping since they were prepared in the Foreign Office and based on considerations of public relations. Suppose, further, that we could, by visiting and closely observing one country, make the corrections to the government estimates that would bring that particular estimate much closer to a true figure. Which method would we choose? Perhaps we would decide to study only one country, or perhaps two or three. Or we might study one country intensively and use our results to reinterpret, and thereby improve, the government-supplied data from the other countries. Our choice should be guided by which data best answer our questions.

To take still another example, suppose we are studying the European Community and want to estimate the expected degree of regulation of an industry throughout the entire Community that will result from actions of the Commission and the Council of Ministers. We could gather data on a large number of rules formally adopted for the industrial sector in question, code these rules in terms of their stringency, and then estimate the average stringency of a rule. If we gather data on 100 rules with similar a priori stringency, the variance of our measure will be the variance of any given rule divided by 100 ($\sigma^2/100$), or less if the rules are related. Undoubtedly, this will be a better measure than using data on one rule as the estimator for regulatory stringency for the industry as a whole.

However, this procedure requires us to accept the formal rule as equivalent to the real regulatory activity in the sector under scrutiny. Further investigation of rule application, however, might reveal a large variation in the extent to which nominal rules are actually enforced. Hence, measures of formal rules might be systematically biased—for instance, in favor of overstating regulatory stringency. In such a case, we would face the bias-efficiency trade-off once again, and it might make sense to carry out three or four intensive case studies of rule implementation to investigate the relationship between formal rules and actual regulatory activity. One possibility would be to substitute an estimator based on these three or four cases—less biased and also less efficient—for the estimator based on 100 cases. However, it might be more creative, if feasible, to use the intensive case-study work for the three or four cases to correct the bias of our 100-case indicator, and then to use a corrected version of the 100-case indicator as our estimator. In this procedure, we would be combining the insights of our intensive case studies with large-n techniques, a practice that we think should be followed much more frequently than is the case in contemporary social science.

The argument for case studies made by those who know a particular part of the world well is often just the one implicit in the previous example. Large-scale studies may depend upon numbers that are not well understood by the naive researcher working on a data base (who may be unaware of the way in which election statistics are gathered in a particular locale and assumes, incorrectly, that they have some real relationship to the votes as cast). The researcher working closely with the materials and understanding their origin may be able to make the necessary corrections. In subsequent sections we will try to explicate how such choices might be made more systematically.

Our formal analysis of this problem in the box below shows precisely how to decide what the results of the trade-off are in the example of British electoral constituencies. The decision in any particular example will always be better when using logic like that shown in the formal analysis below. However, deciding this issue will almost always also require qualitative judgements, too.

Finally, it is worth thinking more specifically about the trade-offs that sometimes exist between bias and efficiency. The sample mean of the first two observations in any larger set of unbiased observations is

Formal Efficiency Comparisons. The variance of the sample mean $\bar{Y}$ is denoted as $V(\bar{Y})$, and the rules for calculating variances of random variables in the simple case of random sampling permit the following:

$$V(\bar{Y}) = V\left(\frac{1}{n}\sum_{i=1}^{n} Y_i\right)$$

$$= \frac{1}{n^2}\sum_{i=1}^{n} V(Y_i)$$

Furthermore, if we assume that the variance across hypothetical replication of each district election is the same as every other district and is denoted by σ^2, then the variance of the sample mean is

$$V(\bar{Y}) = \frac{1}{n^2}\sum_{i=1}^{n} V(Y_i) \tag{2.5}$$

$$= \frac{1}{n^2}\sum_{i=1}^{n} \sigma^2$$

$$= \frac{1}{n^2} n\sigma^2$$

$$= \sigma^2/n$$

In the example above, $n = 650$, so the large-n estimator has variance $\sigma^2/650$ and the case-study estimator has variance σ^2. Unless we can use qualitative, random-error corrections to reduce the variance of the case-study estimator by a factor of at least 650, the statistical estimate is to be preferred on the grounds of efficiency.

---

also unbiased, just as is the sample mean of all the observations. However, using only two observations discards substantial information; this does not change unbiasedness, but it does substantially reduce efficiency. If we did not also use the efficiency criterion, we would have no formal criteria for choosing one estimator over the other.

Suppose we are interested in whether the Democrats would win the next presidential election, and we ask twenty randomly selected American adults which party they plan to vote for. (In our simple version of random selection, we choose survey respondents from all adult Americans, each of which has an equal probability of selection.) Suppose that someone else also did a similar study with 1,000 citizens. Should we include these additional observations with ours to create a single estimate based on 1,020 respondents? If the new observations were randomly selected, just as the first twenty, it should be an easy decision to include the additional data with ours: with the new observations, the estimator is still unbiased and now much more efficient.

However, suppose that only 990 of the 1,000 new observations were randomly drawn from the U.S. population and the other ten were Democratic members of Congress who were inadvertently included in the data after the random sample had been drawn. Suppose further that we found out that these additional observations were included in our data but did not know which ones they were and thus could not remove them. We now know a priori that an estimator based on all 1,020 respondents would produce a slight overestimate of the likelihood that a Democrat would win the nationwide vote. Thus, including these 1,000 additional observations would slightly bias the overall estimate, but it would also substantially improve its efficiency. Whether we should include the observations therefore depends on whether the increase in bias is outweighed by the increase in statistical efficiency. Intuitively, it seems clear that the estimator based on the 1,020 observations will produce estimates fairly close to the right answer much more frequently than the estimator based on only twenty observations. The bias introduced would be small enough, so we would prefer the larger sample estimator even though in practice we would probably apply both. (In addition, we know the direction of the bias in this case and could even partially correct for it.)

If adequate quantitative data are available and we are able to formalize such problems as these, we can usually make a clear decision. However, even if the qualitative nature of the research makes evaluating this trade-off difficult or impossible, understanding it should help us make more reliable inferences.

Formal Comparisons of Bias and Efficiency. Consider two estimators, one a large-n study by someone with a preconception, who is therefore slightly biased, and the other a very small-n study that we believe is unbiased but relatively less efficient and is done by an impartial investigator. As a formal model of this example, suppose we wish to estimate μ and the large-n study produces estimator d:

$$d = \left(\frac{1}{n} \sum_{i=1}^{n} Y_i - 0.01 \right)$$

We model the small-n study with a different estimator of μ, c:

$$c = \left(\frac{Y_1 + Y_2}{2} \right)$$

where districts 1 and 2 are average constituencies, so that $E(Y_1) = \mu$ and $E(Y_2) = \mu$.

Which estimator should we prefer? Our first answer is that we would use neither and instead would prefer the sample mean $\bar{y}$; that is, a large-n study by an impartial investigator. However, the obvious or best estimator is not always applicable. To answer this question, we turn to an evaluation of bias and efficiency.

First, we will assess bias. We can show that the first estimator d is slightly biased according to the usual calculation:

$$E(d) = E\left(\frac{1}{n} \sum_{i=1}^{n} Y_i - 0.01 \right)$$

$$= E\left(\frac{1}{n} \sum_{i=1}^{n} Y_i \right) - E(0.01)$$

$$= \mu - 0.01$$

We can also show that the second estimator c is unbiased by a similar calculation:

$$E(c) = E\left(\frac{Y_1 + Y_2}{2} \right)$$

$$= \frac{E(Y_1) + E(Y_2)}{2}$$

$$= \frac{\mu + \mu}{2}$$

$$= \mu$$

By these calculations alone, we would choose estimator c, the result of the efforts of our impartial investigator's small-n study, since it is unbiased. On average, across an infinite number of hypothetical replications, for the investigator with a preconception, d would give the wrong answer, albeit only slightly so. Estimator c would give the right answer on average.

The efficiency criterion tells a different story. To begin, we calculate the variance of each estimator:

$$V(d) = V\left(\frac{1}{n}\sum_{i=1}^{n}Y_i - 0.01\right)$$

$$= V\left(\frac{1}{n}\sum_{i=1}^{n}Y_i\right) - V(0.01)$$

$$= \sigma^2/n$$

$$= \sigma^2/650$$

This variance is the same as the variance of the sample mean because 0.01 does not change (has zero variance) across samples. Similarly, we calculate the variance of c as follows:[15]

$$V(c) = V\left(\frac{Y_1 + Y_2}{2}\right)$$

$$= \frac{1}{4}[V(Y_1) + V(Y_2)]$$

$$= \frac{1}{4}2\sigma^2$$

$$= \sigma^2/2$$

Thus, c is considerably less efficient than d because $V(c) = \sigma^2/2$ is 325 times larger than $V(d) = \sigma^2/650$. This should be intuitively clear as well, since c discards most of the information in the data set.

Which should we choose? Estimator d is biased but more efficient

---

[15] We assume the absence of spatial correlation across districts in the second line of the preceding and following calculations.

than c, whereas c is unbiased but less efficient. In this particular case, we would probably prefer estimator d. We would thus be willing to sacrifice unbiasedness, since the sacrifice is fairly small (0.01), in order to obtain a significantly more efficient estimator. At some point, however, more efficiency will not compensate for a little bias since we end up guaranteeing that estimates will be farther from the truth. The formal way to evaluate the bias-efficiency trade-off is to calculate the *mean square error* (MSE), which is a combination of bias and efficiency. If g is an estimator for some parameter γ (the Greek letter Gamma), MSE is defined as follows:

$$MSE(g) = V(g) + E(g - \gamma)^2 \tag{2.6}$$

$$= \text{variance} + \text{Squared bias}$$

Mean square error is thus the sum of the variance and the squared bias (see Johnston 1984:27–28). The idea is to choose the estimator with the minimum mean square error since it shows precisely how an estimator with some bias can be preferred if it has a smaller variance.

For our example, the two MSEs are as follows:

$$MSE(d) = \frac{\sigma^2}{650} + (0.01)^2 \tag{2.7}$$

$$= \frac{\sigma^2}{650} + 0.0001$$

and

$$MSE(c) = \frac{\sigma^2}{2} \tag{2.8}$$

Thus, for most values of σ^2, $MSE(d) < MSE(c)$ and we would prefer d as an estimator to c.

In theory, we should always prefer unbiased estimates that are as efficient (i.e., use as much information) as possible. However, in the real research situations we analyze in succeeding chapters, this trade-off between bias and efficiency is quite salient.

CHAPTER 3

Causality and Causal Inference

WE HAVE DISCUSSED two stages of social science research: summarizing historical detail (section 2.5) and making descriptive inferences by partitioning the world into systematic and nonsystematic components (section 2.6). Many students of social and political phenomena would stop at this point, eschewing causal statements and asking their selected and well-ordered facts to "speak for themselves."

Like historians, social scientists need to summarize historical detail and to make descriptive inferences. For some social scientific purposes, however, analysis is incomplete without causal inference. That is, just as causal inference is impossible without good descriptive inference, descriptive inference alone is often unsatisfying and incomplete. To say this, however, is not to claim that all social scientists must, in all of their work, seek to devise causal explanations of the phenomena they study. Sometimes causal inference is too difficult; in many other situations, descriptive inference is the ultimate goal of the research endeavor.

Of course, we should always be explicit in clarifying whether the goal of a research project is description or explanation. Many social scientists are uncomfortable with causal inference. They are so wary of the warning that "correlation is not causation" that they will not state causal hypotheses or draw causal inferences, referring to their research as "studying association and not causation." Others make apparent causal statements with ease, labeling unevaluated hypotheses or speculations as "explanations" on the basis of indeterminate research designs.[1] We believe that each of these positions evades the problem of causal inference.

---

[1] In view of some social scientists' preference for explanation over "mere description," it is not surprising that students of complicated events seek to dress their work in the trappings of explanatory jargon; otherwise, they fear being regarded as doing inferior work. At its core, real explanation is always based on causal inferences. We regard arguments in the literature about "noncausal explanation" as confusing terminology; in virtually all cases, these arguments are really about causal explanation or are internally inconsistent. If social scientists' failures to explain are not due to poor research or lack of imagination, but rather to the nature of the difficult but significant problems that they are examining, such feelings of inferiority are unjustified. Good description of important events is better than bad explanation of anything.

Avoiding causal language when causality is the real subject of investigation either renders the research irrelevant or permits it to remain undisciplined by the rules of scientific inference. Our uncertainty about causal inferences will never be eliminated. But this uncertainty should not suggest that we avoid attempts at causal inference. Rather we should draw causal inferences where they seem appropriate but also provide the reader with the best and most honest estimate of the uncertainty of that inference. It is appropriate to be bold in drawing causal inferences as long as we are cautious in detailing the uncertainty of the inference. It is important, further, that causal hypotheses be disciplined, approximating as closely as possible the rules of causal inference. Our purpose in much of chapters 4–6 is to explicate the circumstances under which causal inference is appropriate and to make it possible for qualitative researchers to increase the probability that their research will provide reliable evidence about their causal hypotheses.

In section 3.1 we provide a rigorous definition of causality appropriate for qualitative and quantitative research, then in section 3.2 we clarify several alternative notions of causality in the literature and demonstrate that they do not conflict with our more fundamental definition. In section 3.3 we discuss the precise assumptions about the world and the hypotheses required to make reliable causal inferences. We then consider in section 3.4 how to apply to causal inference the criteria we developed for judging descriptive inference. In section 3.5 we conclude this chapter with more general advice on how to construct causal explanations, theories, and hypotheses.

3.1 DEFINING CAUSALITY

In this section, we define causality as a *theoretical* concept independent of the data used to learn about it. Subsequently, we consider causal *inference* from our data. (For discussions of specific problems of causal inference, see chapters 4–6.) In section 3.1.1 we give our definition of causality in full detail, along with a simple quantitative example, and in section 3.1.2 we revisit our definition along with a more sophisticated qualitative example.

3.1.1 The Definition and a Quantitative Example

Our theoretical definition of causality applies most simply and clearly to a single unit.[2] As defined in section 2.4, a unit is one of the many elements to be observed in a study, such as a person, country, year, or

---

[2] Our point of departure in this section is Holland's article (1986) on causality and

political organization. For precision and clarity, we have chosen a single running example from quantitative research: the causal effect of incumbency status for a Democratic candidate for the U.S. House of Representatives on the proportion of votes this candidate receives. (Using only a Democratic candidate simplifies the example.) Let the dependent variable be the Democratic proportion of the two-party vote for the House. The key causal explanatory variable is then dichotomous, either the Democrat is an incumbent or not. (For simplicity throughout this section, we only consider districts where the Republican candidate lost the last election.)

Causal language can be confusing and our choice here is hardly unique. The "dependent variable" is sometimes called the "outcome variable." "Explanatory variables" are often referred to as "independent variables." We divide the explanatory variables into the "key causal variable" (also called the "cause" or the "treatment variable") and the "control variables." Finally, the key causal variable always takes on two or more values, which are often denoted by "treatment group" and "control group."

Now consider only the Fourth Congressional District in New York, and imagine an election in 1998 with a Democratic incumbent and one Republican (nonincumbent) challenger. Suppose the Democratic candidate received y_4^I fraction of the vote in this election (the subscript 4 denotes the Fourth District in New York and the superscript I refers to the fact that the Democrat is an Incumbent) y_4^I is then a value of the dependent variable. To *define* the causal effect (a *theoretical* quantity), imagine that we go back in time to the start of the election campaign and everything remains the same, except that the Democratic incumbent decides not to run for re-election and the Democratic Party nominates another candidate (presumably the winner of the primary election). We denote the fraction of the vote that the Democratic (nonincumbent) candidate would receive by y_4^N (where N denotes a Democratic candidate who is a Non-incumbent).[3]

This *counterfactual* condition is the essence behind this definition of causality, and the difference between the actual vote (y_4^I) and the likely

---

what he calls "Rubin's Model." Holland bases his ideas on the work of numerous scholars. Donald Rubin's (1974, 1978) work on the subject was most immediately relevant, but he also cites Aristotle, Locke, Hume, Mill, Suppes, Granger, Fisher, Neyman, and others. We extend Holland's definition of a causal effect by using some ideas expressed clearly by Suppes (1970) and others concerning "probabilistic causality." We found this extension necessary since no existing approach alone is capable of defining causality with respect to a single unit *and* still allowing one to partition causal effects into systematic and nonsystematic components.

[3] See Gelman and King (1990) for details of this example. More generally, I and N can stand for the "treatment" and "control" group or for any two treatments experimentally

vote in this counterfactual situation (y_4^N) is the causal effect, a concept we define more precisely below. We must be very careful in defining counterfactuals; although they are obviously counter to the facts, they must be reasonable and it should be possible for the counterfactual event to have occurred under precisely stated circumstances. A key part of defining the appropriate counterfactual condition is clarifying precisely what we are holding constant while we are changing the value of the treatment variable. In the present example, the key causal (or treatment) variable is incumbency status, and it changes from "incumbent" to "non-incumbent." During this hypothetical change, we hold everything constant up to the moment of the Democratic Party's nomination decision—the relative strength of the Democrats and Republicans in past elections in this district, the nature of the nomination process, the characteristics of the congressional district, and the economic and political climate at the time, etc. We do *not* control for qualities of the candidates, such as name recognition, visibility, and knowledge of the workings of Congress, or anything else that follows the party nomination. The reason is that these are partly *consequences* of our treatment variable, incumbency. That is, the advantages of incumbency include name recognition, visibility, and so forth. If we did hold these constant, we would be controlling for and hence disregarding some of the most important effects of incumbency and as a result, would misinterpret its overall effect on the vote total. In fact, controlling for enough of the consequences of incumbency could make one incorrectly believe that incumbency had no effect at all.[4]

More formally, the causal effect of incumbency in the Fourth District in New York—the proportion of the vote received by the Democratic Party candidate that is attributable to incumbency status—would be the difference between these two vote fractions: ($y_4^I - y_4^N$). For reasons that will become clear shortly, we refer to this difference as the *realized*

---

administered in fact or in theory. Of course, the decision to call one value of an explanatory variable a treatment and the other a control is entirely arbitrary, if this language is used at all.

[4] Jon Elster (1983:34–36) has claimed "the meaning of causality can not be rendered by counterfactual statements" in many situations, such as those in which a third factor accounts for both the apparent explanatory and dependent variables. In our language, Elster is simply pointing to common problems of *inferences*, which are always uncertain to some extent. However, these difficulties of inference do not invalidate a *definition* of causality in terms of counterfactuals. Despite his objections, Elster acknowledges that counterfactual statements "have an important role in causal analysis" (Elster 1983:36). Hence Elster's argument is more cogent, we think, as a set of valuable warnings against careless use of counterfactuals than as a critique of their fundamental definitional importance in causal reasoning.

causal effect and write it in more general notation for unit *i* instead of only district 4:[5]

$$(\text{Realized Causal Effect for unit } i) = y_i^I - y_i^N \tag{3.1}$$

Of course, this effect is defined only in theory since in any one real election we might observe *either* y_4^I *or* y_4^N or neither, but never both. Thus, this simple definition of causality demonstrates that we can never hope to know a causal effect for certain. Holland (1986) refers to this problem as *the fundamental problem of causal inference*, and it is indeed a *fundamental* problem since no matter how perfect the research design, no matter how much data we collect, no matter how perceptive the observers, no matter how diligent the research assistants, and no matter how much experimental control we have, we will never know a causal inference for certain. Indeed, most of the empirical issues of research designs that we discuss in this book involve this fundamental problem, and most of our suggestions constitute partial attempts to avoid it.

Our working definition of causality differs from Holland's, since in section 2.6 we have argued that social science always needs to partition the world into systematic and nonsystematic components, and Holland's definition does not make this distinction clearly.[6] To see the importance of this partitioning, think about what would happen if we could rerun the 1998 election campaign in the Fourth District in New York, with a Democratic incumbent and a Republican challenger. A slightly different total vote would result, due to nonsystematic features of election campaigns—aspects of politics that do not persist from one campaign to the next, even if the campaigns begin on identical footing. Some of these nonsystematic features might include a verbal gaffe, a surprisingly popular speech or position on an issue, an unexpectedly bad performance in a debate, bad weather during one candidate's rally or on election day, or the results of some investigative journalism. We can therefore imagine a variable that would express the values of the Democratic vote across hypothetical replications of this same election.

[5] We can specialize for district 4 by substituting "4" for "*i*" in the following equation.

[6] The reason for this is probably that Holland is a statistician who comes very close to an extreme version of "Perspective 2" random variation, which is described in section 2.6. In his description of the "statistical solution" to the problem of causal inference, he most closely approximates our definition of a causal effect, but this definition is mostly about using different units to solve the Fundamental Problem instead of retaining the definition of causality in just one. In particular, his expected value operator averages over units, whereas ours (described below) averages over hypothetical replications of the same experiment for just a single unit (see Holland 1986:947).

As noted above (see section 2.6), this variable is called a "random variable" since it has nonsystematic features: it is affected by explanatory variables not encompassed in our theoretical analysis or contains fundamentally unexplainable variability.[7] We define the random variable representing the proportion of votes received by the incumbent Democratic candidate as Y_4^I (note the capital Y) and the proportion of votes that would be received in hypothetical replications by a Democratic nonincumbent as Y_4^N.

We now define the *random causal effect* for district 4 as the difference between these two random variables. Since we wish to retain some generality, we again switch notation from district 4 to unit i:

$$\text{(Random Causal Effect for unit } i) = (Y_i^I - Y_i^N) \tag{3.2}$$

(Just as in the definition of a random variable, a random causal effect is a causal effect that varies over hypothetical replications of the same experiment but also represents many interesting systematic features of elections.) *If* we could observe two separate vote proportions in district 4 at the same time, one from an election with and one without a Democratic incumbent running, then we could directly observe the realized causal effect in equation (3.1). Of course, because of the Fundamental Problem of Causal Inference, we cannot observe the realized causal effect. Thus, the realized causal effect in equation 3.1 is a single *unobserved* realization of the random causal effect in equation 3.2. In other words, across many hypothetical replications of the same election in district 4 with a Democratic incumbent, and across many hypothetical replications of the same election but with a Democratic nonincumbent, the (unobserved) realized causal effect becomes a random causal effect.

Describing causality as one of the systematic features of random variables may seem unduly complicated. But it has two virtues. First, it makes our definition of causality directly analogous to those systematic features (such as a mean or variance) of a phenomenon that serve

---

[7] As we explained in more detail in section 2.2, this phrasing can be confusing. A "random variable" contains some systematic component and thus is not always entirely unpredictable. Unfortunately, this language has a specific meaning in statistics and the concepts underlying it are important. The original reason for the terminology is that randomness does not mean "anything goes" or "anything could happen." Instead, it refers to one of many possible very well-specified probabilistic processes. For example, the random process governing which side of a coin lands upward when flipped in the air is a very different random process than the one governing the growth of the European Economic Community's bureaucracy or the uncertain political consequence of a change in Italy's electoral system. The key to our representation is that each of these "random" processes have systematic and probabilistic components.

as objects of descriptive inference: means and variances are also systematic features of random variables (as in section 2.2). Secondly, it enables us to partition a causal inference problem into systematic and nonsystematic components. Although many systematic features of a random variable might be of interest, the most relevant for our running example is the *mean causal effect* for unit i. To explain what we mean by this, we return to our New York election example.

Recall that the random variable refers to the vote fraction received by the Democrat (incumbent or nonincumbent) across a large number of hypothetical replications of the same election. We define the expected value of this random variable—the vote fraction averaged across these replications—for the nonincumbent as

$$E(Y_4^N) = \mu_4^N$$

and for the incumbent as

$$E(Y_4^I) = \mu_4^I.$$

Then, the mean causal effect of incumbency in unit i is a systematic feature of the random causal effect and is defined as the difference between these two expected values (again generalized to unit i instead of to district 4):

$$\text{Mean Causal Effect for unit } i \equiv \beta \qquad (3.3)$$

$$= E(\text{Random Causal Effect for unit } i)$$

$$= E(Y_i^I - Y_i^N)$$

$$= E(Y_i^I) - E(Y_i^N)$$

$$= \mu_i^I - \mu_i^N$$

where in the first line of this equation, β (beta) refers to this mean causal effect. In the second line, we indicate that the mean causal effect for unit i is just the mean (expected value) of the random causal effect, and in the third and fourth lines we show how to calculate the mean. The last line is another way of writing the difference in the means of the two sets of hypothetical elections. (The average of the difference between two random variables equals the difference of the averages.) To summarize in words: *the causal effect is the difference between the systematic component of observations made when the explanatory variable takes one value and the systematic component of comparable observations when the explanatory variable takes on another value.*

The last line of equation 3.3 is similar to equation 3.1, and as such, the Fundamental Problem of Causal Inference still exists in this formulation. Indeed, the problem expressed this way is even more formidable because even if we could get around the Fundamental Problem for a realized causal effect, we would still have all the usual problems of inference, including the problem of separating out systematic and nonsystematic components of the random causal effect. From here on, we use Holland's phrase, the Fundamental Problem of Causal Inference, to refer to the problem that he identified *as well as* to these standard problems of inference, which we have added to his formulation. In the box on page 95, we provide a more general notation for causal effects, which will prove useful throughout the rest of this book.

Many other systematic features of these random causal effects might be of interest in various circumstances. For example, we might wish to know the variance in the possible (realized) causal effects of incumbency status on Democratic vote in unit i, just as with the variance in the vote itself that we described in equation 2.3 in section 2.6. To calculate the variance of the causal effect, we apply the variance operation

$$\text{(variance of the causal effect in unit } i) = V(Y_i^I - Y_i^N)$$

in which we avoid introducing a new symbol for the result of the variance calculation, $V(Y_i^I - Y_i^N)$. Certainly new incumbents would wish to know the variation in the causal effect of incumbency so they can judge how closely their experience will be to that of previous incumbents and how much to rely on their estimated mean causal effect of incumbency from previous elections. It is especially important to understand that this variance in the causal effect is a fundamental part of the world and is not uncertainty due to estimation.

3.1.2 A Qualitative Example

We developed our precise definition of causality in section 3.1. Since some of the concepts in that section are subtle and quite sophisticated, we illustrated our points with a very simple running example from quantitative research. This example helped us communicate the concepts we wished to stress without also having to attend to the contextual detail and cultural sensitivity that characterize good qualitative research. In this section, we proceed through our definition of causality again, but this time via a qualitative example.

Political scientists would learn a lot if they could rerun history with everything constant save for one investigator-controlled explanatory variable. For example, one of the major questions that faces those involved with politics and government has to do with the consequences of a particular law or regulation. Congress passes a tax bill that is intended to have a particular consequence—lead to particular investments, increase revenue by a certain amount, and change consumption patterns. Does it have this effect? We can observe what happens after the tax is passed to see if the intended consequences appear; but even if they do, it is never certain that they *result* from the law. The change in investment policy might have happened anyway. If we could rerun history with and without the new regulation, then we would have much more leverage in estimating the causal effect of this law. Of course, we cannot do this. But the logic will help us design research to give us an approximate answer to our question.

Consider now the following extended example from comparative politics. In the wake of the collapse of the Soviet system, numerous governments in the ex-Soviet republics and in Eastern Europe have instituted new governmental forms. They are engaged—as they themselves realize—in a great political experiment: they are introducing new constitutions, constitutions that they hope will have the intended effect of creating stable democratic systems. One of the constitutional choices is between parliamentary and presidential forms of government. Which system is more likely to lead to a stable democracy is the subject of considerable debate among scholars in the field (Linz 1993; Horowitz 1993; Lijphart 1993). The debate is complex, not the least because of the numerous types of parliamentary and presidential systems and the variety of the other constitutional provisions that might accompany and interact with this choice (such as the nature of the electoral system). It is not our purpose to provide a thorough analysis of these choices but rather a greatly simplified version of the choice in order to define a causal effect in the context of this qualitative example. In so doing, we highlight the distinction between systematic and non-systematic features of a causal effect.

The debate about presidential versus parliamentary systems involves varied features of the two systems. We will focus on two: the extent to which each system represents the varied interests of the citizenry and encourages strong and decisive leadership. The argument is that parliamentary systems do a better job of representing the full range of societal groups and interests in the government since there are many legislative seats to be filled, and they can be filled by representatives elected from various groups. In contrast, the all-or-nothing character of presidential systems means that some groups will feel left out of the government, be disaffected, and cause greater instability. On the other hand, parliamentary systems—especially if they adequately represent the full range of social groups and interests—are likely to be deadlocked and ineffective in providing decisive government. These characteristics, too, can lead to disaffection and instability.[8]

The key purpose of this section is to formulate a precise definition of a causal effect. To do so, imagine that we could institute a parliamentary system and, periodically over the next decade or so, measure the degree of democratic stability (perhaps by actual survival or demise of democracy, attempted coups, or other indicators of instability), and in the same country and at the same time, institute a presidential system, also measuring its stability over the same period with the same measures. The *realized causal effect* would be the difference between the degree of stability observed under a presidential system and that under a parliamentary system. The impossibility of measuring this causal effect directly is another example of the fundamental problem of causal inference.

As part of this definition, we also need to distinguish between systematic and nonsystematic effects of the form of government. To do this, we imagine running this hypothetical experiment many times. We define the *mean causal effect* to be the average of the realized causal effects across replications of these experiments. Taking the average in this way causes the nonsystematic features of this problem to cancel out and leaves the mean causal effect to include only systematic features. Systematic features include indecisiveness in a parliamentary system or disaffection among minorities in a presidential one. Nonsystematic features might include the sudden illness of a president that throws the government into chaos. The latter event would not be a persistent feature of a presidential system; it would appear in one trial of the experiment but not in others.[9]

Another interesting feature of this example is the variance of the causal effect. Any country thinking of choosing one of these political systems would be interested in its mean causal effect on democratic stability; however, this one country gets only one chance—only one replication of this experiment. Given this situation, political leaders may be interested in more than the average causal effect. They may wish to understand what the maximum and minimum causal effects, or at least the *variance* of the causal effects, might be. For example, it may be that presidentialism reduces democratic stability on average

---

[8] These distinctions are themselves debated. Some argue that a presidential system can do a better representational job. And others argue that parliamentary systems can be more decisive.

[9] The distinction between a systematic and nonsystematic feature is by no means always clear-cut. The sudden illness of a president appears to be a nonsystematic feature of the presidential system. On the other hand, the general vulnerability of presidential systems to the vagaries of the health and personality of a single individual is a systematic effect that raises the likelihood that *some* nonsystematic feature will appear.

but that the variability of this effect is enormous—sometimes increasing stability a lot, sometimes decreasing it substantially. This variance translates into risk for a polity. In this circumstance, it may be that citizens and political leaders would prefer to choose an option that produces only slightly less stability on average but has a lower variance in causal effect and thus minimizes the chance of a disastrous outcome.

3.2 CLARIFYING ALTERNATIVE DEFINITIONS OF CAUSALITY

In section 3.1, we defined causality in terms of a causal effect: the mean causal effect is the difference between the systematic component of a dependent variable when the causal variable takes on two different values. In this section, we use our definition of causality to clarify several alternative proposals and apparently complicating ideas. We show that the important points made by other authors about "causal mechanisms" (section 3.2.1), "multiple" causality (section 3.2.2), and "symmetric" versus "asymmetric" causality (section 3.2.3) do not conflict with our more basic definition of causality.

3.2.1 "Causal Mechanisms"

Some scholars argue that the central idea of causality is that of a set of "causal mechanisms" posited to exist between cause and effect (see Little 1991:15). This view makes intuitive sense: any coherent account of causality needs to specify how the effects are exerted. For example, suppose a researcher is interested in the effect of a new bilateral tax treaty on reducing the United States's current account deficit with Japan. According to our definition of causality, the causal effect here is the reduction in the expected current account deficit with the tax treaty in effect as compared to the same situation (at the same time and for the same countries) with the exception that the treaty was not in effect. The causal mechanism operating here would include, in turn, the signing and ratification of the tax treaty, newspaper reports of the event, meetings of the relevant actors within major multinational companies, compensatory actions to reduce their total international tax burden (such as changing its transfer pricing rules or moving manufacturing plants between countries), further actions by other companies and workers to take advantage of the movements of capital and labor between countries, and so on, until we reach the final effect on the balance of payments between the United States and Japan.

From the standpoint of processes through which causality operates, an emphasis on causal mechanisms makes intuitive sense: any coherent account of causality needs to specify how its effects are exerted. Identifying causal mechanisms is a popular way of doing empirical analyses. It has been called, in slightly different forms, "process tracing" (which we discuss in section 6.3.3), "historical analysis," and "detailed case studies." Many of the details of well-done case studies involve identifying these causal mechanisms.

However, identifying the causal mechanisms requires causal inference, using the methods discussed below. That is, to demonstrate the causal status of each potential linkage in such a posited mechanism, the investigator would have to define and then estimate the causal effect underlying it. To portray an internally consistent causal mechanism requires using our more fundamental definition of causality offered in section 3.1 for each link in the chain of causal events.

Hence our definition of causality is logically prior to the identification of causal mechanisms. Furthermore, there always exists in the social sciences an infinity of causal steps between any two links in the chain of causal mechanisms. If we posit that an explanatory variable causes a dependent variable, a "causal mechanisms" approach would require us to identify a list of causal links between the two variables. This definition would also require us to identify a series of causal linkages, to define causality for each pair of consecutive variables in the sequence, and to identify the linkages between any two of these variables and the connections between each pair of variables. This approach quickly leads to infinite regress, and at no time does it alone give a precise definition of causality for any one cause and one effect.

In our example of the effect of a presidential versus parliamentary system on democratic stability (section 3.1.2), the hypothesized causal mechanisms include greater minority disaffection under a presidential regime and lesser governmental decisiveness under a parliamentary regime. These intervening effects—caused by the constitutional system and, in turn, affecting political stability—can be directly observed. We could monitor the attitudes or behaviors of minorities to see how they differ under the two experimental conditions or study the decisiveness of the governments under each system. Yet even if the causal effect of presidential versus parliamentary systems could operate in different ways, our definition of the causal effect would remain valid. We can define a causal effect without understanding all the causal mechanisms involved, but we cannot identify causal mechanisms without defining the concept of causal effect.

In our view, identifying the mechanisms by which a cause has its effect often builds support for a theory and is a very useful operational procedure. Identifying causal mechanisms can sometimes give us more leverage over a theory by making observations at a different level of analysis into implications of the theory. The concept can also create new causal hypotheses to investigate. However, we should not confuse a definition of causality with the nondefinitional, albeit often useful, operational procedure of identifying causal mechanisms.

3.2.2 "Multiple Causality"

Charles Ragin, in a recent work (1987:34–52), argues for a methodology with many explanatory variables and few observations in order that one can take into account what he calls "multiple causation." That is, "The phenomenon under investigation has alternative determinants—what Mill (1843) referred to as the problem of 'plurality of causes.'" This is the problem referred to as "equifinality" in general systems theory (George 1982:11). In situations of multiple causation, these authors argue that the same outcome can be caused by combinations of different independent variables.[10]

Under conditions in which different explanatory variables can account for the same outcome on a dependent variable, according to Ragin, some statistical methods will falsely reject the hypothesis that these variables have causal status. Ragin is correct that some statistical models (or relevant qualitative research designs) could fail to alert an investigator to the existence of "multiple causality," but appropriate statistical models can easily handle situations like these (some of which Ragin discusses).

Moreover, the fundamental features of "multiple causality" are compatible with our definition of causality. They are also no different for quantitative than qualitative research. The idea contains no new features or theoretical requirements. For example, consider the hypothesis that a person's level of income depends *both* on high educational attainment *and* highly educated parents. Having one but not both is insufficient. In this case, we need to compare categories of our causal variable: respondents who have high educational attainment and highly educated parents, the two groups who have one but not the other, and the group with neither. Thus, the concept of "multiple causation" puts greater demands on our data since we now have four cat-

---

[10] This idea is often explained in terms of no explanatory variable being either necessary or sufficient for a particular value of a dependent variable to occur. However, this is misleading terminology because the distinction between necessary and sufficient conditions largely disappears when we allow for the possibility that causes are probabilistic. As Little (1991:27) explains, "Consider the claim that poor communication among superpowers during crisis increases the likelihood of war. This is a probabilistic claim; it identifies a causal variable (poor communication) and asserts that this variable increases the probability of a given outcome (war). It cannot be translated into a claim about the necessary and sufficient conditions for war, however; it is irreducibly probabilistic."

egories of our causal variables, but it does not require a modification of our definition of causality. For our definition, we would need to measure the expected income for the same person, at the same time, experiencing each of the four conditions.

But what happens if different causal explanations generate the same values of the dependent variable? For example, suppose we consider whether or not one graduated from college as our (dichotomous) causal variable in a population of factory workers. In this situation, both groups could quite reasonably earn the same income (our dependent variable). One reason might be that this explanatory variable (college attendance) has no causal effect on income among factory workers, perhaps because a college education does not help one perform better. Alternatively, different explanations might lead to the same level of income for those educated and those not educated. College graduates might earn a particular level of income because of their education, whereas those who had no college education might earn the same level of income because of their four years of additional seniority on the job. In this situation wouldn't we be led to conclude that "college education" has no causal effect on income levels for those who will become factory workers?

Fortunately, our definition of causality requires that we more carefully specify the counterfactual condition. In the present example, the values of the key causal variable to be varied are (1) college education, as compared to (2) no college education but four additional years of job seniority. The dependent variable is starting annual income. Our causal effect is then defined as follows: we record the income of a person graduating from college who goes to work in a factory. Then, we go back in time four years, put this same person to work in the same factory instead of in college and, at the end of four years, measure his or her income "again." The expected difference between these two levels of income for this one individual is our definition of the mean causal effect. In the present situation, we have imagined that this causal effect is zero. But this does not mean that "college education has no effect on income," only that the average difference between treatment groups (1) and (2) is zero. In fact, there is no logically unique definition of "the causal effect of college education" since one cannot define a causal effect without at least two conditions. The conditions need not be the two listed here, but they must be very clearly identified.

An alternative pair of causal conditions is to compare a college graduate with someone without a college degree but with the same level of job seniority as the college graduate. In one sense, this is unrealistic, since the non-college graduate would have to do something for the four years while not attending college, but perhaps we would be willing to imagine that this person had a different, irrelevant job for those four years. Put differently, this alternative counterfactual is the effect of a college education compared to that of none, with job seniority held constant. Failure to hold seniority constant in the two causal conditions would cause any research design to yield estimates of our first counterfactual instead of this revised one. If the latter were the goal, but no controls were introduced, our empirical analysis would be flawed due to "omitted variable bias" (which we introduce in section 5.2).

Thus, the issues addressed under the label "multiple causation" do not confound our definition of causality although they may make greater demands in our subsequent analyses. The fact that some dependent variables, and perhaps all interesting social science-dependent variables, are influenced by many causal factors does not make our definition of causality problematic. The key to understanding these very common situations is to define the counterfactual conditions making up each causal effect very precisely. We demonstrate in chapter 5 that researchers need not identify "all" causal effects on a dependent variable to provide estimates of the one causal effect of interest (even if that were possible). A researcher can focus on only the one effect of interest, establish firm conclusions, and then move on to others that may be of interest (see sections 5.2 and 5.3).[11]

3.2.3 "Symmetric" and "Asymmetric" Causality

Stanley Lieberson (1985:63–64) distinguishes between what he refers to as "symmetrical" and "asymmetrical" forms of causality. He is interested in causal effects which differ when an explanatory variable is increased as compared to when it is decreased. In his words,

> In examining the causal influence of X_1 [an explanatory variable] on Y [a dependent variable], for example, one has also to consider whether shifts to a given value of X_1 from either direction have the same consequences for Y. . . . If the causal relationship between X_1 [an explanatory variable] and Y

[11] Our emphasis on distinguishing systematic from nonsystematic components of observations subject to causal inference reflects our general view that the world, at least as we know it, is probabilistic rather than deterministic. Hence, we also disagree with Ragin's premise (1987:15) that "explanations which result from applications of the comparative method are not conceived in probabilistic terms because every instance of a phenomenon is examined and accounted for if possible." Even if it were possible to collect a census of information on every instance of a phenomenon and every permutation and combination of values of the explanatory variables, the world still would have produced these data according to some probabilistic process (as defined in section 2.6). This

[a dependent variable] is symmetrical or truly reversible, then the effect on Y of an increase in X_1 will disappear if X_1 shifts back to its earlier level (assuming that all other conditions are constant).

As an example of Lieberson's point, imagine that the Fourth Congressional District in New York had no incumbent in 1998 and that the Democratic candidate received 55 percent of the vote. Lieberson would define the causal effect of incumbency as the increase in the vote if the winning Democrat in 1998 runs as an incumbent in the next election in the year 2000. This effect would be "symmetric" if the absence of an incumbent in the subsequent election (in year 2002) caused the vote to return to 55 percent. The effect might be "asymmetric" if, for example, the incumbent Democrat raised money and improved the Democratic party's campaign organization; as a result, if no incumbent were running in 2002, the Democratic candidate might receive more than 55 percent of the vote.

Lieberson's argument is clever and very important. However, in our view, his argument does not constitute a *definition* of causality, but applies only to some causal *inferences*—the process of learning about a causal effect from existing observations. In section 3.1, we defined causality for a single unit. In the present example, a causal effect can be defined theoretically on the basis of hypothetical events occurring only in the 1998 election in the Fourth District in New York. Our definition is the difference in the systematic component of the vote in this district with an incumbent in this election and without an incumbent in the same election, time, and district.

In contrast, Lieberson's example involves no hypothetical quantities and therefore cannot be a causal definition. This example involves only what would actually occur if the explanatory variable changed in two real elections from nonincumbent to incumbent, versus incumbent to nonincumbent in two other elections. Any empirical analysis of this example would involve numerous problems of inference. We discuss many of these problems of causal inference in chapters 4–6. In the present example, we might ask whether the estimated effect seemed larger only because we failed to account for a large number of recently registered citizens in the Fourth District. Or, did the surge in support for the Democrat in the election in which she or he was an incumbent

---

seems to invalidate Ragin's "Boolean Algebra" approach as a general way of designing theoretical explanations or making inferences; to learn from data requires the same logic of scientific inference that we discuss in this book. However, his approach can still be valuable as a form of formal theory (see section 3.5.2): it enables the investigator to specify a theory and its implications in a way that might be much more difficult without it.

seem smaller than it should because we necessarily discarded districts where the Democrat lost the first election?

Thus, Lieberson's concepts of "symmetrical" and "asymmetrical" causality are important to consider in the context of causal inference. However, they should not be confused with a theoretical definition of causality, which we give in section 3.1.

3.3 ASSUMPTIONS REQUIRED FOR ESTIMATING CAUSAL EFFECTS

How do we avoid the Fundamental Problem of Causal Inference and also the problem of separating systematic from nonsystematic components? The full answer to this question will consume chapters 4–6, but we provide an overview here of what is required in terms of the two possible assumptions that enable us to get around the fundamental problem. These are *unit homogeneity* (which we discuss in section 3.3.1) and *conditional independence* (section 3.3.2). These assumptions, like any other attempt to circumvent the Fundamental Problem of Causal Inference, always involve some untestable assumptions. It is the responsibility of all researchers to make the substantive implications of this weak spot in their research designs extremely clear and visible to readers. Causal inferences should not appear like magic. The assumptions can and should be justified with whatever side information or prior research can be mustered, but it always must be explicitly recognized.

3.3.1 Unit Homogeneity

If we cannot rerun history at the same time and the same place with different values of our explanatory variable each time—as a true solution to the Fundamental Problem of Causal Inference would require— we can attempt to make a second-best assumption: we can rerun our experiment in two different units that are "homogeneous." *Two units are homogeneous when the expected values of the dependent variables from each unit are the same when our explanatory variable takes on a particular value.* (That is, $\mu_1^N = \mu_2^N$ and $\mu_1^I = \mu_2^I$.) For example, if we observe $X = 1$ (an incumbent) in district 1 and $X = 0$ (no incumbent) in district 2, an assumption of unit homogeneity means that we can use the observed proportions of the vote in two separate districts for inference about the causal effect β, which we assume is the same in both districts. For a data set with n observations, unit homogeneity is the assumption that all units with the same value of the explanatory variables have the same expected value of the dependent variable. Of course, this is only an assumption and it can be wrong: the two districts might differ in some unknown way that would bias our causal inference. Indeed, any two real districts *will* differ in some ways; application of this assumption requires that these districts must be the same on average over many hypothetical replications of the election campaign. For example, patterns of rain (which might inhibit voter turnout in some areas) would not differ across districts on average unless there were systematic climatic differences between the two areas.

In the following quotation, Holland (1986:947) provides a clear example of the unit homogeneity assumption (defined from his perspective of a realized causal effect instead of the mean causal effect). Since very little randomness exists in the experiment in the following example, his definition and ours are close. (Indeed, as we show in section 4.2, with a small number of units, the assumption of unit homogeneity is most useful when the amount of randomness is fairly low.)

> If [the unit] is a room in a house, *t* [for 'treatment'] means that I flick the light switch in that room, *c* [for 'control'] means that I do not, and [the dependent variable] indicates whether the light is on or not a short time after applying either *t* or *c*, then I might be inclined to *believe* that I can *know* the values of [the dependent variable for both *t* and *c*] by simply flicking the switch. It is clear, however, that it is only because of the plausibility of certain assumptions about the situation that this *belief* of mine can be shared by anyone else. If, for example, the light has been flicking off and on for no apparent reason while I am contemplating beginning this experiment, I might doubt that I would know the values of [the dependent variable for both *t* and *c*] after flicking the switch—at least until I was clever enough to figure out a new experiment!

In this example, the unit homogeneity assumption is that if we had flicked the switch (in Holland's notation, applied *t*) in both periods, the expected value (of whether the light will be on) would be the same. Unit homogeneity also assumes that if we had not flicked the switch (applied *c*) in both periods, the expected value would be the same, although not necessarily the same as when *t* is applied. Note that we would have to reset the switch to the off position after the first experiment to assure this, but we would also have to make the untestable assumption that flipping the switch on in the first period does not effect the two hypothetical expected values in the next period (such as if a fuse were blown after the first flip). In general, the unit homogeneity assumption is untestable for a single unit (although, in this case, we might be able to generate several new hypotheses about the causal mechanism by ripping the wall apart and inspecting the wiring).

A weaker, but also fully acceptable, version of unit homogeneity is the *constant effect* assumption. Instead of assuming that the expected value of the dependent variable is the same for different units with the same value of the explanatory variable, we need only to assume that the causal effect is constant. This is a weaker version of the unit homogeneity assumption, since the causal effect is only the difference between the two expected values. If the two expected values for units with the same value of the explanatory variable vary in the same way, the unit homogeneity assumption would be violated, but the constant effect assumption would still be valid. For example, two congressional districts could vary in the expected proportion of the vote for Democratic nonincumbents (say 45 percent vs. 65 percent), but incumbency could still add an additional ten percent to the vote of a Democratic candidate of either district.

The notion of unit homogeneity (or the less demanding assumption of constant causal effects) lies at the base of all scientific research. It is, for instance, the assumption underlying the method of comparative case studies. We compare several units that have varying values on our explanatory variables and observe the values of the dependent variables. We believe that the differences we observe in the values of the dependent variables are the result of the differences in the values of the explanatory variables that apply to the observations. What we have shown here is that our "belief" in this case necessarily relies upon an assumption of unit homogeneity or constant effects.

Note that we may seek homogeneous units across time or across space. We can compare the vote for the Democratic candidate when there is a Democratic incumbent running with the vote when there is no Democratic incumbent in the same district at different times or across different districts at the same time (or some combination of the two). Since a causal effect can only be estimated instead of known, we should not be surprised that the unit homogeneity assumption is generally untestable. But it is important that the nature of the assumption is made explicit. Across what range of units do we expect our assumption of a uniform incumbency effect to hold? All races for Congress? Congressional but not Senate races? Races in the North only? Races in the past two decades only?

Notice how the unit homogeneity assumption relates to our discussion in section 1.1.3 on complexity and "uniqueness." There we argued that social science generalization depends on our ability to simplify reality coherently. At the limit, simplifying reality for the purpose of making causal inferences implies meeting the standards for unit homogeneity: the observations being analyzed become, for the purposes of analysis, identical in relevant respects. Attaining unit homogeneity is often impossible; congressional elections, not to speak of revolutions, are hardly close analogies to light switches. But understanding the degree of heterogeneity in our units of analysis will help us to estimate the degree of uncertainty or likely biases to be attributed to our inferences.

3.3.2 Conditional Independence

Conditional independence is the assumption that values are assigned to explanatory variables independently of the values taken by the dependent variables. (The term is sometimes used in statistics, but it does not have the same definition as it commonly does in probability theory.) That is, after taking into account the explanatory variables (or controlling for them), the process of assigning values to the explanatory variable is independent of both (or, in general two or more) dependent variables, Y_i^N and Y_i^I. We use the term "assigning values" to the explanatory variables to describe the process by which these variables obtain the particular values they have. In experimental work, the researcher actually *assigns* values to the explanatory variables; some subjects are assigned to the treatment group and others to the control group. In nonexperimental work, the values that explanatory variables take may be "assigned" by nature or the environment. What is crucial in these cases is that the values of the explanatory variables are not caused by the dependent variables. The problem of "endogeneity" that exists when the explanatory variables are caused, at least in part, by the dependent variables is described in section 5.4.

Large-n analyses that involve the procedures of random selection and assignment constitute the most reliable way to assure conditional independence and do not require the unit homogeneity assumption. Random selection and assignment help us to make causal inferences because they *automatically* satisfy three assumptions that underlie the concept of conditional independence: (1) that the process of assigning values to the explanatory variables is independent of the dependent variables (that is, there is no endogeneity problem); (2) that selection bias, which we discuss in section 4.3, is absent; and (3) that omitted variable bias (section 5.2) is also absent. Thus, if we are able to meet these conditions in any way, either through random selection and assignment (as discussed in section 4.2) or through some other procedure, we can avoid the Fundamental Problem of Causal Inference.

Fortunately, random selection and assignment are *not* required to meet the conditional independence assumption. If the process by which the values of the explanatory variables are "assigned" is not independent of the dependent variables, we can still meet the conditional independence assumption if we learn about this process and include a measure of it among our control variables. For example, suppose we are interested in estimating the effect of the degree of residential segregation on the extent of conflict between Israelis and Palestinians in communities on the Israeli-occupied West Bank. Our conditional independence assumption would be severely violated if we looked only at the association between these two variables to find the causal effect. The reason is that the Israelis and Palestinians who choose to live in segregated neighborhoods may do so out of an ideological belief about who ultimately has rights to the West Bank. Ideological extremism (on both sides) may therefore lead to conflict. A measure that we believe to be residential segregation might really be a surrogate for ideology. The difference between the two explanations may be quite important, since a new housing policy might help remedy the conflict if residential segregation were the real cause, whereas this policy would be ineffective or even counterproductive if ideology were really the driving force. We might correct for the problem here by also measuring the ideology of the residents explicitly and controlling for it. For example, we could learn how popular extremist political parties are among the Israelis and PLO affiliation is among the Palestinians. We could then control for the possibly confounding effects of ideology by comparing communities with the same level of ideological extremism but differing levels of residential segregation.

When random selection and assignment are infeasible and we cannot control for the process of assignment and selection, we have to resort to some version of the unit homogeneity assumption in order to make valid causal inferences. Since that assumption will be only imperfectly met in social science research, we will have to be especially careful to specify our degree of uncertainty about causal inferences. This assumption will be particularly apparent when we discuss the procedures used in "matching" observations in section 5.6.

Notation for a Formal Model of a Causal Effect. We now generalize our notation for the convenience of later sections. In general, we will have n realizations of a random variable Y_i. In our running quantitative example, n is the number of congressional districts (435), and the realization y_i of the random variable Y_i is the observed Democratic proportion of the two-party vote in district i (such as 0.56). The expected nonincumbent Democratic proportion of the two-party vote (the average over all hypothetical replications) in district i is μ_i^N. We define the explanatory variable as X_i, which is coded in the present example as zero when district i has no Democratic incumbent and as one when district i has a Democratic incumbent. Then, we can denote the mean causal effect in unit i as

$$\beta = E(Y_i|X_i = 1) - E(Y_i|X_i = 0) = \mu_i^I - \mu_i^N \tag{3.4}$$

and incorporate it into the following simple formal model:

$$E(Y_i) = \mu_i^N + X_i(\mu_i^I - \mu_i^N) \tag{3.5}$$

$$= \mu_i^N + X_i\beta$$

Thus, when district i has no incumbent, and $X_i = 0$, the expected value is determined by substituting zero into equation (3.5) for X_i, and the answer is as before:

$$E(Y_i|X = 0) = \mu_i^N + (0)\beta$$

$$= \mu_i^N$$

Similarly, when a Democratic incumbent is running in district i, the expected value is μ_i^I:

$$E(Y_i|X = 1) = \mu_i^N + (1)\beta$$

$$= \mu_i^N + \beta$$

$$= \mu_i^N + (\mu_i^I - \mu_i^N)$$

$$= \mu_i^I$$

Thus, equation (3.5) provides a useful model of causal inference, and β—the difference between the two theoretical proportions—is our causal effect. Finally, for future reference, we simplify equation (3.5) one last time. If we assume that Y_i has a zero mean (or is written as a deviation from its mean, which does not limit the applicability of the model in any way), then we can drop the intercept from this equation, and write it more simply as

$$E(Y_i) = X_i\beta \tag{3.6}$$

The parameter β is still the theoretical value of the mean causal effect, a systematic feature of the random variables, and one of our goals in causal inference. This model is a special case of "regression analysis," which is common in quantitative research, but regression coefficients are only sometimes coincident with estimates of causal effects.

3.4 CRITERIA FOR JUDGING CAUSAL INFERENCES

Recall that by defining causality in terms of random variables, we were able to draw a strict analogy between it and other systematic features of phenomena, such as a mean or a variance, on which we focus in making descriptive inferences. This analogy enables us to use precisely the same criteria to judge causal inferences as we used to judge descriptive inferences in section 2.7: *unbiasedness* and *efficiency*. Hence, most of what we said on this subject in Chapter 2 applies equally well to the causal inference problems we deal with here. In this section, we briefly formalize the relatively few differences between these two situations.

In section 2.7 the object of our inference was a mean (the expected value of a random variable), which we designate as μ. We conceptualize μ as a fixed, but unknown, number. An estimator of μ is said to be unbiased if it equals μ on average over many hypothetical replications of the same experiment.

As above, we continue to conceptualize the expected value of a random causal effect, denoted as β, as a fixed, but unknown, number. The unbiasedness is then defined analogously: an estimator of β is unbiased if it equals β on average over many hypothetical replications of the same experiment. Efficiency is also defined analogously as the variability across these hypothetical replications. These are very important concepts that will serve as the basis for our studies of many of the problems of causal inference in chapters 4–6. The two boxes that follow provide formal definitions.

A Formal Analysis of Unbiasedness of Causal Estimates. In this box, we demonstrate the unbiasedness of the estimator of the causal effect parameter from section 3.1. The notation and logic of these ideas closely parallel those from the formal definition of unbiasedness in the context of descriptive inference in section 2.7. The simple linear model with one explanatory and one dependent variable is as follows:[12]

---

[12] In order to avoid using a constant term, we assume that all variables have zero mean. This simplifies the presentation but does not limit our conclusions in any way.

$$E(Y_i) = \beta X_i$$

Our estimate of β is simply the least squares regression estimate:

$$b = \frac{\sum_{i=1}^{n} Y_i X_i}{\sum_{i=1}^{n} X_i^2} \tag{3.7}$$

To determine whether b is an unbiased estimator of β, we need to take the expected value, averaging over hypothetical replications:

$$E(b) = E\left(\frac{\sum_{i=1}^{n} X_i Y_i}{\sum_{i=1}^{n} X_i^2}\right) \tag{3.8}$$

$$= \frac{\sum_{i=1}^{n} X_i E(Y_i)}{\sum_{i=1}^{n} X_i^2}$$

$$= \frac{\sum_{i=1}^{n} X_i^2 \beta}{\sum_{i=1}^{n} X_i^2}$$

$$= \beta$$

which proves that b is an unbiased estimator of β.

A Formal Analysis of Efficiency. Here, we assess the efficiency of the standard estimator of the causal effect parameter β from section 3.1. We proved in equation (3.8) that this estimator is unbiased and now calculate its variance:

$$V(b) = V\left(\frac{\sum_{i=1}^{n} X_i Y_i}{\sum_{i=1}^{n} X_i^2}\right) \tag{3.9}$$

$$= \frac{1}{\left(\sum_{i=1}^{n} X_i^2\right)^2} \sum_{i=1}^{n} X_i^2 V(Y_i)$$

$$= \frac{V(Y_i)}{\sum_{i=1}^{n} X_i^2}$$

$$= \frac{\sigma^2}{\sum_{i=1}^{n} X_i^2}$$

Thus, the variance of this estimator is a function of two components. First, the more random *each* unit in our data (the larger is σ^2) is, the more variable will be our estimator b; this should be no surprise. In addition, the larger the observed variance in the explanatory variable ($\sum_{i=1}^{n} X_i^2$), the less variable will be our estimate of b. In the extreme case of no variability in X, nothing can help us estimate the effect of changes in the explanatory variable on the dependent variable, and the formula predicts an infinite variance (complete uncertainty) in this instance. More generally, this component indicates that efficiency is greatest when we have evidence from a larger range of values of the explanatory variable. In general, then, it is best to evaluate our causal hypotheses in as many diverse situations as possible. One way to think of this latter point is to think about drawing a line with a ruler, two dots on a page, and a shaky hand. If the two dots are very close together (small variance of X), errors in the placement of the ruler will be much larger than if the dots are farther apart (the situation of a large variance in X).

3.5 RULES FOR CONSTRUCTING CAUSAL THEORIES

Much sensible advice about improving qualitative research is precise, specific, and detailed; it involves a manageable and therefore narrow aspect of qualitative research. However, even in the midst of solving a host of individual problems, we must keep the big picture firmly in mind: each specific solution must help in solving whatever is the general causal inference problem one aims to solve. Thus far in this chapter, we have provided a precise theoretical definition of a causal effect and discussed some of the issues involved in making causal inferences. We take a step back now and provide a broader overview of some rules regarding theory construction. As we discuss (and have discussed in section 1.2), improving theory does not end when data collection begins.

Causal theories are designed to show the causes of a phenomenon or set of phenomena. Whether originally conceived as deductive or inductive, any theory includes an interrelated set of causal hypotheses. Each hypothesis specifies a posited relationship between variables that creates observable implications: if the specified explanatory variables take on certain values, other specified values are predicted for the dependent variables. Testing or evaluating any causal hypothesis requires causal inference. The overall theory, of which the hypotheses are parts should be *internally consistent*, or else hypotheses can be generated that contradict one another.

Theories and hypotheses that fit these definitions have an enormous range. In this section, we provide five rules that will help in formulating good theories, and we provide a discussion of each with examples.

3.5.1 Rule 1: Construct Falsifiable Theories

By this first rule, we do not only mean that a "theory" incapable of being wrong is not a theory. We also mean that we should design theories so that they can be shown to be wrong as easily and quickly as possible. Obviously, we should not actually try to be wrong, but even an incorrect theory is better than a statement that is neither wrong nor right. The emphasis on falsifiable theories forces us to keep the right perspective on uncertainty and guarantees that we treat theories as tentative and not let them become dogma. We should always be prepared to reject theories in the face of sufficient scientific evidence against them. One question that should be asked about any theory (or of any hypothesis derived from the theory) is simply: what evidence would falsify it? The question should be asked of all theories and hypotheses but, above all, the researcher who poses the theory in the first place should ask it of his or her own.

Karl Popper is most closely identified with the idea of falsifiability (Popper 1968). In Popper's view, a fundamental asymmetry exists between confirming a theory (verification) and disconfirming it (falsification). The former is almost irrelevant, whereas the latter is the key to science. Popper believes that a theory once stated immediately becomes part of the body of accepted scientific knowlege. Since theories are general, and hypotheses specific, theories technically imply an infinite number of hypotheses. However, empirical tests can only be conducted on a finite number of hypotheses. In that sense, "theories are not verifiable" because we can never test all observable implications of a theory (Popper 1968:252). Each hypothesis tested may be shown to be consistent with the theory, but any number of consistent empirical results will not change our opinions since the theory remains accepted scientific knowledge. On the other hand, if even a single hypothesis is shown to be wrong, and thus inconsistent with the theory, the theory is falsified, and it is removed from our collection of scientific knowledge. "The passing of tests therefore makes not a jot of difference to the status of any hypothesis, though the failing of just one test may make a great deal of difference" (Miller 1988:22). Popper did not mean falsification to be a deterministic concept. He recognized that any empirical inference is to some extent uncertain (Popper 1982). In his discussion of disconfirmation, he wrote, "even if the asymmetry [between falsification and verification] is admitted, it is still impossible, for various reasons, that any theoretical system should ever be conclusively falsified" (Popper 1968:42).

In our view, Popper's ideas are fundamental for *formulating* theories. We should always design theories that are vulnerable to falsification. We should also learn from Popper's emphasis on the tentative nature of any theory. However, for *evaluating* existing social scientific theories, the asymmetry between verification and falsification is not as significant. Either one adds to our scientific knowledge. The question is less whether, in some general sense, a theory is false or not—virtually every interesting social science theory has at least one observable implication that appears wrong—than *how much of the world the theory can help us explain*. By Popper's rule, theories based on the assumption of rational choice would have been rejected long ago since they have been falsified in many specific instances. However, social scientists often choose to retain the assumption, suitably modified, because it provides considerable power in many kinds of research problems (see Cook and Levi 1990). The same point applies to virtually every other social science theory of interest. The process of trying to falsify theories in the social sciences is really one of searching for their bounds of applicability. If some observable implication indicates that the theory does not apply, we learn something; similarly, if the theory works, we learn something too.

For scientists (and especially for social scientists) evaluating properly formulated theories, Popper's fundamental asymmetry seems largely irrelevant. O'Hear (1989:43) made a similar point about the application of Popper's ideas to the physical sciences:

> Popper always tends to speak in terms of *explanations* of *universal* theories. But once again, we have to insist that proposing and testing universal theories is only part of the aim of science. There may be no true universal theories, owing to conditions differing markedly through time and space; this is a possibility we cannot overlook. But even if this were so, science could still fulfil [sic] many of its aims in giving us knowledge and true predictions about conditions in and around our spatio-temporal niche.

Surely this same point applies even more strongly to the social sciences.

Furthermore, Popper's evaluation of theories does not fundamentally distinguish between a newly formulated theory and one that has withstood numerous empirical tests. When we are testing for the deterministic distinction between the truth or fiction of a universal theory (of which there exists no interesting examples), Popper's view is appropriate, but from our perspective of searching for the bounds of a theory's applicability, his view is less useful. As we have indicated many times in this book, we require all inferences about specific hypotheses to be made by stating a best guess (an estimate) and a measure of the uncertainty of this guess. Whether we discover that the inference is consistent with our theory or inconsistent, our conclusion will have as much effect on our belief in the theory. Both consistency and inconsistency provide information about the truth of the theory and should affect the certainty of our beliefs.[13]

Consider the hypothesis that Democratic and Republican campaign strategies during American presidential elections have a small net effect on the election outcome. Numerous more specific hypotheses are implied by this one, such as that television commercials, radio commercials, and debates all have little effect on voters. Any test of the theory must really be a test of one of these hypotheses. One test of the theory has shown that forecasts of the outcome can be made very accurately with variables available only at the time of the conventions—and thus before the campaign (Gelman and King 1993). This test is consistent with the theory (if we can predict the election before the campaign, the campaign can hardly be said to have much of an impact), but it does not absolutely verify it. Some aspect of the campaign could have some small effect that accounts for some of the forecasting errors (and few researchers doubt that this is true). Moreover, the prediction could have been luck, or the campaign could have not included any innovative (and hence unpredictable) tactics during the years for which data were collected.

We could conduct numerous other tests by including variables in the forecasting model that measure aspects of the campaign, such as relative amounts of TV and radio time, speaking ability of the candidates, and judgements as to the outcomes of the debates. If all of these hypotheses show no effect, then Popper would say that our opinion is not changed in any interesting way: the theory that presidential campaigns have no effect is still standing. Indeed, if we did a thousand

---

[13] Some might call us (or accuse us of being!) "justificationists" or even "probabilistic justificationists" (see Lakatos 1970), but if we must be labeled, we prefer the more coherent, philosophical Bayesian label (see Leamer 1978; Zellner 1971; and Barnett 1982). In fact, our main difference with Popper is our goals. Given his precise goal, we agree with his procedure; given our goal, perhaps he might agree with ours. However, we believe that our goals are closer to those in use in the social sciences and are also closer to the ones likely to be successful.

similar tests and all were consistent with the theory, the theory could still be wrong since we have not tried every one of the infinite number of possible variables measuring the campaign. So even with a lot of results consistent with the theory, it still *might* be true that presidential campaigns influence voter behavior.

However, if a single campaign event—such as substantial accusations of immoral behavior—is shown to have some effect on voters, the theory would be falsified. According to Popper, even though this theory was not conclusively falsified (which he recognized as impossible), we learn more from it than the thousand tests consistent with the theory.

To us, this is not the way social science is or should be conducted. After a thousand tests in favor and one against, even if the negative test seemed valid with a high degree of certainty, we would not drop the theory that campaigns have no effect. Instead, we might modify it to say perhaps that normal campaigns have no effect except when there is considerable evidence of immoral behavior by one of the candidates—but since this modification would make our theory more restrictive, we would need to evaluate it with a new set of data before being confident of its validity. The theory would still be very powerful, and we would know somewhat more about the bounds to which the theory applied with each passing empirical evaluation. Each test of a theory affects both the estimate of its validity and the uncertainty of that estimate; and it may also affect to what extent we wish the theory to apply.

In the previous discussion, we suggested an important approach to theory, as well as issued a caution. The approach we recommended is one of sensitivity to the contingent nature of theories and hypotheses. Below, we argue for seeking broad application for our theories and hypotheses. This is a useful research strategy, but we ought always to remember that theories in the social sciences are unlikely to be universal in their applicability. Those theories that are put forward as applying to everything, everywhere—some versions of Marxism and rational choice theory are examples of theories that have been put forward with claims of such universality—are either presented in a tautological manner (in which case they are neither true nor false) or in a way that allows empirical disconfirmation (in which case we will find that they make incorrect predictions). Most useful social science theories are valid under particular conditions (in election campaigns without strong evidence of immoral behavior by a candidate) or in particular settings (in industrialized but not less industrialized nations, in House but not Senate campaigns). We should always try to specify the bounds of applicability of the theory or hypothesis. The next step is to raise the question: Why do these bounds exist? What is it about Senate races that invalidates generalizations that are true for House races? What is it about industrialization that changes the causal effects? What variable is missing from our analysis which could produce a more generally applicable theory? By asking such questions, we move beyond the boundaries of our theory or hypothesis to show what factors need to be considered to expand its scope.

But a note of caution must be added. We have suggested that the process of evaluating theories and hypotheses is a flexible one: particular empirical tests neither confirm nor disconfirm them once and for all. When an empirical test is inconsistent with our theoretically based expectations, we do not immediately throw out the theory. We may do various things: We may conclude that the evidence may have been poor due to chance alone; we may adjust what we consider to be the range of applicability of a theory or hypothesis even if it does not hold in a particular case and, through that adjustment, maintain our acceptance of the theory or hypothesis. Science proceeeds by such adjustments; but they can be dangerous. If we take them too far we make our theories and hypotheses invulnerable to disconfirmation. The lesson is that we must be very careful in adapting theories to be consistent with new evidence. We must avoid stretching the theory beyond all plausibility by adding numerous exceptions and special cases.

If our study disconfirms some aspect of a theory, we may choose to retain the theory but add an exception. Such a procedure is acceptable as long as we recognize the fact that we are reducing the claims we make for the theory. The theory, though, is less valuable since it explains less; in our terminology, we have less *leverage* over the problem we seek to understand.[14] Furthermore, such an approach may yield a "theory" that is merely a useless hodgepodge of various exceptions and exclusions. At some point we must be willing to discard theories and hypotheses entirely. Too many exceptions, and the theory should be rejected. Thus, by itself, *parsimony, the normative preference for theories with fewer parts, is not generally applicable*. All we need is our more general notion of maximizing leverage, from which the idea of parsimony can be fully derived when it is useful. The idea that science is largely a process of explaining many phenomena with just a few makes clear that theories with fewer parts are not better or worse. To maximize leverage, we should attempt to formulate theories that explain as much as possible with as little as possible. Sometimes this formulation is achieved via parsimony, but sometimes not. We can con-

[14] As always, when we do modify a theory to be consistent with evidence we have collected, then the theory (or that part of it on which our evidence bears) should be evaluated in a different context or new data set.

ceive of examples by which a slightly more complicated theory will explain vastly more of the world. In such a situation, we would surely use the nonparsimonious theory, since it maximizes leverage more than the more parsimonious theory.[15]

3.5.2 Rule 2: Build Theories That Are Internally Consistent

A theory which is internally inconsistent is not only falsifiable—it is false. Indeed, this is the only situation where the veracity of a theory is known without any empirical evidence: if two or more parts of a theory generate hypotheses that contradict one another, then no evidence from the empirical world can uphold the theory. Ensuring that theories are internally consistent should be entirely uncontroversial, but consistency is frequently difficult to achieve. One method of producing internally consistent theories is with formal, mathematical modeling. *Formal modeling* is a practice most developed in economics but increasingly common in sociology, psychology, political science, anthropology, and elsewhere (see Ordeshook 1986). In political science, scholars have built numerous substantive theories from mathematical models in rational choice, social choice, spatial models of elections, public economics, and game theory. This research has produced many important results, and large numbers of plausible hypotheses. One of the most important contributions of formal modeling is revealing the internal inconsistency in verbally stated theories.

However, as with other hypotheses, formal models do not constitute verified explanations without empirical evaluation of their predic-

---

[15] Another formulation of Popper's view is that "you can't prove a negative." You cannot, he argues, because a result consistent with the hypothesis might just mean that you did the wrong test. Those who try to prove the negative will always run into this problem. Indeed, their troubles will be not only theoretical but professional as well since journals are more likely to publish positive results rather than negative ones.

This has led to what is called *the file drawer problem*, which is clearest in the quantitative literature. Suppose no patterns exist in the world. Then five of every one hundred tests of any pattern will fall outside the 95 percent confidence interval and thus produce incorrect inferences. If we were to assume that journals publish positive rather than negative results, they will publish only those 5 percent that are "significant"; that is, they will publish only the papers that come to the wrong conclusions, and our file drawers will be filled with all the papers that come to the right conclusions! (See Iyengar and Greenhouse (1988) for a review of the statistical literature on this problem.) In fact, these incentives are well known by researchers, and it probably affects their behaviors as well. Even though the acceptance rate at many major social science journals is roughly 5 percent, the situation is not quite this bad, but it is still a serious problem. In our view, the file drawer problem could be solved if everyone adopted our alternative position. *A negative result is as useful as a positive one; both can provide just as much information about the world.* So long as we present our estimates and a measure of our uncertainty, we will be on safe ground.

tions. Formality does help us reason more clearly, and it certainly ensures that our ideas are internally consistent, but it does not resolve issues of empirical evaluation of social science theories. An assumption in a formal model in the social sciences is generally a convenience for mathematical simplicity or for ensuring that an equilibrium can be found. Few believe that the political world is mathematical in the same way that some physicists believe the physical world is. Thus, formal models are merely models—abstractions that should be distinguished from the world we study. Indeed, some formal theories make predictions that depend on assumptions that are vastly oversimplified, and these theories are sometimes not of much empirical value. They are only more precise in the abstract than are informal social science theories: they do not make more specific predictions about the real world, since the conditions they specify do not correspond, even approximately, to actual conditions.

Simplifications are essential in formal modeling, as they are in all research, but we need to be cautious about the inferences we can draw about reality from the models. For example, assuming that all omitted variables have no effect on the results can be very useful in modeling. In many of the formal models of qualitative research that we present throughout this book, we do precisely this. Assumptions like this are not usually justified as a feature of the world; they are only offered as a convenient feature of our model of the world. The results, then, apply exactly to the situation in which these omitted variables are irrelevant and may or may not be similar to results in the real world. We do not have to check the assumption to work out the model and its implications, but it is *essential* that we check the assumption during empirical evaluation. The assumption need not be correct for the formal model to be useful. But we cannot take untested or unjustified theoretical assumptions and use them in constructing empirical research designs. Instead, we must generally supplement a formal theory with additional features to make it useful for empirical study.

A good formal model should be abstract so that the key features of the problem can be apparent and mathematical reasoning can be easily applied. Consider, then, a formal model of the effect of proportional representation on political party systems, which implies that proportional representation fragments party systems. The key causal variable is the type of electoral system—whether it is a proportional representation system with seats allocated to parties on the basis of their proportion of the vote or a single-member district system in which a single winner is elected in each district. The dependent variable is the number of political parties, often referred to as the degree of party-system fragmentation. The leading hypothesis is that electoral systems based on proportional representation generate more political parties than do district-based electoral systems. For the sake of simplicity, such a model might well include only variables measuring some essential features of the electoral system and the degree of party-system fragmentation. Such a model would generate only a *hypothesis*, not a conclusion, about the relationship between proportional representation and party-system fragmentation in the real world. Such a hypothesis would have to be tested through the use of qualitative or quantitative empirical methods.

However, even though an implication of this model is that proportional representation fragments political parties, and even though no other variables were used in the model, using only two variables in an empirical analysis would be foolish. A study that indicates that countries with proportional representation have more fragmented party systems would ignore the problem of endogeneity (section 5.4), since countries which establish electoral systems based on a proportional allocation of seats to the parties may well have done so because of their already existent fragmented party systems. Omitted variable bias would also be a problem since countries with deep racial, ethnic, or religious divisions are probably also likely to have fragmented party systems, and countries with divisions of these kinds are more likely to have proportional representation.

Thus, both of the requirements for omitted variable bias (section 5.2) seem to be met: the omitted variable is correlated both with the explanatory and the dependent variable, and any analysis ignoring the variable of social division would therefore produce biased inferences.

The point should be clear: formal models are extremely useful for clarifying our thinking and developing internally consistent theories. For many theories, especially complex, verbally stated theories, it may be that only a formal model is capable of revealing and correcting internal inconsistencies. At the same time, formal models are unlikely to provide the correct empirical model for empirical testing. They certainly do not enable us to avoid any of the empirical problems of scientific inference.

3.5.3 Rule 3: Select Dependent Variables Carefully

Of course, we should do everything in research carefully, but choosing variables, especially dependent variables, is a particularly important decision. We offer the following three suggestions (based on mistakes that occur all too frequently in the quantitative and qualitative literatures):

First, *dependent variables should be dependent*. A very common mistake is to choose a dependent variable which in fact causes changes in our explanatory variables. We analyze the specific consequences of endogeneity and some ways to circumvent the problem in section 5.4, but we emphasize it here because the easiest way to avoid it is to choose explanatory variables that are clearly exogenous and dependent variables that are endogenous.

Second, *do not select observations based on the dependent variable so that the dependent variable is constant*. This, too, may seem a bit obvious, but scholars often choose observations in which the dependent variable does not vary at all (such as in the example discussed in section 4.3.1). Even if we do not deliberately design research so that the dependent variable is constant, it may turn out that way. But, as long as we have not predetermined that fact by our selection criteria, there is no problem. For example, suppose we select observations in two categories of an explanatory variable, and the dependent variable turns out to be constant across the two groups. This is merely a case where the estimated causal effect is zero.

Finally we should *choose a dependent variable that represents the variation we wish to explain*. Although this point seems obvious, it is actually quite subtle, as illustrated by Stanley Lieberson (1985:100):

> A simple gravitational exhibit at the Ontario Science Centre in Toronto inspires a heuristic example. In the exhibit, a coin and a feather are both released from the top of a vacuum tube and reach the bottom at virtually the same time. Since the vacuum is not a total one, presumably the coin reaches the bottom slightly ahead of the feather. At any rate, suppose we visualize a study in which a variety of objects is dropped without the benefit of such a strong control as a vacuum—just as would occur in nonexperimental social research. If social researchers find that the objects differ in the time that they take to reach the ground, typically they will want to know what characteristics determine these differences. Probably such characteristics of the objects as their density and shape will affect speed of the fall in a nonvacuum situation. If the social researcher is fortunate, such factors together will fully account for all of the differences among the objects in the velocity of their fall. If so, the social researcher will be very happy because all of the variation between objects will be accounted for. The investigator, applying standard social research-thinking will conclude that there is a complete understanding of the phenomenon *because all differences among the objects under study have been accounted for*. Surely there must be something faulty with our procedures if we can approach such a problem without even considering gravity itself.

The investigator's procedures in this example would be faulty only if the variable of interest were gravity. If gravity were the explanatory variable we cared about, our experiment does not vary it (since the experiment takes place in only one location) and therefore tells us nothing about it. However, the experiment Lieberson describes would be of great interest if we sought to understand variations in the time it will take for different types of objects to hit the ground when they are dropped from the same height under different conditions of air pressure. Indeed, even if we knew all about gravity, this experiment would still yield valuable information. But if, as Lieberson assumes, we were really interested in an inference about the causal effect of gravity, we would need a dependent variable which varied over observations with differing degrees of gravitational attraction. Likewise, in social science, we must be careful to ensure that we are really interested in understanding our dependent variable, rather than the background factors that our research design holds constant.

Thus, we need the entire range of variation in the dependent variable to be a possible outcome of the experiment in order to obtain an unbiased estimate of the impact of the explanatory variables. Artificial limits on the range or values of the dependent variable produce what we define (in section 4.3) as selection bias. For instance, if we are interested in the conditions under which armed conflict breaks out, we cannot choose as observations only those instances where the result is armed conflict. Such a study might tell us a great deal about variations among observations of armed conflict (as the gravity experiment tells us about variations in speed of fall of various objects) but will not enable us to explore the sources of armed conflict. A better design if we want to understand the sources of armed conflict would be one that selected observations according to our explanatory variables and allowed the dependent variable the *possibility* of covering the full range from there being little or no threat of a conflict through threat situations to actual conflict.

3.5.4 Rule 4: Maximize Concreteness

Our fourth rule, which follows from our emphasis on falsifiability, consistency, and variation in the dependent variable is to maximize concreteness. We should choose observable, rather than unobservable, concepts wherever possible. Abstract, unobserved concepts such as utility, culture, intentions, motivations, identification, intelligence, or the national interest are often used in social science theories. They can play a useful role in theory *formulation*; but they can be a hindrance to empirical *evaluation* of theories and hypotheses unless they can be defined in a way such that they, or at least their implications, can be observed and measured. Explanations involving concepts such as culture or national interest or utility or motivation are suspect unless we can measure the concept independently of the dependent variable that we are explaining. When such terms are used in explanations, it is too easy to use them in ways that are tautological or have no differentiating, observable implications. An act of an individual or a nation may be explained as resulting from a desire to maximize utility, to fulfill intentions, or to achieve the national interest. But the evidence that the act maximized utility or fulfilled intentions or achieved the national interest is the fact that the actor or the nation engaged in it. It is incumbent upon the researcher formulating the theory to specify clearly and precisely what observable implications of the theory would indicate its veracity and distinguish it from logical alternatives.

In no way do we mean to imply by this rule that concepts like intentions and motivations are unimportant. We only wish to recognize that the standard for explanation in any *empirical* science like ours must be *empirical* verification or falsification. Attempting to find empirical evidence of abstract, unmeasurable, and unobservable concepts will necessarily prove more difficult and less successful than for many imperfectly conceived specific and concrete concepts. The more abstract our concepts, the less clear will be the observable consequences and the less amenable the theory will be to falsification.

Researchers often use the following strategy. They begin with an abstract concept of the sort listed above. They agree that it cannot be measured directly; therefore, they suggest specific indicators of the abstract concept that can be measured and use them in their explanations. The choice of the specific indicator of the more abstract concept is justified on the grounds that it is observable. Sometimes it is the *only thing* that is observable (for instance, it is the only phenomenon for which data are available or the only type of historical event for which records have been kept). This is a perfectly respectable, indeed usually necessary, aspect of empirical investigation.

Sometimes, however, it has an unfortunate side. Often the specific indicator is far from the original concept and has only an indirect and uncertain relationship to it. It may not be a valid indicator of the abstract concept at all. But, after a quick apology for the gap between the abstract concept and the specific indicator, the researcher labels the indicator with the abstract concept and proceeds onward as if he were measuring that concept directly. Unfortunately, such reification is common in social science work, perhaps more frequently in quantitative than in qualitative research, but all too common in both. For example, the researcher has figures on mail, trade, tourism and student exchanges and uses these to compile an index of "societal integration" in Europe. Or the researcher asks some survey questions as to whether respondents are more concerned with the environment or making money and labels different respondents as "materialists" and "post-materialists." Or the researcher observes that federal agencies differ in the average length of employment of their workers and converts this into a measure of the "institutionalization" of the agencies.

We should be clear about what we mean here. The gap between concept and indicator is inevitable in much social science work. And we use general terms rather than specific ones for good reasons: they allow us to expand our frame of reference and the applicability of our theories. Thus we may talk of legislatures rather than of more narrowly defined legislative categories such as parliaments or specific institutions such as the German Bundestag. Or we may talk of "decision-making bodies" rather than legislatures when we want our theory to apply to an even wider range of institutions. (In the next section we, in fact, recommend this.) Science depends on such abstract classifications—or else we revert to summarizing historical detail. But our abstract and general terms must be connected to specific measureable concepts at some point to allow empirical testing. The fact of that connection—and the distance that must be traversed to make it—must always be kept in mind and made explicit. Furthermore, the choice of a high level of abstraction must have a real justification in terms of the theoretical problem at hand. It must help make the connection between the specific research at hand—in which the particular indicator is the main actor—and the more general problem. And it puts a burden on us to see that additional research using other specific indicators is carried on to bolster the assumption that our specific indicators really relate to some broader concept. The abstract terms used in the examples above—"societal integration," "post-materialism," and "institutionalization"—may be measured reasonably by the specific indicators cited. We do not deny that the leap from specific indicator to general abstract concept must be made—we have to make such a leap to carry on social science research. The leap must, however, be made with care, with justification, and with a constant "memory" of where the leap began.

Thus, we do not argue against abstractions. But we do argue for a language of social research that is as concrete and precise as possible. If we have no alternative to using unobservable constructs, as is usually the case in the social sciences, then we should at least *choose ideas with observable consequences*. For example, "intelligence" has never been directly observed but it is nevertheless a very useful concept. We have numerous tests and other ways to evaluate the implications of intelligence. On the other hand, if we have the choice between "the institutionalization of the presidency" and "size of the White House staff," it is usually better to choose the latter. We may argue that the size of the White House staff is related to the general concept of the institutionalization of the presidency, but we ought not to reify the narrower concept as identical to the broader. And, if size of staff means institutionalization, we should be able to find other measures of institutionalization that respond to the same explanatory variables as does size of staff. Below, we shall discuss "maximizing leverage" by expanding our dependent variables.

Our call for concreteness extends, in general, to the words we use to describe our theory. If a reader has to spend a lot of time extracting the precise meanings of the theory, the theory is of less use. There should be as little controversy as possible over what we mean when we describe a theory. To help in this goal of specificity, even if we are not conducting empirical research ourselves, we should spend time explicitly considering the observable implications of the theory and even possible research projects we could conduct. The vaguer our language, the less chance we will be wrong—but the less chance our work will be at all useful. It is better to be wrong than vague.

In our view, eloquent writing—a scarce commodity in social science—should be encouraged (and savored) in presenting the rationale for a research project, arguing for its significance, and providing rich descriptions of events. Tedium never advanced any science. However, as soon as the subject becomes causal or descriptive inference, where we are interested in observations and generalizations that are expected to persist, we require concreteness and specificity in language and thought.[16]

---

[16] The rules governing the best questions to ask in interviews are almost the same as those used in designing explanations: Be as concrete as possible. We should not ask conservative, white Americans, "Are you racist?", rather, "Would you mind if your daughter married a black man?" We should not ask someone if he or she is knowledgeable about politics; we should ask for the names of the Secretary of State and Speaker of the House. In general and wherever possible, *we must not ask an interviewee to do our work for us*. It is best not to ask for estimates of causal effects; we must ask for measures of the explanatory and dependent variables, and estimate the causal effect ourselves. We must not ask for motivations, but rather for facts.

This rule is not meant to imply that we should never ask people why they did something. Indeed, asking about motivations is often a productive means of generating hypotheses. Self-reported motivations may also be a useful set of observable implications. However, the answer given must be interpreted as the interviewee's response to the researcher's question, not necessarily as the correct answer. If questions such as these are to be of use, we should design research so that a particular answer given (with whatever justifications, embellishments, lies, or selective memories we may encounter) is an observable implication.

3.5.5 Rule 5: State Theories in as Encompassing Ways as Feasible

Within the constraints of guaranteeing that the theory will be falsifi able and that we maximize concreteness, the theory should be formulated so that it explains as much of the world as possible. We realize that there is some tension between this fifth rule and our earlier injunction to be concrete. We can only say that both goals are important, though in many cases they may conflict, and we need to be sensitive to both in order to draw a balance.

For example, we must not present our theory as if it only applies to the German Bundestag when there is reason to believe that it might apply to all independent legislatures. We need not provide evidence for all implications of the theory in order to state it, so long as we provide a reasonable estimate of uncertainty that goes along with it. It may be that we have provided strong evidence in favor of the theory in the German Bundestag. Although we have no evidence that it works elsewhere, we have no evidence against it either. The broader reference is useful if we remain aware of the need to evaluate its applicability. Indeed, expressing it as a hypothetically broader reference may force us to think about the structural features of the theory that would make it apply or not to other independent legislatures. For example, would it apply to the U.S. Senate, where terms are staggered, to the New Hampshire Assembly, which is much larger relative to the number of constituents, or to the British House of Commons, in which party voting is much stronger? An important exercise is stating what we think are systematic features of the theory that make it applicable in different areas. We may learn that we were wrong, but that is considerably better than not having stated the theory with sufficient precision in the first place.

This rule might seem to conflict with Robert Merton's ([1949] 1968) preference for "theories of the middle-range," but even a cursory reading of Merton should indicate that this is not so. Merton was reacting to a tradition in sociology where "theories" such as Parson's "theory of action" were stated so broadly that they could not be falsified. In political science, Easton's "systems theory" (1965) is in this same tradition (see Eckstein 1975:90). As one example of the sort of criticism he was fond of making, Merton ([1949] 1968: 43) wrote, "So far as one can tell, the theory of role-sets is not inconsistent with such broad theoretical orientations as Marxist theory, functional analysis, social behaviorism, Sorokin's integral sociology, or Parson's theory of action." Merton is not critical of the theory of role-sets, which he called a middle-range theory, rather he is arguing against those "broad theoretical orientations," with which almost any more specific theory or empirical observation is consistent. Merton favors "middle-range" theories but we believe he would agree that theories should be stated as broadly as possible as long as they remain falsifiable and concrete. Stating theories as broadly as possible is, to return to a notion raised earlier, a way of maximizing leverage. If the theory is testable—and the danger of very broad theories is, of course, that they may be phrased in ways that are not testable—then the broader the better; that is, the broader, the greater the leverage.

CHAPTER 4

Determining What to Observe

UP TO THIS POINT, we have presented our view of the standards of scientific inference as they apply to both qualitative and quantitative research (chapter 1), defined descriptive inference (chapter 2), and clarified our notion of causality and causal inference (chapter 3). We now proceed to consider specific practical problems of qualitative research design. In this and the next two chapters, we will use many examples, both drawn from the literature and constructed hypothetically, to illustrate our points. This chapter focuses on how we should select cases, or observations, for our analysis. Much turns on these decisions, since poor case selection can vitiate even the most ingenious attempts, at a later stage, to make valid causal inferences. In chapter 5, we identify some major sources of bias and inefficiency that should be avoided, or at least understood, so we can adjust our estimates. Then in chapter 6, we develop some ideas for increasing the number of observations available to us, often already available within data we have collected. We thus pursue a theme introduced in chapter 1: we should seek to derive as many observable implications of our theories as possible and to test as many of these as are feasible.

In section 3.3.2, we discussed "conditional independence": the assumption that observations are chosen and values assigned to explanatory variables independently of the values taken by the dependent variables. Such independence is violated, for instance, if explanatory variables are chosen by rules that are correlated with the dependent variables or if dependent variables cause the explanatory variables. Randomness in selection of units and in assigning values to explanatory variables is a common procedure used by some quantitative researchers working with large numbers of observations to ensure that the conditional independence assumption is met. Statistical methods are then used to mitigate the Fundamental Problem of Causal Inference. Unfortunately, random selection and assignment have serious limitations in small-n research. If random selection and assignment are not appropriate strategies, we can seek to achieve unit homogeneity through the use of intentional selection of observations (as discussed in section 3.3.1). In a sense, intentional selection of observations is our "last line of defense" to achieve conditions for valid causal inference.

Recall the essence of the unit homogeneity assumption: if two units have the same value of the key explanatory variable, the expected value of the dependent variable will be the same. The stricter version of the unit homogeneity assumption implies, for example, that if turning on one light switch lights up a 60-watt bulb, so will turning a second light switch to the "on" position. In this example, the position of the switch is the key explanatory variable and the status of the light (on or off) is the dependent variable. The unit homogeneity assumption requires that the expected status of each light is the same as long as the switches are in the same positions. The less strict version of the unit homogeneity assumption—often more plausible but equally acceptable—is the assumption of *constant effect*, in which similar variation in values of the explanatory variable for the two observations leads to the same causal effect in different units, even though the levels of the variables may be different. Suppose, for instance, that our light switches have three settings and we measure the dependent variable according to wattage generated. If one switch is changed from "off" to "low," and the other from "low" to "high," the assumption of constant effect is met if the increase in wattage is the same in the two rooms, although in one observation it goes from zero to 60, in the other from 60 to 120.

When neither the assumption of conditional independence nor the assumption of unit homogeneity is met, we face serious problems in causal inference. However, we face even more serious problems—indeed, we can literally make no valid causal inferences—when our research design is indeterminate. A determinate research design is the sine qua non of causal inference. Hence we begin in section 4.1 by discussing indeterminate research designs. After our discussion of indeterminate research designs, we consider the problem of selection bias as a result of the violation of the assumptions of conditional independence and unit homogeneity. In section 4.2, we analyze the limits of using random selection and assignment to achieve conditional independence. In section 4.3, we go on to emphasize the dangers of selecting cases intentionally on the basis of values of dependent variables and provide examples of work in which such selection bias has invalidated causal inferences. Finally, in section 4.4, we systematically consider ways to achieve unit homogeneity through intentional case selection, seeking not only to provide advice about ideal research designs but also offering suggestions about "second-best" approaches when the ideal cannot be attained.

The main subject of this chapter: issues involved in selecting cases, or observations, for analysis deserves special emphasis here. Since terminology can be confusing, it is important to review some terminological issues at the outset. Much discussion of qualitative research design speaks of "cases"—as in discussions of case studies or the "case method." However, the word "case" is often used ambiguously. It can mean a single observation. As explained in section 2.4, an "observation" is defined as one measure on one unit for one dependent variable and includes information on the values of the explanatory variables. However, a case can also refer to a single unit, on which many variables are measured, or even to a large domain for analysis.

For example, analysts may write about a "case study of India" or of World War II. For some purposes, India and World War II may constitute single observations; for instance, in a study of the population distribution of countries or the number of battle deaths in modern wars. But with respect to many questions of interest to social scientists, India and World War II each contain many observations that involve several units and variables. An investigator could compare electoral outcomes by parties across Indian states or the results of battles during World War II. In such a design, it can be misleading to refer to India or World War II as case studies, since they merely define the boundaries within which a large number of observations are made.

In thinking about choosing what to observe, what really concern us are the *observations* used to draw inferences at whatever level of analysis is of interest. Hence we recommend that social scientists think in terms of the observations they will be able to make rather than in the looser terminology of cases. However, what often happens in qualitative research is that researchers begin by choosing what they think of as "cases," conceived of as observations at a highly aggregated level of analysis, and then they find that to obtain enough observations, they must disaggregate their cases.

Suppose, for example, that a researcher seeks to understand how variations in patterns of economic growth in poor democratic countries affect political institutions. The investigator might begin by thinking of India between 1950 and 1990 as a single case, by which he might have in mind observations for one unit (India) on two variables—the rate of economic growth and a measure of change or stability in political institutions. However, he might only be able to find a very small number of poor democracies, and at this level of analysis have too few observations to make any valid causal inferences. Recognizing this problem, perhaps belatedly, he could decide to use each of the Indian states as a unit of analysis, perhaps also disaggregating his time period into four or five subperiods. If these disaggregated observations were implications of the same theory he set out to test, such a procedure would give him many observations within his "case study" of India. The resulting study might then yield enough information to support valid causal inferences about Indian politics and would be very different from a conventional case study that is narrowly conceived in terms of observations on one unit for several variables.

Since "observation" is more precisely defined than "case," in this chapter we will usually write of "selecting observations." However, since investigators often begin by choosing domains for study that contain multiple potential observations, and conventional terminology characteristically denotes these as "cases," we often speak of selecting cases rather than observations when we are referring to the actual practice of qualitative researchers.

4.1 INDETERMINATE RESEARCH DESIGNS

A *research design* is a plan that shows, through a discussion of our model and data, how we expect to use our evidence to make inferences. Research designs in qualitative research are not always made explicit, but they are at least implicit in every piece of research. However, some research designs are indeterminate; that is, virtually nothing can be learned about the causal hypotheses.

Unfortunately, indeterminate research designs are widespread in both quantitative and qualitative research. There is, however, a difference between indeterminacy in quantitative and qualitative research. When quantitative research is indeterminate, the problem is often obvious: the computer program will not produce estimates.[1] Yet computer programs do not always work as they should and many examples can be cited of quantitative researchers with indeterminate statistical models that provide meaningless substantive conclusions. Unfortunately, nothing so automatic as a computer program is available to discover indeterminant research designs in qualitative research. However, being aware of this problem makes it easier to identify indeterminate research designs and devise solutions. Moreover, qualitative researchers often have an advantage over quantitative researchers since they often have enough information to do something to make their research designs determinant.

Suppose our purpose in collecting information is to examine the validity of a hypothesis. The research should be designed so that we have maximum leverage to distinguish among the various possible out-

---

[1] The literature on "identification" in econometrics and statistics is concerned with determining when quantitative research designs are indeterminate and how to adjust the model or collect different types of data to cope with the problem. See Hsiao (1983) and King (1989: section 8.1).

comes relevant to the hypothesis. Two situations exist, however, in which a research design is indeterminate and, therefore, gives us no such leverage:

1. We have more inferences to make than implications observed.
2. We have two or more explanatory variables in our data that are perfectly correlated with each other—in statistical terms, this is the problem of multicollinearity. (The variables might even differ, but if we can predict one from the other without error in the cases we have, then the design is indeterminate).

Note that these situations, and the concept of indeterminate research designs in general, apply only to the goal of making causal inferences. A research design for summarizing historical detail cannot be indeterminate unless we literally collect no relevant observations. Data-collection efforts designed to find interesting questions to ask (see section 2.1.1) cannot be indeterminate if we have at least some information. Of course, indeterminancy may still occur later on when reconceptualizing our data (or collecting new data) to evaluate a causal hypothesis.

4.1.1 More Inferences than Observations

Consider the first instance, in which we have more inferences than implications observed. Inference is the process of using facts we know to learn something about facts we do not know. There is a limit to how much we can learn from limited information. It turns out that the precise rule is that one fact (or observable implication) cannot give *independent* information about more than one other fact. More generally, each observation can help us make one inference at most; n observations will help us make fewer than n inferences if the observations are not independent. In practice, we usually need many more than one observation to make a reasonably certain causal inference.

Having more inferences than implications observed is a common problem in qualitative case studies. However, the problem is not inherent in qualitative research, only in that research which is improperly conceptualized or organized into many observable implications of a theory. We will first describe this problem and then discuss solutions.

For example, suppose we have three case studies, each of which describes a pair of countries' joint efforts to build a high-technology weapons system. The three case studies include much interesting description of the weapons systems, the negotiations between the countries, and the final product. In the course of the project, we list seven important reasons that lead countries to successful joint collaboration on capital-defense projects. These might all be very plausible explanatory variables. We might also have interviewed decision-makers in the different countries and learned that they, too, agreed that these are the important variables. Such an approach would give us not only seven plausible hypotheses, but observations on eight variables: the seven explanatory variables and the dependent variable. However in this circumstance, the most careful collection of data would not allow us to avoid a fundamental problem. Valuable as it is, such an approach—which is essentially the method of structured, focused comparison—does not provide a methodology for causal inference with an indeterminate research design such as this. With seven causal variables and only three observations, the research design cannot determine which of the hypotheses, if any, is correct.

Faced with indeterminate explanations, we sometimes seek to consider additional possible causes of the event we are trying to explain. This is exactly the opposite of what the logic of explanation should lead us to do. Better or more complete description of each case study is not the solution, since with more parameters than observations, almost any answer about the impact of each of the seven variables is as consistent with the data as any other. No amount of description, regardless of how thick and detailed; no method, regardless of how clever; and no researcher, regardless of how skillful, can extract much about any of the causal hypotheses with an indeterminate research design. An attempt to include all possible explanatory variables can quickly push us over the line to an indeterminate research design.

A large number of additional case studies might solve the problem of the research design in the previous paragraph, but this may take more time and resources than we have at our disposal, or there may be only three examples of the phenomena being studied. One solution to the problem of indeterminacy would be to refocus the study on the effects of particular explanatory variables across a range of state action rather than on the causes of a particular set of effects, such as success in joint projects. An alternative solution that doesn't change the focus of the study so drastically might be to add a new set of observations measured at a different level of analysis. In addition to using the weapons system, it might be possible to identify every major decision in building each weapon system. This procedure could help considerably if there were significant additional information in these decisions relevant to the causal inference. And, as long as our theory has some implication for what these decisions should be like, we would not need to change the purpose of the project at all. If properly specified, then, our theory may have many observable implications and our data, especially if qualitative, may usually contain observations for many of these implications. If so, each case study may be converted into many observations by looking at its subparts. By adding new observations from different levels of analysis, we can generate multiple tests of these implications. This method is one of the most helpful ways to redesign qualitative research and to avoid (to some extent) both indeterminacy and omitted variable bias, which will be discussed in section 5.2. Indeed, expanding our observations through research design is the major theme of chapter 6 (especially section 6.3).

A Formal Analysis of the Problem of More Inferences than Observations. The easiest way to understand this problem is by taking a very simple case. We avoid generality in the proof that follows in order to maximize intuition. Although we do not provide the more general proof here, the intuition conveyed by this example applies much more generally.

Suppose we are interested in making inferences about two parameters in a causal model with two explanatory variables and a single dependent variable

$$E(Y) = X_1\beta_1 + X_2\beta_2, \tag{4.1}$$

but we have only a single observation to do the estimation (that is, $n = 1$). Suppose further that, for the sake of clarity, our observation consists of $X_1 = 3$, $X_2 = 5$, and $Y = 35$. Finally, let us suppose that in this instance Y happens to equal its expected value (which would occur by chance or if there were no random variability in Y). Thus, $E(Y) = 35$. We never know this last piece of information in practice (because of the randomness inherent in Y), so if we have trouble estimating β_1 and β_2 in this case, we will surely fail in the general case when we do not have this information about the expected value.

The goal, then, is to estimate the parameter values in the following equation:

$$E(Y) = X_1\beta_1 + X_2\beta_2 \tag{4.2}$$

$$35 = 3\beta_1 + 5\beta_2$$

The problem is that this equation has no unique solution. For example, the values ($\beta_1 = 10$, $\beta_2 = 1$) satisfy this equation, but so does ($\beta_1 = 5$, $\beta_2 = 4$) and ($\beta_1 = -10$, $\beta_2 = 13$). This is quite troubling since the different values of the parameters can indicate very different substantive implications about the causal effects of these two variables; in the last case, even a sign changed. Indeed, these solutions and an infinite number of others satisfy this equation equally well. Thus nothing in the problem can help us to distinguish among the solutions because all of them are equally consistent with our one observation.

4.1.2 Multicollinearity

Suppose we manage to solve the problem of too few observations by focusing on the effects of pre-chosen causes, instead of on the causes of observed effects, by adding observations at different levels of analysis or by some other change in the research design. We will still need to be concerned about the other problem that leads to indeterminate research designs—multicollinearity. We have taken the word "multicollinearity" from statistical research, especially regression analysis, but we mean to apply it much more generally. In particular, our usage includes any situation where we can perfectly predict one explanatory variable from one or more of the remaining explanatory variables. We apply no linearity assumption, as in the usual meaning of this word in statistical research.

For example, suppose two of the hypotheses in the study of arms collaboration mentioned above are as follows: (1) collaboration between countries that are dissimilar in size is more likely to be successful than collaboration among countries of similar size; and (2) collaboration is more successful between nonneighboring than neighboring countries. The explanatory variables behind these two hypotheses both focus on the negative impact of rivalry on collaboration; both are quite reasonable and might even have been justified by intensive interviews or by the literature on industrial policy. However, suppose we manage to identify only a small data set where the unit of analysis is a pair of countries. Suppose, in addition, we collect only two types of observations: (1) neighboring countries of dissimilar size and (2) nonneighboring countries of similar size. If all of our observations happen (by design or chance) to fall in these categories, it would be impossible to use these data to find any evidence whatsoever to support or deny either hypothesis. The reason is that the two explanatory variables are perfectly correlated: every observation in which the potential partners are of similar size concerns neighboring countries and vice versa. Size and geographic proximity are conceptually very different variables, but in this data set at least, they cannot be distinguished from each other. The best course of action at this point would be to collect additional observations in which states of similar size were neighbors. If this is impossible, then the only solution is to search for observable implications at some other level of analysis.

Even if the problem of an indeterminate research design has been solved, our causal inferences may remain highly uncertain due to problems such as insufficient numbers of observations or collinearity among our causal variables. To increase confidence in our estimates, we should always seek to *maximize leverage* over our problem. Thus, we should always observe as many implications of our theory as possible. Of course, we will always have practical constraints on the time and resources we can devote to data collection. But the need for more observations than inferences should sensitize us to the situations in which we should stop collecting detailed information about a particular case and start collecting information about other similar cases. Concerns about indeterminacy should also influence the way we define our unit of analysis: we will have trouble making valid causal inferences if nearly unique events are the only unit of analysis in our study, since finding many examples will be difficult. Even if we are interested in Communism, the French Revolution, or the causes of democracy, it will also pay to break the problem down into manageable and more numerous units.

Another recommendation is to maximize leverage by limiting the number of explanatory variables for which we want to make causal inferences. In limiting the explanatory variables, we must be careful to avoid omitted variable bias (section 5.2). The rules in section 5.3 should help in this. A successful project is one that explains a lot with a little. At best, the goal is to use a single explanatory variable to explain numerous observations on dependent variables.

A research design that explains a lot with a lot is not very informative, but an indeterminate design does not allow us to separate causal effects at all. The solution is to select observations on the same variables or others that are implications of our theory to avoid the problem. After formalizing multicollinearity (see box), we will turn to a more detailed analysis of methods of selecting observations and the problem of selection bias.

A Formal Analysis of Multicollinearity. We will use the same strategy as we did in the last formal analysis by providing a proof of only a specific case in order to clarify understanding. The intuition also applies far beyond the simple example here. We also use an example very similar to the one above.

Let us use the model in equation (4.1), but this time we have a very large number of observations and our two explanatory variables are perfect linear combinations of one another. In fact, to make the problem even more transparent, suppose that the two variables are the same, so that $X_1 = X_2$. We might have coded X_1 and X_2 as two substantively different variables (like gender and pregnancy), but in a sample of data they might turn out to be the same (if all women surveyed happened to be pregnant). Can we distinguish the causal effects of these different variables?

Note that equation (4.1) can be written as follows:

$$E(Y) = X_1\beta_1 + X_2\beta_2, \tag{4.3}$$

$$= X_1(\beta_1 + \beta_2)$$

As should be obvious from the second line of this equation, regardless of what $E(Y)$ and X_1 are, numerous values of β_1 and β_2 can satisfy it. (For example, if $\beta_1 = 5$ and $\beta_2 = -20$ satisfy equation (4.3), then so does $\beta_1 = -20$ and $\beta_2 = 5$.) Thus, although we now have many more observations than parameters, multicollinearity leaves us with the same problem as when we had more parameters than units: no estimation method can give us unique estimates of the parameters.

4.2 The Limits of Random Selection

We avoid selection bias in large-n studies if observations are randomly selected, because a random rule is uncorrelated with all possible explanatory or dependent variables.[2] Randomness is a powerful approach because it provides a selection procedure that is *automatically* uncorrelated with all variables. That is, with a large n, the odds of a selection rule correlating with any observed variable are extremely small. As a result, random selection of observations automatically eliminates selection bias in large-n studies. In a world in which there are many potential confounding variables, some of them unknown, randomness has many virtues for social scientists. If we have to abandon randomness, as is usually the case in political science research, we must do so with caution.

[2] We emphasize again that we should not confuse randomness with haphazardness. Random selection in this context means that every potential unit has an equal probability of selection into our sample and successive choices are independent, just as when names are picked out of a hat with replacements. This is only the simplest version of randomness, but all require specific probabilistic processes.

Controlled experiments are only occasionally constructed in the social sciences.[3] However, they provide a useful model for understanding certain aspects of the design of nonexperimental research. The best experiments usually combine random selection of observations and random assignments of values of the explanatory variables with a large number of observations (or experimental trials). Even though no experiment can solve the Fundamental Problem of Causal Inference, experimenters are often able to select their observations (rather than having them provided through social processes) and can assign treatments (values of the explanatory variables) to units. Hence it is worthwhile to focus on these two advantages of experiments: control over *selection of observations* and *assignment of values of the explanatory variables to units*. In practice, experimenters often do not select randomly, choosing instead from a convenient population such as college sophomores, but here we focus on the ideal situation. We discuss selection here, postponing our discussion of assignment of values of the explanatory variables until the end of chapter 5.

In qualitative research, and indeed in much quantitative research, random selection may not be feasible because the universe of cases is not clearly specified. For instance, if we wanted a random sample of foreign policy elites in the United States, we would not find an available list of all elites comparable to the list of congressional districts. We could put together lists from various sources, but there would always be the danger that these lists would have built in biases. For instance, the universe for selection might be based on government lists of citizens who have been consulted on foreign policy issues. Surely such citizens could be considered to be members of a foreign policy elite. But if the research problem had to do with the relationship between social background and policy preferences, we might have a list that was biased toward high-status individuals who are generally supportive of government policy. In addition, we might not be able to study a sample of elites chosen at random from a list because travel costs might be too high. We might have to select only those who lived in the local region—thus possibly introducing other biases.

Even when random selection is feasible, it is not necessarily a wise technique to use. Qualitative researchers often balk (appropriately) at the notion of random selection, refusing to risk missing important cases that might not have been chosen by random selection. (Why study revolutions if we don't include the French Revolution?) Indeed, if we have only a small number of observations, random selection may not solve the problem of selection bias but may even be worse than

[3] For some examples, see Roth (1988), Iyengar and Kinder (1987), Fiorina and Plott (1978), Plott and Levine (1978), and Palfrey (1991).

other methods of selection. We believe that many qualitative researchers understand this point intuitively when they complain about what they perceive as the misguided preaching of some quantitative researchers about the virtues of randomness. In fact, using a very simple formal model of qualitative research, we will now prove that random selection of observations in small-n research will often cause very serious biases.

Suppose we have three units that have observations on the dependent variable of (High, Medium, Low), but only two of these three are to be selected into the analysis ($n = 2$). We now need a selection rule. If we let 1 denote a unit selected into the analysis and 0 denote an omitted unit, then only three selection rules are possible: (1,1,0), which means that we select the High and Medium choices but not the Low case, (0,1,1), and (1,0,1). The problem is that only the last selection rule, in which the second unit is omitted, is uncorrelated with the dependent variable.[4] Since random selection of observations is equivalent to a random choice of one of these three possible selection rules, random selection of units in this small-n example will produce selection bias with two-thirds probability! More careful selection of observations using a priori knowledge of the likely values of the dependent variable might be able to choose the third selection rule with much higher probability and thus avoid bias.

Qualitative researchers rarely resort explicitly to randomness as a selection rule, but they must be careful to ensure that the selection criteria actually employed do not have similar effects. Suppose, for example, that a researcher is interested in those East European countries with Catholic heritage that were dominated by the Soviet Union after World War II: Czechoslovakia, Hungary, and Poland. This researcher observes substantial variation in their politics during the 1970s and 1980s: in Poland, a well-organized antigovernment movement (Solidarity) emerged; in Czechoslovakia a much smaller group of intellectuals was active (Charter 77); while in Hungary, no such large national movement developed. The problem is to explain this discrepancy.

Exploring the nature of antigovernment movements requires close analysis of newspapers, recently declassified Communist Party documents, and many interviews with participants—hence, knowledge of the language. Furthermore, the difficulty of doing research in contemporary Eastern Europe means that a year of research will be required to study each country. It seems feasible, therefore, to study only two

---

[4] The (1,1,0) selection rule omits the low end of the scale (the Low unit), and the second (0,1,1) omits the unit at the high end (the High unit). Only the third case, in which "Medium" is not selected, is uncorrelated with the dependent variable.

countries for this work. Fortunately, for reasons unconnected with this project, the researcher already knows Czech and Polish, so she decides to study Charter 77 in Czechoslovakia and Solidarity in Poland. This is obviously different from random assignment, but at least the reason for selecting these countries is probably unrelated to the dependent variable. However, in our example it turns out that her selection rule (linguistic knowledge) *is* correlated with her dependent variable and that she will therefore encounter selection bias. In this case, a non-random, informed selection might have been better—if it were not for the linguistic requirement.

This researcher could avoid selection bias by forgetting her knowledge of Czech and learning Hungarian instead. But this solution will hardly seem an attractive option! In this observation, the more realistic alternative is that she use her awareness of selection bias to judge the direction of bias, at least partially correct for it, and qualify her conclusions appropriately. At the outset, she knows that she has reduced the degree of variance on her dependent variable in a systematic manner, which should tend to cause her to underestimate her causal estimates, at least on average (although other problems with the same research might change this).

Furthermore she should at least do enough secondary research on Hungary to know, for any plausible explanatory variable, whether the direction of selection bias will be in favor of, or against, her hypothesis. For example, she might hypothesize on the basis of the Czech and Polish cases that mass-based antigovernment movements arise under lenient, relatively nonrepressive communist regimes but not under strong, repressive ones. She should know that although Hungary had the most lenient of the East European communist governments, it lacked a mass-based antigovernment movement. Thus, if possible, the researcher should expand the number of observations to avoid selection bias; but even if more observations cannot be studied thoroughly, some knowledge of additional observations can at least mitigate the problem. A very productive strategy would be to supplement these two detailed case studies with a few much less detailed cases based on secondary data and, perhaps, a much more aggregate (and necessarily superficial) analysis of a large number of cases. If the detailed case studies produce a clear causal hypothesis, it may be much easier to collect information on just those few variables identified as important for a much larger number of observations across countries. (See section 4.3 for an analogous discussion and more formal treatment.) Another solution might be to reorganize the massive information collected in each of the two case studies into numerous observable implications of the theory. For example, if the theory that government repression successfully inhibited the growth of antigovernment movements was correct, such movements should have done poorly in cities or regions where the secret police were zealous and efficient, as compared to those ares in which the secret police were more lax—controlling for the country involved.

4.3 SELECTION BIAS

How should we select observations for inclusion in a study? If we are interviewing city officials, which ones should we interview? If we are doing comparative case studies of major wars, which wars should we select? If we are interested in presidential vetoes, should we select all vetoes, all since World War II, a random sample, or only those overridden by Congress? No issue is so ubiquitous early in the design phase of a research project as the question: which cases (or more precisely, which observations) should we select for study? In qualitative research, the decision as to which observations to select is crucial for the outcome of the research and the degree to which it can produce determinate and reliable results.

As we have seen in section 4.2, random selection is not generally appropriate in small-n research. But abandoning randomness opens the door to many sources of bias. The most obvious example is when we, knowing what we want to see as the outcome of the research (the confirmation of a favorite hypothesis), subtly or not so subtly select observations on the basis of combinations of the independent and dependent variables that support the desired conclusion. Suppose we believe that American investment in third world countries is a prime cause of internal violence, and then we select a set of nations with major U.S. investments in which there has been a good deal of internal violence and another set of nations where there is neither investment nor violence. There are other observations that illustrate the other combinations (large investment and no violence, or no small investment and large violence) but they are "conveniently" left out. Most selection bias is not as blatant as this, but since selection criteria in qualitative research are often implicit and selection is often made without any self-conscious attempt to evaluate potential biases, there are many opportunities to allow bias subtly to intrude on our selection procedures.[5]

[5] This example is a good illustration of what makes science distinctive. When we introduce this bias in order to support the conclusion we want, we are not behaving as social scientists ought to behave, but rather the way many of us behave when we are in political arguments in which we are defending a political position we cherish. We often select examples that prove our point. When we engage in research, we should try to get all

4.3.1 Selection on the Dependent Variable

Random selection with a large-n allows us to ignore the relationship between the selection criteria and other variables in our analysis. Once we move away from random selection, we should consider how the criteria used relate to each variable. That brings us to a basic and obvious rule: *selection should allow for the possibility of at least some variation on the dependent variable*. This point seems so obvious that we would think it hardly needs to be mentioned. How can we explain variations on a dependent variable if it does not vary? Unfortunately, the literature is full of work that makes just this mistake of failing to let the dependent variable vary; for example, research that tries to explain the outbreak of war with studies only of wars, the onset of revolutions with studies only of revolutions, or patterns of voter turnout with interviews only of nonvoters.[6]

We said in chapter 1 that good social scientists frequently thrive on anomalies that need to be explained. One consequence of this orientation is that investigators, particularly qualitative researchers, may select observations having a common, puzzling outcome, such as the social revolutions that occurred in France in the eighteenth century and those that occurred in France and China in the twentieth (Skocpol 1979). Such a choice of observations represents selection on the dependent variable, and therefore risks the selection bias discussed in this section. When observations are selected on the basis of a particular value of the dependent variable, nothing whatsoever can be learned about the causes of the dependent variable without taking into account other instances when the dependent variable takes on other values. For example, Theda Skocpol (1979) partially solves this problem in her research by explicitly including some limited information about "moments of revolutionary crisis" (Skocpol 1984:380) in seventeenth-century England, nineteenth-century Prussia/Germany, and nineteenth-century Japan. She views these observations as "control cases," although they are discussed in much less detail than her principal cases. The bias induced by selecting on the dependent variable does not imply that we should never take into account values of the dependent variable when designing research. What it does mean, as we

---

observations if possible. If selection is required, we should attempt to get those observations which are pivotal in deciding the question of interest, not those which merely support our position.

[6] In this section, we do not consider the possibility that a specific research project that is designed not to let the dependent variable change at all is part of a larger research program and therefore can provide useful information about causal hypotheses. We explain this point in section 4.4.

discuss below and in chapter 6, is that we must be aware of the biases introduced by such selection on the dependent variable and seek insofar as possible to correct for these biases.

There is also a milder and more common version of the problem of selection on the dependent variable. In some instances, the research design does allow variation on the dependent variable but that variation is truncated: that is, we limit our observations to less than the full range of variation on the dependent variable that exists in the real world. In these cases, something can be said about the causes of the dependent variable; but the inferences are likely to be biased since, if the explanatory variables do not take into account the selection rule, *any selection rule correlated with the dependent variable attenuates estimates of causal effects on average* (see Achen, 1986; King 1989: chapter 9). In quantitative research, this result means that numerical estimates of causal effects will be closer to zero than they really are. In qualitative research, selection bias will mean that the true causal effect is larger than the qualitative researcher is led to believe (unless of course the researcher is aware of our argument and adjusts his or her estimates accordingly). If we know selection bias exists and have no way to get around it by drawing a better sample, these results indicate that our estimate at least gives, on average, a lower bound to the true causal effect. The extent to which we underestimate the causal effect depends on the severity of the selection bias (the extent to which the selection rule is correlated with the dependent variable), about which we should have at least some idea, if not detailed evidence.

The cases of extreme selection bias—where there is by design no variation on the dependent variable—are easy to deal with: avoid them! We will not learn about causal effects from them. The modified form of selection bias, in which observations are selected in a manner related to the dependent variable, may be harder to avoid since we may not have access to all the observations we want. But fortunately the effects of this bias are not as devastating since we can learn something; our inferences might be biased but they will be so in a predictable way that we *can* compensate for. The following examples illustrate this point.

Given that we will often be forced to choose observations in a manner correlated with the dependent variable, and we therefore have selection bias, it is worthwhile to see whether we can still extract some useful information. Figure 4.1, a simple pictorial model of selection bias, shows that we can. Each dot is an observation (a person, for example). The horizontal axis is the explanatory variable (for example, number of accounting courses taken in business school). The vertical axis is the dependent variable (for example, starting salary in the first

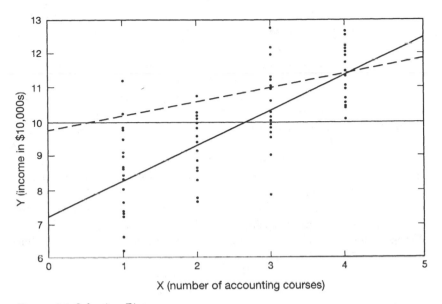

Figure 4.1 Selection Bias

full-time job, in units of $10,000). The regression line showing the relationship between these two variables is the solid line fit to the scatter of points. Each additional accounting course is worth on average about an additional $10,000 in starting salary. The scatter of points around this line indicates that, as usual, the regression line does not fit each student's situation perfectly. In figures like these, the *vertical* deviations between the points and the line represent the errors in predictions (given particular values of the explanatory variables) and are therefore minimized in fitting a line to the points.

Now suppose an incoming business-school student were interested in studying how he could increase his starting salary upon graduation. Not having learned about selection bias, this student decides to choose for study a sample of previous students composed only of those who did well in their first job—the ones who received jobs he would like. It may *seem* that if he wants to learn about how to earn more money it would be best to focus only on those with high earnings, but this reasoning is fallacious. For simplicity, suppose the choice included only those making at least $100,000. This sample selection rule is portrayed in figure 4.1 by a solid horizontal line at $Y = 10$, where only the points above the line are included in this student's study. Now, instead of fitting a regression line to all the points, he fits a line (the dashed line) only to the points in his sample. Selection bias exerts its effect by decreasing this line's slope compared to that of the solid line.

As a result of the selection bias, this student would incorrectly conclude that each additional accounting course is worth only about $5,000.

This is a specific example of the way in which we can underestimate a causal effect when we have selection on the dependent variable. Luckily, there *is* something our student can do about his problem. Suppose after this student completes business school, he gets bored with making money and goes to graduate school in one of the social sciences where he learns about selection bias. He is very busy preparing for comprehensive examinations, so he does not have the time to redo his study properly. Nevertheless, he does know that his starting salary would have increased by some amount significantly *more* than his estimate of $5,000 for each additional accounting class. Since his selection rule was quite severe (indeed it was deterministic), he concludes that he would have made more money in business if he had taken additional accounting classes—but having decided not to maximize his income (who would enter graduate school with that in mind?)—he is thankful that he did not learn about selection bias until his values had changed.

4.3.1.1 EXAMPLES OF INVESTIGATOR-INDUCED SELECTION BIAS

The problem just described is common in qualitative research (see Geddes 1990). It can arise from a procedure as apparently innocuous as selecting cases based on available data, if data availability is related to the dependent variable. For instance, suppose we are interested in the determinants of presidential involvement in significant foreign policy decisions during recent years and that we propose to study those decisions on which information about the president's participation in meetings is available. The problem with this research design is that the selection rule (information availability) is probably correlated with relatively low levels of presidential involvement (the dependent variable) since the more secret meetings, which will not be available to us, are likely to have involved the president more fully than those whose deliberations have become public. Hence the set of observations on which information is available will overrepresent events with lower presidential involvement, thus biasing our inferences about the determinants of presidential involvement.

The reasoning used in our business-school example can help us learn about the consequences of unavoidable selection bias in qualitative research. Suppose, in the study just mentioned, we were interested in whether presidents are more involved when the events entail threats of force than when no such threats were made. Suppose also that existing evidence, based on perhaps two dozen observations, indicates that such a relationship does exist, but that its magnitude is surprisingly small. To assess the degree of selection bias in this research, we would first compile a list of foreign policy situations in which the president took action or made public pronouncements, regardless of whether we had any information on decision-making processes. This list would avoid one source of selection bias that we had identified: greater secrecy with respect to decision-making involving threats of force. Our new list would not be a complete census of issues in which the president was engaged, since it would miss covert operations and those on which no actions were taken, but it would be a larger list than our original one, which required information about decision-making. We could then compare the two lists to ascertain whether (as we suspect) cases on which we had decision-making information were biased against those in which force was used or threatened. If so, we could reasonably infer that the true relationship was probably even stronger than it seemed from our original analysis.

The problem of selection bias appears often in comparative politics when researchers need to travel to particular places to study their subject matter. They often have limited options when it comes to choosing what units to study since some governments restrict access by foreign scholars. Unfortunately, the refusal to allow access may be correlated with the dependent variable in which the scholar is interested. A researcher who wanted to explain the liberalization of authoritarian regimes on the basis of the tactics used by dissident groups might produce biased results, especially if she only studied those places that allowed her to enter, since the factors that led the regime to allow her in would probably be correlated with the dependent variable, liberalization. We obviously do not advise clandestine research in inhospitable places. But we do advise self-conscious awareness of these problems and imagination in finding alternative data sources when on-site data are unavailable. Recognition of these difficulties could also lead to revision of our research designs to deal with the realities of scholarly access around the world. If no data solution is available, then we might be able to use these results on selection bias at least to learn in which direction our results will be biased—and thus perhaps provide a partial correction to the inevitable selection bias in a study like this. That is, if selection bias is unavoidable, we should analyze the problem and ascertain the direction and, if possible, the magnitude of the bias, then use this information to adjust our original estimates in the right direction.

Selection bias is such an endemic problem that it may be useful to consider some more examples. Consider a recent work by Michael Porter (1990). Porter was interested in the sources of what he called "competitive advantage" for contemporary industries and firms. He designed a large-scale research project with ten national teams to study the subject. In selecting the ten nations for analysis, he chose, in his words, "ones that already compete successfully in a range of such industries, or, in the case of Korea and Singapore, show signs of an improving ability to do so" (Porter 1990:22). In his eagerness to explore the puzzle that interested him, Porter intentionally selected on his dependent variable, making his observed dependent variable nearly constant. As a result, any attempts by Porter, or anyone else using these data at this level of analysis, to explain variations in success among his ten countries will produce seriously biased causal effects.

But what Porter did—try to determine the circumstances and policies associated with competitive success—was somewhat related to Mill's method of agreement. This method is not a bad first attempt at the problem, in that it enabled Porter to develop some hypotheses about the causes of competitive advantage by seeing what these nations have in common; however, his research design made it impossible to evaluate any individual causal effect.

More serious is the logical flaw in the method: without a control group of nations (that is, with his explanatory variable set to other values), he cannot determine whether the absence of the hypothesized causal variables is associated with competitive failure. Thus, he has no way of knowing whether the conditions he has associated with success are not also associated with failure. In his provocative work, Porter has presented a fascinating set of *hypotheses* based on his cases of success, but without a range of competitive successes and failures (or selection based on something other than his dependent variable) he has no way of knowing whether he is totally right, completely wrong, or somewhere in between.[7]

A striking example of selection bias is found in the foreign policy literature dealing with deterrence: that is, "the use of threats to induce the opponents to behave in desirable ways" (Achen and Snidal 1989: 151). Students of deterrence have often examined "acute crises"—that is, those that have not been deterred at an earlier stage in the process of political calculation, signalling, and action. For descriptive pur-

[7] Porter claims to have numerous examples of countries which were not successful; however, these are introduced in his analyses by way of selectively chosen anecdotes and are not studied with similar methods as his original ten. When nonsystematically selecting supporting examples from the infinite range of supporting and nonsupporting possibilities, it is much too easy to fool ourselves into finding a relationship when none exists. We take no position on whether Porter's hypotheses are correct and only wish to point out that the information needed to make this decision must be collected more systematically.

poses, there is much to be said for such a focus, at least initially: as in Porter's emphasis on competitive success, the observer is able to describe the most significant episodes of interest and may be enabled to formulate hypotheses about the causes of observed outcomes. But as a basis for inference (and without appropriate corrections), such a biased set of observations is seriously flawed because instances in which deterrence has worked (at earlier stages in the process) have been systematically excluded from the set of observations to be analyzed. "When the cases are then misused to estimate the success rate of deterrence, the design induces a 'selection bias' of the sort familiar from policy-evaluation research" (Achen and Snidal 1989:162).

4.3.1.2 EXAMPLES OF SELECTION BIAS INDUCED BY THE WORLD

Does choosing a census of observations, instead of a sample, enable us to avoid selection bias? We might think so since there was apparently no selection at all, but this is not always correct. For example, suppose we wish to make a descriptive inference by estimating the strength of support for the Liberal party in New York State. Our dependent variable is the percent of the vote in New York State Assembly districts cast for the candidate (or candidates) endorsed by the Liberal party. The problem here is that the party often chooses not to endorse candidates in many electoral districts. If they do not endorse candidates in districts where they feel sure that they will lose (which seems to be the case), then we will have selection bias even if we choose every district in which the Liberal party made an endorsement. *The selection process in this example is performed as part of the political process we are studying, but it can have precisely the same consequences for our study as if we caused the problem ourselves.*

This problem of bias when the selection of cases is correlated with the dependent variable is one of the most general difficulties faced by those scholars who use the historical record as the source of their evidence, and they include virtually all of us. The reason is that the processes of "history" differentially select that which remains to be observed according to a set of rules that are not always clear from the record. However, it is *essential* to discover the process by which these data are produced. Let us take an example from another field: some cultures have created sculptures in stone, others in wood. Over time, the former survive, the latter decay. This pattern led some European scholars of art to underestimate the quality and sophistication of early African art, which tended to be made of wood, because the "history" had selectively eliminated some examples of sculpture while maintaining others. The careful scholar must always evaluate the possible selection biases in the evidence that is available: what kinds of events are likely to have been recorded; what kinds of events are likely to have been ignored?

Consider another example. Social scientists often begin with an end point that they wish to "explain"—for example, the peculiar organizational configurations of modern states. The investigator observes that at an early point in time (say, A.D. 1500) a wide variety of organizational units existed in Europe, but at a later time (say, A.D. 1900), all, or almost all, important units were national states. What the researcher should do is begin with units in 1500 and explain later organizational forms in terms of a limited number of variables. Many of the units of analysis would have disappeared in the interim, because they lost wars or were otherwise amalgamated into larger entities; others would have survived. Careful categorization could thus yield a dependent variable that would index whether the entity that became a national state is still in existence in 1900; or if not, when it disappeared.

However, what many historical researchers inadvertently do is quite different. They begin, as Charles Tilly (1975: 15) has observed, by doing *retrospective* research: selecting "a small number of West European states still existing in the nineteenth and twentieth centuries for comparison." Unfortunately for such investigators, "England, France, and even Spain are *survivors* of a ruthless competition in which most contenders lost." The Europe of 1500 included some five hundred more or less independent political units, the Europe of 1900 about twenty-five. The German state did not exist in 1500, or even 1800. Comparing the histories of France, Germany, Spain, Belgium, and England (or, for that matter, any other set of modern Western European countries) for illumination on the processes of state-making weights the whole inquiry toward a certain kind of outcome which was, in fact, quite rare.

Such a procedure therefore selects on the basis of one value of the dependent variable—survival in the year 1900. It will bias the investigator's results, on average reducing the attributed effects of explanatory variables that distinguish the surviving states from their less durable counterparts. Tilly and his colleagues (1975), recognizing the selection bias problem, moved from a *retrospective* toward a *prospective* formulation of their research problem. Suppose, however, that such a huge effort had not been possible, or suppose they wished to collect the best available evidence in preparation for their larger study. They could have reanalyzed the available retrospective studies, inferring that those studies' estimates of causal effects were in most observations biased downward. They would need to remember that, even if the criteria described above do apply exactly, any one application might overestimate or underestimate the causal effect. The best guess of the true causal effect, based on the flawed retrospective studies, however, would be that the causal effects were underestimated at least on average—if we assume that the rules above do apply and the criteria for selection were correlated with the dependent variable.

4.3.2 Selection on an Explanatory Variable

Selecting observations for inclusion in a study according to the categories of the key causal explanatory variable causes no inference problems. The reason is that our selection procedure does not predetermine the outcome of our study, since we have not restricted the degree of possible variation in the dependent variable. By limiting the range of our key causal variable, we may limit the generality of our conclusion or the certainty with which we can legitimately hold it, but we do not introduce bias. By selecting cases on the basis of values of this variable, we can control for that variable in our case selection. Bias is not introduced even if the causal variable is correlated with the dependent variable since we have already controlled for this explanatory variable.[8] Thus, it is possible to avoid bias while selecting on a variable that is correlated with the dependent variable, so long as we control for that variable in the analysis.

It is easy to see that selection on an explanatory variable causes no bias by referring again to figure 4.1. If we restricted this figure to exclude all the observations for which the explanatory variable equaled one, the logic of this figure would remain unchanged, and the correct line fit to the points would not change. The line would be somewhat less certain, since we now have fewer observations and less information to bear on the inference problem, but on average there would be no bias.[9]

Thus, one can avoid bias by selecting cases based on the key causal variable, but we can also achieve the same objective by selecting according to the categories of a control variable (so long as it is causally prior to the key causal variable, as all control variables should be). Experiments almost always select on the explanatory variables. Units are created when we manipulate the explanatory variables (administering a drug, for example) and watch what happens to the dependent variable (whether the patient's health improves). It would be difficult to select on the dependent variable in this case, since its value is not even

[8] In general, selection bias occurs when selecting on the dependent variable, after taking into account (or controlling for) the explanatory variables. Since one of these explanatory variables is the method of selection, we control for it and do not introduce bias.

[9] The inference would also be less certain if the range of values of the explanatory variables were limited through this selection. See section 6.2.

known until after the experiment. However, most experiments are far from perfect, and we can make the mistake of selecting on the dependent variable by inadvertently giving some treatments to patients based on their expected response.

For another example, if we are researching the effect of racial discrimination on black children's grades in school, it would be quite reasonable to select several schools with little discrimination and some with a lot of discrimination. Even though our selection rule will be correlated with the dependent variable (blacks get lower grades in schools with more discrimination), it will not be correlated with the dependent variable *after* taking into account the effect of the explanatory variables, since the selection rule is determined by the values of one of the explanatory variables.

We can also avoid bias by selecting on an explanatory variable that is irrelevant to our study (and has no effect on our dependent variable). For example, to study the effects of discrimination on grades, suppose someone chose all schools whose names begin with the letter "A." This, of course, is not recommended, but it would cause no bias as long as this irrelevant variable is not a proxy for some other variable that is correlated with the dependent variable.

One situation in which selection by an irrelevant variable can be very useful involves secondary analysis of existing data. For example, suppose we are interested in what makes for a successful coup d'etat. Our key hypothesis is that coups are more often successful when led by a military leader rather than a civilian one. Suppose we find a study of attempted coups that selected cases based on the extent to which the country had a hierarchical bureaucracy before a coup. We could use these data even if hierarchical bureaucratization is irrelevant to our research. To be safe, however, it would be easy enough to include this variable as a control in our analysis of the effects of military versus civilian leaders. We would include this control by studying the frequency of coup success for military versus civilian leaders in countries with and then without hierarchical bureaucratization. The presence of this control will help us avoid selection bias and its causal effect will indicate some possibly relevant information about the process by which the observations were really selected.

4.3.3 Other Types of Selection Bias

In all of the above examples, selection bias was introduced when the units were chosen according to some rule correlated with the dependent variable or correlated with the dependent variable after the explanatory variables were taken into account. With this type of selection effect, estimated causal effects are always underestimates. This is by far the most common type of selection bias in both qualitative and quantitative research. However, it is worth mentioning another type of selection bias, since its effects can be precisely the opposite and cause *overestimation* of a causal effect.

Suppose the causal effect of some variable varies over the observations. Although we have not focused on this possibility, it is a real one. In section 3.1, we defined a causal effect for a single unit and allowed the effect to differ across units. For example, suppose we were interested in the causal effect of poverty on political violence in Latin American countries. This relationship might be stronger in some countries, such as those with a recent history of political violence, than in others. In this situation, where causal effects vary over the units, a selection rule correlated with the size of the causal effect would induce bias in estimates of *average* causal effects. Hence if we conducted our study only in countries with recent histories of political violence but sought to generalize from our findings to Latin America as a whole, we would be likely to overestimate the causal effect under investigation. If we selected units with large causal effects and averaged these effects during estimation, we would get an overestimate of the average causal effect. Similarly, if we selected units with small effects, the estimate of the average causal effect would be smaller than it should be.

4.4 Intentional Selection of Observations

In political science research, we typically have no control over the values of our explanatory variables; they are assigned by "nature" or "history" rather than by us. In this common situation, the main influence we can have at this stage of research design is in selecting cases and observations. As we have seen in section 4.2, when we are able to focus on only a small number of observations, we should rarely resort to random selection of observations. Usually, selection must be done in an *intentional* fashion, consistent with our research objectives and strategy.

Intentional selection of observations implies that we know in advance the values of at least some of the relevant variables, and that random selection of observations is ruled out. We are least likely to be fooled when cases are selected based on categories of the explanatory variables. The research itself, then, involves finding out the values of the dependent variable. However, in practice, we often have fragmentary evidence about the values of many of our variables, even before selection of observations. This can be dangerous, since we can inadvertently and unknowingly introduce selection bias, perhaps favoring our prior hypothesis. We will now discuss the various methods of intentional selection of observations.

4.4.1 Selecting Observations on the Explanatory Variable

As just noted, the best "intentional" design selects observations to ensure variation in the explanatory variable (and any control variables) without regard to the values of the dependent variables. Only during the research do we discover the values of the dependent variable and then make our initial causal inference by examining the differences in the distribution of outcomes on the dependent variable for given values of the explanatory variables.

For example, suppose we are interested in the effect of formal arms-control treaties on United States and Soviet decisions to procure armaments during the Cold War. Our key causal variable, then, is the existence of a formal arms-control treaty covering a particular weapons sytem in a country. We could choose a set of weapons types—some of which are covered by treaty limitations and some of which are not—that vary in relation to our explanatory variable. Our dependent variable, on which we did not select, might be the rate of change in weapons procurement. Insofar as the two sets of observations were well matched on the control variables and if problems such as that of endogeneity are successfully resolved, such a design could permit valid inferences about the effects of arms control agreements.

Sometimes we are interested in only one of several explanatory variables that seems to have a substantial effect on the dependent variable. In such a situation, it is appropriate to control for the variable in which we are not primarily (or currently) interested. An example of this procedure was furnished by Jack Snyder (1991). Snyder selected nations he described as the "main contenders for power" in the modern era in order to study their degree of "overexpansion" (his dependent variable). A very important variable affecting overexpansion is military power, but this cause is so obvious and well documented that Snyder was not interested in investing more resources in estimating its effects again. Instead, he controlled for military power by choosing only nations with high levels of this variable. By holding this important control variable nearly constant, Snyder could make no inference about the effect of power on overexpansion, but he could focus on the explanatory variables of interest to him without suffering the effects of omitted variable bias. Beyond these aspects of his research design, Snyder's was an exploratory study. He did not identify all his explanatory variables before commencing his research (Snyder 1991:61–65). Such an open-ended research design probably led him to ideas he would not have otherwise considered, but it also meant that the questions he eventually asked were not as efficiently answered as they could have been. In particular, the range of variation on the explanatory variables that did interest him was probably not as large as it could have been. In addition, he did not evaluate the theory in a set of data other than the one in which it was formulated.

As we have emphasized throughout in this book, "purist" advice—always select on explanatory variables, never on dependent variables—is often unrealistic for qualitative research. When we must take into account the values of the dependent variable in gathering data, or when the data available already take into account these values, all is not lost. Information about causal effects can still be gained. But bias is likely to be introduced if we are not especially careful.

4.4.2 Selecting a Range of Values of the Dependent Variable

An alternative to choosing observations on the explanatory variable would be to select our observations across a range of values of the dependent variable. Research often begins this way: we find some fascinating instances of variation in behavior that we want to explain. In such a retrospective research design (in epidemiology, this is called a "case-control" study), we select observations with particularly high and particularly low values of the dependent variable. As we have emphasized, although this selection process may help with causal inferences, this design is useless for making *descriptive* inferences about the dependent variable. Furthermore, the absence of systematic descriptive data, and the increased possibility of other problems caused by possible nonlinearities or variable causal effects, means that this procedure will not generally yield valid causal inferences.

A retrospective research design may help us to gain some valuable information about the empirical plausibility of a *causal* inference, since we might well find that high and low values of the dependent variable are associated with high and low values, respectively, of potential explanatory variables. However, if this design is to lead to meaningful—albeit necessarily limited—causal inferences, it is crucial to select observations without regard to values of the explanatory variables. We must not search for those observations that fit (or do not fit) our a priori theory. The observations should be as representative as possible of the population of observations to which we wish to generalize. If we found that high and low values of potential explanatory variables are associated with high and low values of the dependent variable, we might then want to design a study in which observations are selected only on the explanatory variable(s) to assess whether our hypothesis is correct. At a minimum, the results must be uncertain at the outset or else we can learn nothing. To have uncertainty about causal inferences, we must leave values of the explanatory or dependent variable to be determined by the research situation.

For example, we might observe puzzling variations in violent conflict among states and speculate that they were caused by different forms of government. It might be worthwhile to begin, in an exploratory way, by carefully examining some bilateral relationships in which war was frequent and others that were characterized by exceptional degrees of peace. Suppose we found that the observations of war were associated with relationships involving at least one modernizing autocracy and that observations of peace were associated with both states being stable democracies. Such an exploratory investigation would generate a more precise hypothesis than we began with. We could not pronounce our hypothesis confirmed, since we would not yet have a clear picture of the general patterns (having selected observations on the dependent variable), but we might be encouraged to test it with a design that selected observations on the basis of the explanatory variable. In such a design, we would choose observations without regard to the degree of military conflict observed. We would seek to control for other potentially relevant causal variables and attempt to determine whether variations in regime type were associated with degree of military conflict.

4.4.3 Selecting Observations on Both Explanatory and Dependent Variables

It is dangerous to select observations intentionally on the basis of both the explanatory and dependent variables, because in so doing, it is easy to bias the result inadvertently. The most egregious error is to select observations in which the explanatory and dependent variables vary together in ways that are known to be consistent with the hypothesis that the research purports to test. For instance, we may want to test whether it is true that authoritarian rule (which suppresses labor organization and labor demands) leads to high rates of economic growth. We might select observations that vary on both variables but select them deliberately so that all the authoritarian observations have high growth rates and all the nonauthoritarian observations have low growth rates. Such a research design can describe or explain nothing, since without examining a representative set of observations, we cannot determine whether economic growth may be as, or more, likely in observations where a democratic regime allows labor organization.

Despite the risk involved in selection on *both* the explanatory and dependent variables, there may be rare instances in limited-n observation studies when it makes some sense to follow procedures that take into account information about the values of dependent as well as explanatory variables, although this is a dangerous technique that requires great caution in execution. For example, suppose that the distribution of the values of our dependent variable was highly skewed such that most observations took one value of that variable. If we selected observations on the basis of variation in the explanatory variable and allowed the values of the dependent variable to "fall where they may," we might be left with no variation in the latter. Nothing about this result would disqualify the data from being analyzed. In fact, when the values of the dependent variable turn out to be the same regardless of the values of the explanatory variables, we have a clear case of zero causal effect. The only situation where this might be worrisome is if we believe that the true causal effect is very small, but not zero. In small-n research, we are unlikely to be able to distinguish our estimated zero effect from a small but nonzero effect with much certainty. The most straightforward solution in this situation is to increase the number of observations. Another possibility is to select observations based on very extreme values of the explanatory variables, so that a small causal effect will be easier to spot. If these are not sufficient, then selection on the explanatory and dependent variables (but not both simultaneously) could increase the power of the research design sufficiently to find the effect we are looking for. (See section 6.3 for additional suggestions.)

Thus, it might make sense to use sampling techniques to choose observations on the basis first of variation in the explanatory variable, but also such that a number of observations having the rare value of the dependent variable would be included. In doing so, however, it is important not to predetermine the value of the explanatory variable with which the dependent variable is associated. Furthermore, in using this procedure, we must be aware of the potential introduced for bias, and therefore, of the limited value of our inferences. In other words, in these rare cases, we can select based on the values of the explanatory variables and on the values of the dependent variable, but not on both simultaneously.[10]

---

[10] In still other words, if we select based on the marginal distributions of the dependent and explanatory variables, we can still learn about the joint distribution by doing the study.

For example, suppose we hypothesized that a particular pattern of joint membership in certain international organizations significantly inhibited the outbreak of violent conflict between any pair of states. Following our preferred method of selecting only on the explanatory variable, our observations would be pairs of nations that varied over specified periods of time in their international organizational memberships. Suppose also that it was difficult to establish whether the specified membership patterns exist, so that we could only examine a relatively small number of observations—not hundreds or thousands but only scores of pairs of states. The difficulty for our preferred method would arise if conflict were rare—for example, it broke out in the specified time period for only one pair of states in a thousand. In such a situation, we might select pairs of nations that varied on the explanatory variable (institutional membership) but find that no selected pair of states experienced violent conflict.

Under such conditions, a mixed-selection procedure might be wise. We might choose observations on the basis of some variation in the explanatory variable (some pairs of nations with specified membership patterns and some without) and select more observations than we had intended to study. We might then divide these potential observations into two categories on the basis of whether there was armed conflict between the nations in a particular time period and then choose disproportionate numbers of observations in the category with armed conflict in order to get examples of each in our final set of observations. Such a procedure would have to be carried out *in some manner that was independent of our knowledge about the observations in terms of the explanatory variable*. For example, we might choose from the no-conflict observations randomly and select all of the conflict observations. Then, if there was a strong association between organizational membership patterns and military conflict in the final set of observations, we might be willing to make tentative causal inferences.

Atul Kohli's study of the role of the state in poverty policy in India (1987) illustrates the constraints on the selection of observations in small-*n* research, the consequences of these constraints for valid causal inference, and some ways of overcoming the constraints. Kohli was interested in the effect of governmental authority structures and regime types on the prevalence of policies to alleviate poverty in developing countries. His argument, briefly stated, is that regimes that have a clear ideological commitment to aid the poor, that bar the participation of upper-class groups in the regime, and that have a strong organizational capacity will create effective policies to achieve their goal. Regimes that lack such ideological commitment, that have a broad class base, and that lack tight organization will be ineffective in developing such policies even if ostensibly committed to do so.

Kohli focuses on India, where his research interests lie and for which he has linguistic skills. His primary observations are Indian states. As he notes, "The federal nature of the Indian polity allows for a disaggregated and comparative analysis within India. Below the federal government, the state (or provincial) governments in India play a significant role in the formulation and execution of agrarian policies. Variations in the nature of political rule at the state level can lead to differential effectiveness in the pursuit of antipoverty programs" (1987:3–4). Kohli assumes a less strict (but appropriate) version of unit homogeneity, that of "constant effect": that the causal effect is identical in states with different levels of his key explanatory factors—that is, the degree of ideology, class basis, and organization hypothesized as conducive to antipoverty policies. He can evaluate his causal hypothesis only by comparing his dependent variable across different states while making this "constant effect" assumption in each.

A sample of Indian states is useful, he argues, because they are, relatively speaking, similar. At least they "approximate the ceteris paribus assumption . . . better than most independent nations" (Kohli 1987:4). But which states to choose? The intensive studies that he wanted to carry out (based on two long-planned field trips to India) precluded studying all states. Given his constraints, three states were all he could choose. To have selected the three states at random would have been unwise since random selection is only guaranteed to help with a large-n. Most of the Indian states have regimes with the features that impede the development of poverty-alleviating policies and therefore have few of these policies. Indeed, only West Bengal has a regime with the features that would foster antipoverty policies. As Kohli points out, West Bengal had to be in his sample. He then added two more states, Uttar Pradesh, which has few antipoverty programs and Karnatake, a state in between these two extremes. These states were selected entirely on the dependent variable "because they represent a continuum of maximum to minimum governmental efforts in mitigating rural poverty" (Kohli 1987:7).

The problem with the study is that the values of the explanatory variables are also known; the selection, in effect, is on both the explanatory and dependent variables. Under these circumstances the design is indeterminate and provides no information about his causal hypothesis. That is, the hypothesis cannot be evaluated with observations selected in a manner known in advance to fit the hypothesis.

Is the study, then, of any value? Not much, if Kohli is only evaluating his hypothesis at the level of these three states. Fortunately, he does considerably more. He conceptualizes his study as having only three observations, but as with many studies that at first seem to have a small *n*, he has many more observations. It is, in fact, a large-*n* study. Kohli goes beyond the simple finding that the explanatory and dependent variables at the state level in the three cases are consistent with his hypothesis. He does so by looking at the numerous observable implications of his hypothesis both within the states he studies and in other countries. Since these approaches to *apparently* small-*n* research form the subject of the next chapter, we will describe his strategy for dealing with a small *n* in section 6.3.1.

At the aggregate level of analysis, however, Kohli could have done more to improve his causal inferences. For example, he probably knew or could have ascertained the values of his explanatory and dependent variables for virtually all of the Indian states. A valuable addition to his book would have been a short chapter briefly surveying all the states. This would have provided a good sense of the overall veracity of his causal hypothesis, as well as making it possible to select his three case studies according to more systematic rules.

4.4.4 Selecting Observations So the Key Causal Variable Is Constant

Sometimes social scientists design research in such a way that the explanatory variable that forms the basis of selection is constant. Such an approach is obviously deficient: the causal effect of an explanatory variable that does not vary cannot be assessed. Hence, a research design that purports to show the effect of a constant feature of the environment is unlikely to be very productive—at least by itself. However, most research is part of a literature or research tradition (see section 1.2.1), and so some useful prior information is likely to be known. For example, the usual range of the dependent variable might be very well known when the explanatory variable takes on, for instance, one particular value. The researcher who conducts a study to find out the range of the dependent variable for one other different value of the explanatory variable can be the first to estimate the causal effect.

Consider the following example where research conducted with no variation in the explanatory variable led to a reasonable, though tentative, hypothesis for a causal effect, which was in turn refuted by further research in which the explanatory variable took another value. In some early research on the impact of industrialization, Inkeles and Rossi (1956) compared a number of industrialized nations in terms of the prestige assigned to various occupations. They found a great deal of similarity across a set of nations that was quite varied except that they all were industrialized. They concluded that industrialization was the causal variable that led to the particular prestige hierarchy they observed. In the absence of variation in their explanatory variable (all the nations studied were industrialized), a firm inference of causality would have been inappropriate, though a more tentative conclusion which made the hypothesis more plausible was reasonable. However, other researchers replicated the study in the Phillipines and Indonesia (which are not industrialized)—thereby varying the value of the explanatory variable—and found a similar prestige hierarchy, thus calling into question the causal effect of industrialization (see Zelditch 1971).

The previous example shows how a sequence of research projects can overcome the problems of valid inference when the original research lacked variation in the explanatory variable. David Laitin (1986) provides an enlightening example of the way in which a single researcher can, in a sequence of studies, overcome such a problem. In his study of the impact of religious change on politics among the Yoruba in Nigeria, Laitin discusses why he was not able to deal with this issue in his previous study of Somalia. As he points out, religion, his explanatory variable, is a constant throughout Somalia and is, in addition, multicollinear (see section 4.1) with other variables, thereby making it impossible to isolate its causal effect. "Field research in Somalia led me to raise the question of the independent impact of religious change on politics; but further field research in Somalia would not have allowed me to address that question systematically. How is one to measure the impact of Islam on a society where everyone is a Muslim? Everyone there also speaks Somali. Nearly everyone shares a nomadic heritage. Nearly every Somali has been exposed to the same poetic tradition. Any common orientation toward action could be attributed to the Somali's poetic, or nomadic, or linguistic traditions rather than their religious tradition" (1986:186). Laitin overcomes this problem by turning his research attention to the Yoruba of Nigeria, who are divided into Muslims and Christians. We will see in chapter 5 how he does this.

4.4.5 Selecting Observations So the Dependent Variable Is Constant

We can also learn nothing about a causal effect from a study which selects observations so that the dependent variable does not vary. But sufficient information may exist in the literature to use with this study to produce a valid causal inference.

Thus a study of why a certain possible outcome never occurred should, if possible, be changed to create variation on the dependent as well as explanatory variables. For instance, if the research question is why antebellum South Carolina plantation owners failed to use fertilizer in optimal amounts to maintain soil fertility, we can learn little at the level of the state from a study limited to South Carolina if all of the plantation owners behaved that way. There would, in that case, be no variance on the dependent variable, and the lack of variation would be entirely due to the researcher and thus convey no new information. If some Virginia plantations did use fertilizer, it could make sense to look at both states in order to account for the variation in fertilizer use—at least one difference between the states which would be our key causal variable might account for the use of fertilizer. On the other hand, if all prior studies had been conducted in states which did not use fertilizer, a substantial contribution to the literature could be made by studying a state in which farmers did use fertilizer. This would at least raise the possibility of estimating a causal effect.

As another example, despite the fears of a generation and the dismal prognosis of many political scientists, nuclear weapons have not been exploded in warfare since 1945. Yet even if nuclear war has never occurred, it seems valuable to try to understand the conditions under which it could take place. This is clearly an extreme case of selection on the dependent variable where the variable appears constant. But, as many in the literature fervently argue, nuclear weapons may not have been used because the value of a key explanatory variable (a world with at least two nuclear superpowers) has remained constant over this entire period. Trying to estimate a causal inference with explanatory and dependent "variables" that are both constant is hopeless unless we reconceptualize the problem. We will show how to solve this problem, for the present example, in section 6.3.3.

Social science researchers sometimes pursue a retrospective approach exemplified by the Centers for Disease Control (CDC). It selects based on extreme but constant values of a dependent variable. The CDC may identify a "cancer cluster"—a group of people with the same kind of cancer in the same geographic location. The CDC then searches for some chemical or other factor in the environment (the key explanatory variable) that might have caused all the cancers (the dependent variable). These studies, in which observations are selected on the basis of extreme values of the dependent variable, are reasonably valid because there is considerable data on the normal levels of these explanatory variables. Although almost all of the CDC studies are either negative or inconclusive, they occasionally do find some suspect chemical. If there is no previous evidence that this chemical causes cancer, the CDC will then usually commission a study in which observations are selected, if possible, on the explanatory variable (variation in the presence or absence of this chemical) in order to be more confident about the causal inference.

Social science researchers sometimes pursue such an approach. We notice a particular "political cluster"—a community or region in which there is a long history of political radicalism, political violence, or other characteristic and seek to find what it is that is "special" about that region. As in the CDC's research, if such a study turns up suggestive correlations, we should not take these as confirming the hypothesis, but only as making it worthwhile to design a study that selects on the basis of the putative explanatory variable while letting the dependent variable—political radicalism or political violence—vary.

CONCLUDING REMARKS

In this chapter we have discussed how we can select observations in order to achieve a determinate research design that minimizes bias as a result of the selection process. Since perfect designs are unattainable, we have combined our critique of selection processes with suggestions for imperfect but helpful strategies that can provide some leverage on our research problem. Ultimately, we want to be able to design a study that selects on the basis of the explanatory variables suggested by our theory and let the dependent variable vary. However, en route to that goal, it may be useful to employ research designs that take into account observed values of the dependent variable; but for any researcher doing this, we advise utmost caution. Our overriding goal is to obtain more information relevant to evaluation of our theory without introducing so much bias as to jeopardize the quality of our inferences.

CHAPTER 5

Understanding What to Avoid

IN CHAPTER 4, we discussed how to construct a study with a determinate research design in which observation selection procedures make valid inferences possible. Carrying out this task successfully is necessary but not sufficient if we are to make valid inferences: analytical errors later in the research process can destroy the good work we have done earlier. In this chapter, we discuss how, once we have selected observations for analysis, we can understand sources of inefficiency and bias and reduce them to manageable proportions. We will then consider how we can control the research in such a way as to deal effectively with these problems.

In discussing inefficiency and bias, let us recall our criteria that we introduced in sections 2.7 and 3.4 for judging inferences. If we have a determinate research design, we then need to concern ourselves with the two key problems that we will discuss in this chapter: *bias* and *inefficiency*. To understand these concepts, it is useful to think of any inference as an estimate of a particular point with an interval around it. For example, we might guess someone's age as forty years, plus or minus two years. Forty years is our best guess (the estimate) and the interval from thirty-eight to forty-two includes our best guess at the center, with an estimate of our uncertainty (the width of the interval). We wish to choose the interval so that the true age falls within it a large proportion of the time. *Unbiasedness refers to centering the interval around the right estimate whereas efficiency refers to narrowing an appropriately centered interval.*

These definitions of unbiasedness and efficiency apply regardless of whether we are seeking to make a descriptive inference, as in the example about age or a causal inference. If we were, for instance, to estimate the effect of education on income (the number of dollars in income received for each additional year of education), we would have a point estimate of the effect surrounded by an interval reflecting our uncertainty as to the exact amount. We would want an interval as narrow as possible (for efficiency) and centered around the right estimate (for unbiasedness). We also want the estimate of the width of the interval to be an honest representation of our uncertainty.

In this chapter, we focus on four sources of bias and inefficiency, beginning with the stage of research at which we seek to improve the quality of information and proceeding through the making of causal inferences. In section 5.1, we discuss measurement error, which can bias our results as well as make them less efficient. We then consider in section 5.2 the bias in our causal inferences that can result when we have omitted explanatory variables that we should have included in the analysis. In section 5.3 we take up the inverse problem: controlling for irrelevant variables that reduce the efficiency of our analysis. Finally, we study the problem that results when our "dependent" variable affects our "explanatory" variables. This problem is known as endogeneity and is introduced in section 5.4. Finally, in sections 5.5 and 5.6 we discuss, respectively, random assignment of values of the explanatory variables and various methods of nonexperimental control.

5.1 MEASUREMENT ERROR

Once we have selected our observations, we have to measure the values of variables in which we are interested. Since all observation and measurement in the social sciences is imprecise, we are immediately confronted with issues of measurement error.

Much analysis in social science research attempts to estimate the amount of error and to reduce it as much as possible. Quantitative research produces more precise (numerical) measures, but not necessarily more accurate ones. Reliability—different measurements of the same phenomenon yield the same results—is sometimes purchased at the expense of validity—the measurements reflect what the investigator is trying to measure. Qualitative researchers try to achieve accurate measures, but they generally have somewhat less precision.

Quantitative measurement and qualitative observation are in essential respects very similar. To be sure, qualitative researchers typically label their categories with words, whereas quantitative researchers assign numerical values to their categories and measures. But both quantitative and qualitative researchers use nominal, ordinal, and interval measurements. With nominal categories, observations are grouped into a set of categories without the assumption that the categories are in any particular order. The relevant categories may be based on legal or institutional forms; for instance, students of comparative politics may be interested in patterns of presidential, parliamentary, and authoritarian rule across countries. Ordinal categories divide phenomena according to some ordering scheme. For example, a qualitative researcher might divide nations into three or four categories according to their degree of industrialization or the size of their military forces. Finally, interval measurement uses continuous variables, as in studies of transaction flows across national borders.

The differences between quantitative and qualitative measurement involve how data are represented, not the theoretical status of measurement. Qualitative researchers use words like "more" or "less," "larger" or "smaller," and "strong" or "weak" for measurements; quantitative researchers use numbers.

For example, most qualitative researchers in international relations are acutely aware that "number of battle deaths" is not necessarily a good index of how significant wars are for subsequent patterns of world politics. In balance-of-power theory, not the severity of war but a "consequential" change in the major actors is viewed as the relevant theoretical concept of instability to be measured (see Gulick 1967 and Waltz 1979:162). Yet in avoiding invalidity, the qualitative researcher often risks unreliability due to measurement error. How are we to know what counts as "consequential," if that term is not precisely defined? Indeed, the very language seems to imply that such a judgment will be made depending on the systemic outcome—which would bias subsequent estimates of the relationship in the direction of the hypothesis.

No formula can specify the tradeoffs between using quantitative indicators that may not validly reflect the underlying concepts in which we are interested, or qualitative judgments that are inherently imprecise and subject to unconscious biases. But both kinds of researchers should provide estimates of the uncertainty of their inferences. Quantitative researchers should provide standard errors along with their numerical measurements; qualitative researchers should offer uncertainty estimates in the form of carefully worded judgments about their observations. The difference between quantitative and qualitative measurement is in the style of representation of essentially the same ideas.

Qualitative and quantitative measurements are similar in another way. For each, the categories or measures used are usually artifacts created by the investigator and are not "given" in nature. The division of nations into democratic and autocratic regimes or into parliamentary and presidential regimes depends on categories that are intellectual constructs, as does the ordering of nations along such dimensions as more or less industrialized.

Obviously, a universally right answer does not exist: all measurement depends on the problem that the investigator seeks to understand. The closer the categorical scheme is to the investigator's original theoretical and empirical ideas, the better; however, this very fact emphasizes the point that the categories are artifacts of the investigator's purposes. The number of parliamentary regimes in which proportional representation is the principal system of representation depends on the investigator's classification of "parliamentary regimes" and of what counts as a system of proportional representation. Researchers in international relations may seek to study recorded monetary flows across national borders, but their use of a continuous measure depends on decisions as to what kinds of transactions to count, on rules as to what constitutes a single transaction, and on definitions of national borders. Similarly, the proportion of the vote that is Democratic in a Congressional district is based on classifications made by the analyst assuming that the "Democratic" and "Republican" party labels have the same meaning, for his or her purposes, across all 435 congressional districts.

Even the categorization schemes we have used in this section for measurements (nominal, ordinal, and interval) depend upon the theoretical purpose for which a measure is used. For example, it might seem obvious that ethnicity is a prototypical nominal variable, which might be coded in the United States as black, white, Latino, Native American and Asian-American. However, there is great variation across nominal ethnic groups in how strongly members of such groups identify with their particular group. We could, therefore, categorize ethnic groups on an ordinal scale in terms of, for example, the proportion of a group's members who strongly identify with it. Or we might be interested in the size of an ethnic group, in which case ethnicity might be used as an interval-level measure. The key point is to *use the measure that is most appropriate to our theoretical purposes.*

Problems in measurement occur most often when we measure without explicit reference to any theoretical structure. For example, researchers sometimes take a naturally continuous variable that could be measured well, such as age, and categorize it into young, middle-aged, and old. For some purposes, these categories might be sufficient, but as a theoretical representation of a person's age, this is an unnecessarily imprecise procedure. The *grouping error* created here would be quite substantial and should be avoided. Avoiding grouping error is a special case of the principle: do not discard data unnecessarily.

However, we can make the opposite mistake—assigning continuous, interval-level numerical values to naturally discrete variables. Interval-level measurement is *not* generally better than ordinal or nominal measurement. For example, a survey question might ask for religious affiliation and also intensity of religious commitment. Intensity of religious commitment could—if the questions are asked properly—be measured as an ordinal variable, maybe even an interval one, depending on the nature of the measuring instrument. But it would make less sense to assign a numerical ranking to the particular religion to which an individual belonged. In such a case, an ordinal or continuous variable probably does not exist and measurement error would be created by such a procedure.

The choice between nominal categories, on one hand, and ordinal or interval ones, on the other, may involve a tradeoff between descriptive richness and facilitation of comparison. For example, consider the voting rules used by international organizations. The institutional rule governing voting is important because it reflects conceptions of state sovereignty, and because it has implications for the types of resolutions that can pass, for resources allocated to the organization, and for expectations of compliance with the organization's mandates.

A set of nominal categories could distinguish among systems in which a single member can veto any resolution (as in the League of Nations Council acting under the provisions of Article 15 of the Covenant); in which only certain members can veto resolutions (as in the Security Council of the United Nations); in which some form of supermajority voting prevails (as in decisions concerning the internal market of the European Community); and in which simple majority voting is the rule (as for many votes in the United Nations General Assembly). Each of these systems is likely to generate distinct bargaining dynamics, and if our purpose is to study the dynamics of one such system (such as a system in which any member can exercise a veto), it is essential to have our categories defined, so that we do not inappropriately include other types of systems in our analysis. Nominal categories would be appropriate for such a project.

However, we could also view these categories in an ordinal way, from most restrictive (unanimity required) to least (simple majority). Such a categorization would be necessary were we to test theoretical propositions about the relationship between the restrictiveness of a voting rule and patterns of bargaining or the distributive features of typical outcomes. However, at least two of our categories—vetoes by certain members and qualified majority voting—are rather indistinct because they include a range of different arrangements. The first category includes complete veto by only one member, which verges on dictatorship, and veto by all but a few inconsequential members; the second includes the rule in the European Community that prevents any two states from having a blocking minority on issues involving the internal market. The formula used in the International Monetary Fund is nominally a case of qualified majority voting, but it gives such a blocking minority both to the United States and, recently, to the European Community acting as a bloc. Hence, it seems to belong in both of these categories.

We might, therefore, wish to go a step further to generate an interval-level measure based on the proportion of states (or the proportion of resources, based on gross national product, contributions to the organization, or population represented by states) required for passage of resolutions, measuring international organizations on a scale of voting restrictiveness.

However, different bases for such a measure—for example, whether population or gross national product were used as the measure of resources—would generate different results. Hence, the advantages of precision in such measurements might be countered by the liabilities either of arbitrariness in the basis for measurement or of the complexity of aggregate measures. Each category has advantages and limitations: the researcher's purpose must determine the choice that is made.

In the following two subsections, we will analyze the specific consequences of measurement error for qualitative research and reach some conclusions that may seem surprising. Few would disagree that *systematic* measurement error, such as a consistent overestimate of certain units, causes bias and, since the bias does not disappear with more error-laden observations, inconsistency. However, a closer analysis shows that only some types of systematic measurement error will bias our causal inferences. In addition, the consequences of *nonsystematic* measurement error may be less clear. We will discuss nonsystematic measurement error in two parts: in the dependent variable and then in the explanatory variable. As we will demonstrate, error in the dependent variable causes inefficiencies, which are likely to produce incorrect results in any one instance and make it difficult to find persistent evidence of systematic effects. In other words, nonsystematic measurement error in the dependent variable causes no bias but can increase inefficiency substantially. More interesting is nonsystematic error in the key causal variable, which unfailingly biases inferences in predictable ways. Understanding the nature of these biases will help ameliorate or possibly avoid them.

5.1.1 Systematic Measurement Error

In this section, we address the consequences of *systematic* measurement error. Systematic measurement error, such as a measure being a consistent overestimate for certain types of units, can sometimes cause bias and inconsistency in estimating causal effects. Our task is to find out what types of systematic measurement error result in which types of bias. In both quantitative and qualitative research, systematic error can derive from choices on the part of researchers that slant the data in favor of the researcher's prior expectations. In quantitative work, the researcher may use such biased data because it is the only numerical series available. In qualitative research, systematic measurement error can result from subjective evaluations made by investigators who have already formed their hypotheses and who wish to demonstrate their correctness.

It should be obvious that *any systematic measurement error will bias descriptive inferences.*[1] Consider, for example, the simplest possible case in which we inadvertently overestimate the amount of annual income of every survey respondent by $1,000. Our estimate of the average annual income for the whole sample will obviously be overestimated by the same figure. If we were interested in estimating the causal effect of a college education on average annual income, the systematic measurement error would have no effect on our causal inference. If, for example, our college group really earns $30,000 on average, but our control group of people who did not go to college earn an average of $25,000, our estimate of the causal effect of a college education on annual income would be $5,000. If the income of every person in both groups was overestimated by the same amount (say $1,000 again), then our causal effect—now calculated as the difference between $31,000 and $26,000—would still be $5,000. Thus, *systematic measurement error which affects all units by the same constant amount causes no bias in causal inference.* (This is easiest to see by focusing on the constant effects version of the unit homogeneity assumption described in section 3.3.1.)

However, suppose there is a systematic error in one part of the sample: college graduates systematically overreport their income because they want to impress the interviewer, but the control group reports its income more accurately. In this case, both the descriptive inference *and* our inference about the causal effect of education on income would be biased. If we knew of the reporting problem, we might be able to ask better survey questions or elicit the information in other ways. If the information has already been collected and we have no opportunity to collect more, then we may at least be able to ascertain the direction of the bias to make a post hoc correction.

To reinforce this point, consider an example from the literature on regional integration in international relations. That literature sought, more than most work in international relations, to test specific hypotheses, sometimes with quantitative indicators. However, one of the most important concepts in the literature—the degree to which policy authority is transferred to an international organization from nation-states—is not easily amenable to valid quantitative measurement. Researchers therefore devised qualitative measurements of this variable, which they coded on the basis of their own detailed knowledge of

---

[1] An exception is when positive systematic errors cancel out negative systematic ones, but this odd case is more properly described as a type of nonsystematic measurement error.

the issues involved (e.g., Lindberg and Scheingold 1970:71, table 3.1). Their explanatory variables included subjective categorizations of such variables as "elite value complementarity" and "decision-making style" (see Nye 1971 or Lindberg and Sheingold 1971). They tried to examine associations between the explanatory and dependent variables, when the variables were measured in this manner.

This approach was a response to concerns about validity: expert researchers coded the information and could examine whether it was relevant to the concepts underlying their measurements. But the approach ran the risk of subjective measurement error. The researchers had to exercise great self-discipline in the process and refrain from coding their explanatory variables in light of their theoretical positions or expectations. In any given case, they may have done so, but it is difficult for their readers to know to what extent they were successful.

Our advice in these circumstances is, first, to try to use judgments made for entirely different purposes by *other researchers*. This element of arbitrariness in qualitative or quantitative measurement guarantees that the measures will not be influenced by your hypotheses, which presumably were not formed until later. This strategy is frequently followed in quantitative research—a researcher takes someone else's measures and applies them to his or her own purposes—but it is also an excellent strategy in qualitative research. For example, it may be possible to organize joint coding of key variables by informed observers with different preferred interpretations and explanations of the phenomena. Qualitative data banks having standard categories may be constructed on the basis of shared expertise and discussion. They can then be used for evaluating hypotheses. If you are the first person to use a set of variables, it is helpful to let *other informed people* code your variables without knowing your theory of the relationship you wish to evaluate. Show them your field notes and taped interviews, and see if their conclusions about measures are the same as yours. Since replicability in coding increases confidence in qualitative variables, the more highly qualified observers who cross-check your measures, the better.

5.1.2 *Nonsystematic Measurement Error*

Nonsystematic measurement error, whether quantitative or qualitative, is another problem faced by all researchers.[2] Nonsystematic error does not bias the variable's measurement. In the present context, we

[2] Whether this is due to our inability to measure the real world accurately or due to randomness in nature is a philosophical question to which different answers can be given. (section 2.6). Whichever position we accept, the consequence is the same.

define variables with nonsystematic, or random, measurement error as having values that are sometimes too high and sometimes too low, but correct on average. Random error obviously creates inefficiencies but not bias in making descriptive inferences. This point has already been discussed in section 2.7.1. Here, we go beyond the consequence of random measurement error for descriptive inference to its conseqence for causal inference.

In the estimation of causal effects, random measurement error has a different effect when the error is in an explanatory variable than when the error is in the dependent variable. Random measurement error in the dependent variable reduces the efficiency of the causal estimate but does not bias it. It can lead to estimates of causal relationships that are at times too high and at times too low. However, the estimate will be, on average, correct. Indeed, random measurement error in a dependent variable is not different or even generally distinguishable from the usual random error present in the world as reflected in the dependent variable.

Random error in an explanatory variable can also produce inefficiencies that lead to estimates that are uncertainly high or low. But it also has an effect very different from random error in the dependent variable: random error in an explanatory variable produces bias in the estimate of the relationship between the explanatory and the dependent variable. That bias takes a particular form: it results in the estimation of a weaker causal relationship than is the case. If the true relationship is positive, random error in the explanatory variable will bias the estimate downwards towards a smaller or zero relationship. If the relationship is negative it will bias the relationship upwards towards zero.

Since this difference between the effect of random error in an explanatory variable and random error in a dependent variable is not intuitively obvious, we present formal proofs of each effect as well as a graphic presentation and an illustrative example. We begin with the effect of random error in a dependent variable.

5.1.2.1 NONSYSTEMATIC MEASUREMENT ERROR IN THE
DEPENDENT VARIABLE

Nonsystematic or random measurement error in a dependent variable does not bias the usual estimate of the causal effect, but it does make the estimate less efficient. In any one application, this inefficiency will yield unpredictable results, sometimes giving causal inferences that are too large and sometimes too small. Measurement error in the dependent variable thus increases the uncertainty of our inferences. In other words, random measurement error in a dependent variable creates a problem similar to that created by a small number of observations; in both cases, the amount of information we can bring to bear on a problem is less than we would like. The result is that *random measurement error in the dependent variable produces estimates of causal effects that are less efficient and more uncertain.*

When we use several data sets, as we should when feasible, estimates based on dependent variables with random measurement error will be unstable. Some data sets will produce evidence of strong relationships while others will yield nonexistent or negative effects, even if the true relationship has not changed at all. This inefficiency makes it harder, sometimes considerably harder, to find systematic descriptive or causal features in one data set or (perhaps more obviously) across different data sets. Estimates of uncertainty will often be larger than the estimated size of relationships among our variables. Thus, we may have insufficient information to conclude that a causal effect exists when it may actually be present but masked by random error in the dependent variable (and represented in increased uncertainty of an inference). Qualitative and quantitative researchers who are aware of this general result will have no additional tools to deal with measurement error—except a stronger impetus to improve the measurements of the observations they have or collect new observations with the same (or lower) levels of measurement error. Understanding these results with a fixed amount of data will enable scholars to more appropriately qualify their conclusions. Such an explicit recognition of uncertainty may motivate these investigators or others to conduct follow-up studies with more carefully measured dependent variables (or with larger numbers of observations). It should be of even more help in designing research, since scholars frequently face a trade-off between attaining additional precision for each measurement and obtaining more observations. The goal is more information relevant to our hypothesis: we need to make judgments as to whether this information can best be obtained by more observations within existing cases or collecting more data.

Consider the following example of random measurement error in the dependent variuable. In studying the effects of economic performance on violent crime in developing countries or across the regions of a single developing country, we may measure the dependent variable (illegal violence) by observing each community for a short period of time. Of course, these observations will be relatively poor measurements: correct on average, but, in some communities, we will miss much crime and underestimate the average violence; in other communities, we will see a lot of crime and will overestimate average violence.

Suppose our measurement of our explanatory variable—the state of the economy—is the percentage unemployed in the community and we measure that quite well (perhaps from good government data). If we studied the effect of the economy as indicated by the percentage unemployed on the average amount of violent crime, we would expect very uncertain results—results that are also unstable across several applications—precisely because the dependent variable was measured imperfectly, even though the measurement technique was correct on average. Our awareness that this was the source of the problem, combined with a continuing belief that there should be a strong relationship, provides a good justification for a new study in which we might observe community crime at more sites or for longer periods of time. Once again, we see that measurement error and few observations lead to similar problems. We could improve efficiency either by increasing the accuracy of our observations (perhaps by using good police records and, thus, reducing measurement error) or by increasing the number of imperfectly measured observations in different communities. In either case, the solution is to increase the amount of information that we bring to bear on this inference problem. This is another example of why the amount of *information* we bring to bear on a problem is more important than the raw number of observations we have (the number of observations being our measure of information).

To show why this is the case, we use a simplified version of this example first in a graphic presentation and then offer a more formal proof. In figure 5.1, the horizontal axis represents unemployment. We imagine that the two categories ("4 percent" and "7 percent") are perfectly measured. The vertical axis is a measure of violent crime.

In figure 5.1, the two solid circles can be viewed as representing an example of a simple study with no measurement error in either variable. We can imagine that we have a large number of observations, all of which happen to fall exactly on the two solid dots, so that we know the position of each dot quite well. Alternatively, we can imagine that we have only two observations, but they have very little nonsystematic error of any kind. Of course, neither of these cases will likely occur in reality, but this model highlights the essential problems of measurement error in a dependent variable for the more general and complicated case. Note how the solid line fits these two points.

Now imagine another study where violent crime was measured with nonsystematic error. To emphasize that these measures are correct on average, we plot the four open circles, each symmetrically above and below the original solid circles.[3] A new line fit to all six data

---

[3] We imagine again that the open circles are either a large number of observations that happen to fall exactly on these four points or that there happens to be little stochastic variability.

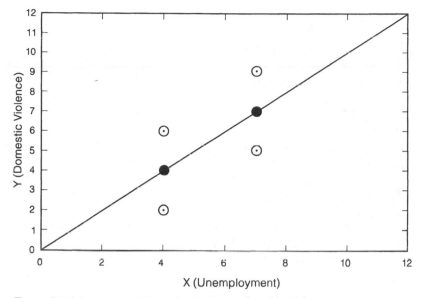

Figure 5.1 Measurement Error in the Dependent Variable

points is exactly the same line as originally plotted. Note again that this line is drawn by minimizing the prediction errors, the *vertical* deviations from the line.

However, the new line is more uncertain in several ways. For example, a line with a moderately steeper or flatter slope would fit these points almost as well. In addition, the vertical position of the line is also more uncertain, and the line itself provides worse predictions of where the individual data points should lie. The result is that measurement error in the dependent variable produces more inefficient estimates. Even though they are still unbiased—that is, on average across numerous similar studies—they might be far off in any one study.

A Formal Analysis of Measurement Error in y. Consider a simple linear model with a dependent variable measured with error and one errorless explanatory variable. We are interested in estimating the effect parameter β:

$$E(Y^*) = \beta X$$

We also specify a second feature of the random variables, the variance:

$$V(Y_i^*) = \sigma^2$$

which we assume to be the same for all units $i = 1, \ldots, n.$[4]

Although these equations define our model, we unfortunately do not observe Y^* but instead Y, where

$$Y = Y^* + U$$

That is, the observed dependent variable Y is equal to the true dependent variable Y^* plus some random measurement error U. To formalize the idea that U contains only *nonsystematic* measurement error, we require that the error cancels on average across hypothetical replications, $E(U) = 0$, and that it is uncorrelated with the true dependent variable, $C(U,Y^*) = 0$, and with the explanatory variable, $C(U,X) = 0.$[5] We further assume that the measurement error has variance $V(U_i) = \tau^2$ for each and every unit i. If τ^2 is zero, Y contains no measurement error and is equal to Y^*; the larger this variance, the more error our measure Y contains.

How does random measurement error in the dependent variable affect one's estimates of β? To see, we use our usual estimator but with Y instead of Y^*:

$$b = \frac{\sum_{i=1}^{n} Y_i X_i}{\sum_{i=1}^{n} X_i^2}$$

and then calculate the average across hypothetical replications:

$$E(b) = E\left(\frac{\sum_{i=1}^{n} X_i Y_i}{\sum_{i=1}^{n} X_i^2}\right)$$

$$= \frac{\sum_{i=1}^{n} X_i E(Y_i)}{\sum_{i=1}^{n} X_i^2}$$

$$= \frac{\sum_{i=1}^{n} X_i E(Y_i + U)}{\sum_{i=1}^{n} X_i^2}$$

[4] Statistical readers will recognize this as the property of homoskedasticity, or constant variance.

[5] These error assumptions imply that the expected value of the observed dependent variable is the same as the expected value of the true dependent variable:

$$E(Y) = E(Y^* + U) = E(Y^*) + E(U) = E(Y^*) = \beta X$$

$$= \frac{\sum_{i=1}^{n} X_i^2 \beta}{\sum_{i=1}^{n} X_i^2}$$

$$= \beta$$

This analysis demonstrates that even with measurement error in the dependent variable, the standard estimator will be unbiased (equal to β on average), just as we showed for a dependent variable without measurement error in equation (3.8).

However, to complete this analysis, we must assess the efficiency of our estimator in the presence of a dependent variable measured with error. We use the usual procedure:

$$V(b) = V \left(\frac{\sum_{i=1}^{n} X_i Y_i}{\sum_{i=1}^{n} X_i^2} \right) \tag{5.1}$$

$$= \frac{1}{\left(\sum_{i=1}^{n} X_i^2 \right)^2} \sum_{i=1}^{n} X_i^2 V(Y_i^* + U)$$

$$- \frac{\sigma^2 + \tau^2}{\sum_{i=1}^{n} X_i^2}$$

Note that this estimator is *less* efficient than the same estimator applied to data without measurement error in the dependent variable (compare equation [3.9]) by the amount of the measurement error in the dependent variable τ^2.

5.1.2.2 NONSYSTEMATIC MEASUREMENT ERROR IN AN EXPLANATORY VARIABLE

As we pointed out above, nonsystematic error in the explanatory variable has the same consequences for estimates of the value of that variable—for descriptive inferences—as it has for estimates of the value of the dependent variable: the measures will sometimes be too high, sometimes too low, but on average they will be right. As with nonsystematic error in the dependent variable, random error in the explanatory variable can also make estimates of causal effects uncertain and inefficient. But the random error in the explanatory variable has another, quite different consequence from the case in which the random error is in the dependent variable. When it is the explanatory variable that is measured with random error, there is a systematic bias in the estimates of the causal relationship, a bias in the direction of zero or no relationship. In other words, when there is a true causal connection between an explanatory variable and a dependent variable, random error in the former can serve to mask that fact by depressing the relationship. If we were to test our hypothesis across several data sets we would not only find great variation in the results, as with random error in the dependent variable, we would also encounter a systematic bias across the several data sets towards a weaker relationship than is in fact the case.

Just as with measurement error in the dependent variable, even if we recognize the presence of measurement error in the explanatory variables, more carefully analyzing the variables measured with error will not ameliorate the *consequences* of this measurement error unless we follow the advice given here. Better measurements would of course improve the situation.

Consider again our study of the effects of unemployment on crime in various communities of an underdeveloped country. However, suppose the data situation is the opposite of that mentioned above: in the country we are studying, crime reports are accurate and easy to obtain from government offices, but unemployment is a political issue and hence not accurately measurable. Since systematic sample surveys are not permitted, we decide to measure unemployment by direct observation (just as in our earlier example, where we measured crime by direct observation). We infer the rate of unemployment from the number of people standing idle in the center of various villages as we drive through. Since the hour and day when we observe the villages would vary, as would the weather, we would have a lot of random error in our estimates of the degree of unemployment. Across a large number of villages, our estimates would not be systematically high or low. An estimate based on any pair of villages would be quite inefficient: any pair might be based on observations on Sunday (when many people may linger outside) or on a rainy day (when few would). But many observations of pairs of villages at different times on different days, in rain or shine, would produce, on average, correct estimates of the effect. However, as indicated above, the consequence will be very different from the consequence of similar error in our measure of the dependent variable, violent crime.

Figure 5.2 illustrates this situation. The two solid dots represent one study with no measurement error in either variable.[6] The slope of the

---

[6] We also continue to assume that each point represents data either with almost no stochastic variation or numerous points that happen to fall in the same place. As in section 5.1, the purpose of this assumption is to keep the focus on the problem.

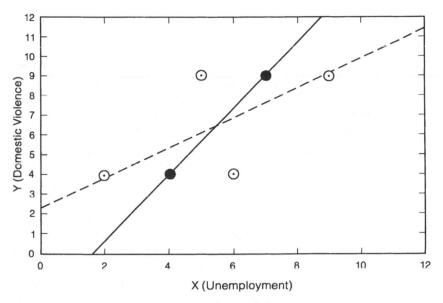

Figure 5.2 Measurement Error in the Explanatory Variable

solid line is then the correct estimate of the causal effect of unemployment on crime. To show the consequences of measurement error, we
add two additional points (open circles) to the right and the left of each
of the solid dots, to represent measurement error in the explanatory
variable that is correct on average (that is, equal to the filled dot on
average). The dashed line is fit to the open circles, and the difference
between the two lines is the bias due to random measurement error in
the explanatory variable. We emphasize again that the lines are drawn
so as to minimize the errors in predicting the dependent variable (the
errors appear in the figure as *vertical* deviations from the line being fit),
given each value of the explanatory variables.

Thus, the estimated effect of unemployment, made here with considerable random measurement error, will be much smaller (since the
dashed line is flatter) than the true effect. We could infer from our
knowledge of the existence of measurement error in the explanatory
variable that the true effect of unemployment on crime is larger than
the observed correlation found in this research project.

The analysis of the consequences of measurement error in an explanatory variable leads to two practical guidelines:

1. If an analysis suggests no effect to begin with, then the true effect is difficult to ascertain since the direction of bias is unknown; the analysis will
   then be largely indeterminate and should be described as such. The true

effect may be zero, negative, or positive, and nothing in the data will provide an indication of which it is.

2. However, if an analysis suggests that the explanatory variable with random measurement error has a small positive effect, then we should use the results in this section as justification for concluding that the true effect is probably even larger than we found. Similarly, if we find a small negative effect, the results in this section can be used as evidence that the true effect is probably an even larger negative relationship.

Since measurement error is a fundamental characteristic of all qualitative research, these guidelines should be widely applicable.

We must qualify these conclusions somewhat so that researchers know exactly when they do and do not apply. First, the analysis in the box below, on which our advice is based, applies to models with only a single explanatory variable. Similar results do apply to many situations with multiple explanatory variables, but not to all. The analysis applies just the same if a researcher has many explanatory variables, but only one with substantial random measurement error. However, if one has multiple explanatory variables and is simultaneously analyzing their effects, and if each has different kinds of measurement error, we can only ascertain the kinds of biases likely to arise by extending the formal analysis below. It turns out that although qualitative researchers often have many explanatory variables, they most frequently study the effect of each variable sequentially rather than simultaneously. Unfortunately, as we describe in section 5.2, this procedure can cause other problems, such as omitted variable bias, but it does mean that results similar to those analyzed here apply quite widely in qualitative research.

A Formal Analysis of Random Measurement Error in X. We first define a model as follows:

$$E(Y) = \beta X^*$$

where we do not observe the true explanatory variable X^* but instead observe X where

$$X = X^* + U$$

and the random measurement error U has similar properties as before: it is zero on average, $E(U) = 0$, and is uncorrelated with the true explanatory variable, $C(U,X^*) = 0$, and with the dependent variable, $C(U,Y) = 0$.

What happens when we use the standard estimator for β with the error-ridden X, instead of the unobserved X^*? This situation corresponds to the usual one in qualitative research in which we have measurement error but do not make any special adjustment for the results that follow. To analyze the consequences of this procedure, we evaluate bias, which will turn out to be the primary consequence of this sort of measurement problem. We thus begin with the standard estimator in equation (3.7) applied to the observed X and Y for the model above.

$$b = \frac{\sum_{i=1}^{n} X_i Y_i}{\sum_{i=1}^{n} X_i^2} \tag{5.2}$$

$$= \frac{\sum_{i=1}^{n} (X_i^* + U_i) Y_i}{\sum_{i=1}^{n} (X_i^* + U_i)^2}$$

$$= \frac{\sum_{i=1}^{n} X_i^* Y_i + \left(\sum_{i=1}^{n} U_i Y_i\right)}{\sum_{i=1}^{n} X_i^{*2} + \sum_{i=1}^{n} U_i^2 + \left(2\sum_{i=1}^{n} X_i^* U_i\right)}$$

It should be clear that b will be biased, $E(b) \neq \beta$. Furthermore, the two parenthetical terms in the last line of equation (5.2) will be zero on average because we have assumed that U and Y, and U and X^*, are uncorrelated (that is, $C(U_i, Y_i) = E(U_i, Y_i) = 0$). This equation therefore reduces to approximately[7]

$$b \approx \frac{\sum_{i=1}^{n} X_i^* Y_i}{\sum_{i=1}^{n} X_i^{*2} + \sum_{i=1}^{n} U_i^2}$$

This equation for the estimator of β in the model above is the same as the standard one, except for the extra term in the denominator, $\sum_{i=1}^{n} U_i^2$ (compare equation [3.7]). This term represents the amount of measurement error in X, the sample variance of the error U. In the absence of measurement error, this term is zero, and the equation reduces to the standard estimator in equation (3.7), since we would have actually observed the true values of the explanatory variable.

In the general case with some measurement error, $\sum_{i=1}^{n} U_i^2$ is a sum of squared terms and so will always be positive. Since this term is added to the denominator, b will approach zero. If the correct esti-

---

[7] Since this equation holds exactly only in large samples, we are really analyzing consistency instead of unbiasedness (section 2.7.1). More precisely, the parenthetical terms in equation (5.2), when divided by n, vanish as n approaches infinity.

mator would produce a large positive number, random measurement error in the explanatory variable would incorrectly cause the researcher to think b was positive but smaller. If the estimate based on X^* were a large negative number, a researcher analyzing data with random measurement error would think the estimate was a smaller negative number.

It would be straightforward to use this formal analysis to show that random measurement error in the explanatory variables also causes inefficiencies, but bias is generally a more serious problem, and we will deal with it first.

5.2 EXCLUDING RELEVANT VARIABLES: BIAS

Most qualitative social scientists appreciate the importance of controlling for the possibly spurious effects of other variables when estimating the effect of one variable on another. Ways to effect this control include, among others, John Stuart Mill's (1843) methods of difference and similarity (which, ironically, are referred to by Przeworski and Teune (1982) as most similar and most different systems designs, respectively), Verba's (1967) "disciplined-configurative case comparisons," (which are similar to George's [1982] "structured-focused comparisons"), and diverse ways of using ceteris paribus assumptions and similar counterfactuals. These phrases are frequently invoked, but researchers often have difficulty applying them effectively. Unfortunately, qualitative researchers have few tools for expressing the precise consequences of failing to take into account additional variables in particular research situations: that is, of "omitted variable bias." We provide these tools in this section.

We begin our discussion of this issue with a verbal analysis of the consequences of omitted variable bias and follow it with a formal analysis of this problem. Then we will turn to broader questions of research design raised by omitted variable bias.

5.2.1 Gauging the Bias from Omitted Variables

Suppose we wish to estimate the causal effect of our explanatory variable X_1 on our dependent variable Y. If we are undertaking a quantitative analysis, we denote this causal effect of X_1 on Y as β_1. One way of estimating β_1 is by running a regression equation or another form of analysis, which yields an estimate b_1 of β_1. If we are carrying out qualitative research, we will also seek to make such an estimate of the causal effect; however, this estimate will depend on verbal argument and the investigator's assessment, based on experience and judgment.

Suppose that after we have made these estimates (quantitatively or qualitatively) a colleague takes a look at our analysis and objects that we have omitted an important control variable, X_2. We have been estimating the effect of campaign spending on the proportion of the votes received by a congressional candidate. Our colleague conjectures that our finding is spurious due to "omitted variable bias." That is, she suggests that our estimate b_1 of β_1 is incorrect since we have failed to take into account another explanatory variable X_2 (such as a measure of whether or not the candidate is an incumbent). The true model should presumably control for the effect of the new variable.

How are we to evaluate her claim? In particular, under what conditions would our omission of the variable measuring incumbency affect our estimate of the effect of spending on votes and under what conditions would it have no effect? Clearly, the omission of a term measuring incumbency will not matter if incumbency has no effect on the dependent variable; that is, if X_2 is irrelevant, because it has no effect on Y, it will not cause bias. This is the first special case: irrelevant omitted variables cause no bias. Thus, if incumbency had no electoral consequences we could ignore the fact that it was omitted.

The second special case, which also produces no bias, occurs when the omitted variable is uncorrelated with the included explanatory variable. Thus, there is also no bias if incumbency status is uncorrelated with our explanatory variable, campaign spending. Intuitively, when an omitted variable is uncorrelated with the main explanatory variable of interest, controlling for it would not change our estimate of the causal effect of our main variable, since we control for the portion of the variation that the two variables have in common, if any. Thus, *we can safely omit control variables, even if they have a strong influence on the dependent variable, as long as they do not vary with the included explanatory variable.*[8]

---

[8] Note the difference between the two cases in which omitting a variable is acceptable. In the first case, in which the omitted variable is unrelated to the dependent variable, there is no bias and we lose no power in predicting future values of the dependent variable. In the latter case, in which the omitted variable is unrelated to the independent variable though related to the dependent variable, we have no bias in our estimate of the *relationship* of the included explanatory variable and the dependent variable, but we lose some accuracy in forecasting future values of the dependent variable. Thus, if incumbency were unrelated to campaign spending, omitting it would not bias our estimate of the relationship of campaign spending to votes. But if our goal were forecasting, we would wish to map all of the systematic variation in the dependent variable, and omitting incumbency would prevent that since we are leaving out an important causal variable. However, even if our long-term goal were the fullest systematic explanation of the

If these special cases do not hold for some omitted variable (i.e., this variable is correlated with the included explanatory variable and has an effect on the dependent variable), then failure to control for it will bias our estimate (or perception) of the effect of the included variable. In the case at hand, our colleague would be right in her criticism since incumbency is related to both the dependent variable and the independent variable: incumbents get more votes and they spend more.

This insight can be put in formal terms by focusing on the last line of equation (5.5) from the box below:

$$E(b_1) = \beta_1 + F\beta_2 \tag{5.3}$$

This is the equation used to calculate the bias in the estimate of the effect of X_1 on the dependent variable Y. In this equation, F represents the degree of correlation between the two explanatory variables X_1 and X_2.[9] If the estimator calculated by using only X_1 as an explanatory variable (that is b_1) was unbiased, it would equal β_1 on average; that is, it would be true that $E(b_1) = \beta_1$. This estimator is unbiased in the two special cases where the *bias term* $F\beta_2$ equals zero. It is easy to see that this formalizes the conditions for unbiasedness that we stated above. That is, we can omit a control variable if either

- The omitted variable has no causal effect on the dependent variable (that is, $\beta_2 = 0$, regardless of the nature of the relationship between the included and excluded variables F); or
- The omitted variable is uncorrelated with the included variable (that is, $F = 0$, regardless of the value of β_2.)

If we discover an omitted variable that we suspect might be biasing our results, our analysis should *not* end here. If possible, we should control for the omitted variable. And even if we cannot, because we have no good source of data about the omitted variable, our model can help us to ascertain the direction of bias, which can be extremely helpful. Having an underestimate or an overestimate may substantially bolster or weaken an existing argument.

For example, suppose we study a few sub-Saharan African states and find that coups d'etat appear more frequently in politically repressive regimes—that β_1 (the effect of repression on the likelihood of a coup) is positive. That is, the explanatory variable is the degree of po-

---

vote, it might prove difficult to be very confident of several causal effects within the framework of a single study. Thus, it might pay to focus on one causal effect (or just a few), whatever our long-term goal.

[9] More precisely, F is the coefficient estimate produced when X_1 is regressed on X_2.

litical repression, and the dependent variable is the likelihood of a coup. The unit of analysis is the sub-Saharan African countries. We might even expand the sample to other African states and come to the same conclusion. However, suppose that we did not consider the possible effects of economic conditions on coups. Although we might have no data on economic conditions, it is reasonable to hypothesize that unemployment would probably increase the probability of a coup d'etat ($\beta_2 > 0$), and it also seems likely that unemployment is positively correlated with political repression ($F > 0$). We also assume, for the purposes of this illustration that economic conditions are prior to our key causal variable, the degree of political repression. If this is the case, the degree of bias in our analysis could be severe. Since unemployment has a positive correlation with both the dependent variable and the explanatory variable ($F\beta_2 > 0$ in this case), excluding that variable would mean that we were inadvertently estimating the effect of repression and unemployment on the likelihood of a coup instead of just repression ($\beta_1 + F\beta_2$ instead of β_1). Furthermore, because the joint impact of repression and unemployment is greater than the effect of repression alone ($\beta_1 + F\beta_2$ is greater than β_1), the estimate of the effect of repression (b_1) will be too large on average. Therefore, this analysis shows that by excluding the effects of unemployment, we overestimated the effects of political repression. (This is different from the consequences of measurement error in the explanatory variables since omitted variable bias can sometimes cause a negative relationship to be estimated as a positive one.)

Omitting relevant variables does not always result in overestimates of causal effects. For example, we could reasonably hypothesize that in some other countries (perhaps the subject of a new study), political repression and unemployment were inversely related (that F is negative). In these countries, political repression might enable the government to control warring factions, impose peace from above, and put most people to work. This in turn means that the effect of bias introduced by the negative relationship of unemployment and repression ($F\beta_2$) will also be negative, so long as we are still willing to assume that more unemployment will increase the probability of a coup in these countries. The substantive consequence is that the estimated effect of repression on the likelihood of a coup ($E(b_1)$) will now be less than the true effect (β_1). Thus, if economic conditions are excluded, b_1 will generally be an *underestimate* of the effect of political repression. If F is sufficiently negative and β_2 is sufficiently large, then we might routinely estimate a positive β_1 to be negative and incorrectly conclude that more political repression decreases the probability of a coup d'etat! Even if we had insufficient information on unemployment rates to include it in the original study, an analysis like this can still help us generate reasonable substantive conclusions.

As these examples should make clear, we need not actually run a regression to estimate parameters, to assess the degrees and directions of bias, or to arrive at such conclusions. Qualitative and intuitive estimates are subject to the same kinds of biases as are strictly quantitative ones. This section shows that in both situations, information outside the existing data can help substantially in estimating the degree and direction of bias.

If we know that our research design might suffer from omitted variables but do not know what those variables are, then we may very well have flawed conclusions (and some future researcher is likely to find them). The incentives to find out more are obvious. Fortunately, in most cases, researchers have considerable information about variables outside their analysis. Sometimes this information is detailed but available for only some subunits, or partial but widely applicable, or even from previous research studies. Whatever the source, even incomplete information can help one focus on the likely degree and direction of bias in our causal effects.

Of course, even scholars who understand the consequences of omitted variable bias may encounter difficulties in identifying variables that might be omitted from their analysis. No formula can be provided to deal with this problem, but we do advise that all researchers, quantitative and qualitative, systematically look for omitted control variables and consider whether they should be included in the analysis. We suggest some guidelines for such a review in this section.

Omitted variables can cause difficulties even when we have adequate information on all relevant variables. Scholars sometimes have such information, and believing the several variables to be positively related to the dependent variable, they estimate the causal effects of these variables sequentially, in separate "bivariate" analyses. It is particularly tempting to use this approach in studies with a small number of observations, since including many explanatory variables simultaneously creates very imprecise estimates or even an indeterminate research design, as discussed in section 4.1. Unfortunately, however, each analysis excludes the other relevant variables, and this omission leads to omitted variable bias in each estimation. The ideal solution is not merely to collect information on all relevant variables, but explicitly and *simultaneously* to control for all relevant variables. The qualitative researcher must recognize that failure to take into account all relevant variables at the same time leads to biased inferences. Recognition of the sources of bias is valuable, even if small numbers of observations make it impossible to remove them.

Concern for omitted variable bias, however, should *not* lead us automatically to include every variable whose omission might cause bias because it is correlated with the independent variable and has an effect on the dependent variable. In general, *we should not control for an explanatory variable that is in part a consequence of our key causal variable.*

Consider the following example. Suppose we are interested in the causal effect of an additional $10,000 in income (our treatment variable) on the probability that a citizen will vote for the Democratic candidate (our dependent variable). Should we control for whether this citizen reports planning to vote Democratic in an interview five minutes before he arrives at the polls? This control variable certainly affects the dependent variable and is probably correlated with the explanatory variable. Intuitively, the answer is no. If we did control for it, the estimated effect of income on voting Democratic would be almost entirely attributed to the control variable, which in this case is hardly an alternative causal explanation. A blind application of the omitted variable bias rules, above, might incorrectly lead one to control for this variable. After all, this possible control variable certainly has an effect on the dependent variable—voting Democratic—and it is correlated with the key explanatory variable—income. But including this variable would attribute part of the causal effect of our key explanatory variable to the control variable.

To take another example, suppose we are interested in the causal effect of a sharp increase in crude-oil prices on public opinion about the existence of an energy shortage. We could obtain measures of oil prices (our key causal variable) from newspapers and use opinion polls as our dependent variable to gauge the public's perception of whether there is an energy shortage. But we might ask whether we should control for the effects of television coverage of energy problems. Certainly television coverage of energy problems is correlated with both the included explanatory variable (crude oil prices) and the dependent variable (public opinion about an energy shortage). However, since television coverage is in part a consequence of real-world oil prices, we should not control for that coverage in assessing the causal influence of oil prices on public opinion about an energy shortage. If instead we were interested in the causal effect of television coverage, we would control for oil prices, since these prices come *before* the key explanatory variable (which is now coverage).[10]

---

[10] It is worth considering just what it means to look at the estimated causal effect of crude-oil prices on public opinion about an energy shortage, while controlling for the amount of television coverage about energy shortages. Consider two descriptions, both of which are important in that they enable us to further analyze and study the causal processes in greater depth. First, this estimated effect is just the effect of that aspect of oil

Thus, to estimate the total effect of an explanatory variable, we should list all variables that, according to our theoretical model, could cause the dependent variable. To repeat the point made above: in general, we should not control for an explanatory variable that is in part a consequence of our key explanatory variable. Having eliminated these possible explanatory variables, we should then control for other potential explanatory variables that would otherwise cause omitted variable bias—those that are correlated with both the dependent variable and with the included explanatory variables.[11]

The argument that we should not control for explanatory variables that are consequences of our key explanatory variables has a very important implication for the role of theory in research design. Thinking about this issue, we can see why we should begin with or at least work towards a theoretically-motivated model rather than "data-mining": running regressions or qualitative analyses with whatever explanatory variables we can think of. Without a theoretical model, we cannot decide which potential explanatory variables should be included in our analysis. Indeed, in the absence of a model, we might get the strongest results by using a trivial explanatory variable—such as intention to vote Democratic five minutes before entering the polling place—and controlling for all other factors correlated with it. We cannot determine whether to control for or ignore possible explanatory variables that are correlated with each other without a theoretically motivated model, without which we have serious dangers either of omitted variable bias or triviality in research design.

Choosing when to add additional explanatory variables to our analysis is by no means simple. The number of additional variables is always unlimited, our resources are limited, and, above all, the more

---

prices that *directly* affects public opinion about an energy shortage, apart from the aspect of the causal effect that affects public opinion indirectly with changing television coverage. That is, it is the direct and not the indirect effect of oil on opinion. The total effect can be found by not controlling for the extent of television coverage of energy shortages at all. An alternative description of this effect is the effect of energy prices on the variable "public opinion about energy shortages given a fixed degree of television coverage about energy shortages." As an example of the latter, imagine the experiment in which we controlled network television coverage of oil shortages and forced it to remain at the same level while crude oil prices varied naturally. Since coverage is a constant in this experiment, it is controlled for without any other explicit procedure. Even if we could not do an experiment, we could still estimate this conditional effect of oil prices on public opinion about energy shortages by controlling for television coverage.

[11] In addition, we might be interested in just the direct or indirect effect of a variable, or even in the causal effect of some other variable in an equation. In this situation, a perfectly reasonable procedure is to run several different analyses on the same data, as long as we understand the differences in interpretation.

explanatory variables we include, the less leverage we have for estimating any of the individual causal effects. Avoiding omitted variable bias is one reason to add additional explanatory variables. If relevant variables are omitted, our ability to estimate causal inferences correctly is limited.

A Formal Analysis of Omitted Variable Bias. Let us begin with a simple model with two explanatory variables

$$E(Y) = X_1\beta_1 + X_2\beta_2 \tag{5.4}$$

Suppose now that we came upon an important analysis which reported the effect of X_1 on Y without controlling for X_2. Under what circumstances would we have grounds for criticizing this work or justification for seeking funds to redo the study? To answer this question, we formally evaluate the estimator with the omitted control variable.

The estimator of β_1 where we omit X_2 is

$$b_1 - \frac{\sum_{i=1}^{n} X_{1i}Y_i}{\sum_{i=1}^{n} X_{1i}^2}$$

To evaluate this estimator, we take the expectation of b_1 across hypothetical replications under the model in equation (5.4):

$$E(b_1) = E\left(\frac{\sum_{i=1}^{n} X_{1i}Y_i}{\sum_{i=1}^{n} X_{1i}^2}\right) \tag{5.5}$$

$$= \frac{\sum_{i=1}^{n} X_{1i}E(Y_i)}{\sum_{i=1}^{n} X_{1i}^2}$$

$$= \frac{\sum_{i=1}^{n} X_{1i}(X_{1i}\beta_1 + X_{2i}\beta_2)}{\sum_{i=1}^{n} X_{1i}^2}$$

$$= \frac{\sum_{i=1}^{n} X_{1i}^2\beta_1 + \sum_{i=1}^{n} X_{1i}X_{2i}\beta_2)}{\sum_{i=1}^{n} X_{1i}^2}$$

$$= \beta_1 + F\beta_2$$

where $F = \dfrac{\sum_{i=1}^{n} X_{1i} X_{2i}}{\sum_{i=1}^{n} X_{1i}^2}$, the slope coefficient from the regression of X_1 on X_2. The last line of this equation is reproduced in the text in equation (5.3) and is discussed in some detail above.

5.2.2 Examples of Omitted Variable Bias

In this section, we consider several quantitative and qualitative examples, some hypothetical and some from actual research. For example, educational level is one of the best predictors of political participation. Those who have higher levels of education are more likely to vote and more likely to take part in politics in a number of other ways. Suppose we find this to be the case in a new data set but want to go further and see whether the relationship between the two variables is causal and, if so, how education leads to participation.

The first thing we might do would be to see whether there are omitted variables antecedent to education that are correlated with education and at the same time cause participation. Two examples might be the political involvement of the individual's parents and the race of the individual. Parents active in politics might inculcate an interest in participation in their children and at the same time be the kind of parents who foster educational attainment in their children. If we did not include this variable, we might have a spurious relationship between education and political activity or an estimate of the relationship that was too strong.

Race might play the same role. In a racially discriminatory society, blacks might be barred from both educational opportunities and political participation. In such a case, the apparent effect of education on participation would not be real. Ideally, we would want to eliminate all possible omitted variables that might explain away part or all of the relationship between education and participation.

But the fact that the relationship between education and participation diminishes or disappears when we control for an antecedent variable does not necessarily mean that education is irrelevant. Suppose we found that the education-participation link diminished when we controlled for race. One reason might be, as in the example above, that discrimination against blacks meant that race was associated separately with both educational attainment and participation. Under these conditions, no real causal link between education and participation would exist. On the other hand, race might affect political participation *through* education. Racial discrimination might reduce the access of blacks to education. Education might, in turn, be the main factor leading to participation. In this case, the reduction in the relationship between education and participation that is introduced when the investigator adds race to the analysis does not diminish the importance of education. Rather, it explains how race and education interact to affect participation.

Note that these two situations are fundamentally different. If lower participation on the part of blacks was due to a lack of education, we might expect participation to increase if their average level of education increased. But if the reason for lower participation was direct political discrimination that prevented the participation of blacks as citizens, educational improvement would be irrelevant to changes in patterns of participation.

We might also look for variables that are simultaneous with education or that followed it. We might look for omitted variables that show the relationship between education and participation to be spurious. Or we might look for variables that help explain how education works to foster participation. In the former category might be such a variable as the general intelligence level of the individual (which might lead to doing well in school and to political activity). In the latter category might be variables measuring aspects of education such as exposure to civics courses, opportunities to take part in student government, and learning of basic communications skills. If it were found that one or more of the latter, when included in the analysis, reduced the relationship between educational attainment and participation (when we controlled for communications skills, there was no independent effect of educational attainment on participation), this finding would not mean that education was irrelevant. The requisite communications skills were learned in school and there would be a difference in such skills across educational levels. What the analysis would tell us would be how education influenced participation.

All of these examples illustrate once again why it is necessary to have a theoretical model in mind to evaluate. There is no other way to choose what variables to use in our analysis. A theory of how education affected civic activity would guide us to the variables to include. Though we do not add additional variables to a regression equation in qualitative research, the logic is much the same when we decide what other factors to take into account. Consider the research question we raised earlier: the impact of summit meetings on cooperation between the superpowers. Suppose we find that cooperation between the United States and the USSR was higher in years following a summit than preceding one. How would we know that the effect is real and not the result of some omitted variable? And if we are convinced it is real, can we explicate further how it works?

We might want to consider antecedent variables that would be related to the likelihood of a summit and might also be direct causes of cooperation. Perhaps when leaders in each country have confidence in each other, they meet frequently and their countries cooperate. Or perhaps when the geopolitical ambitions of both sides are limited for domestic political reasons, they schedule meetings and they cooperate. In such circumstances, summits themselves would play no direct role in fostering cooperation, though the scheduling of a summit might be a good indicator that things were going well between the superpowers. It is also possible that summits would be part of a causal sequence, just as race might have affected educational level which in turn affected participation. When the superpower leaders have confidence in one another, they call a summit to reinforce that mutual confidence. This, in turn, leads to cooperation. In this case, the summit is far from irrelevant. Without it, there would be less cooperation. Confidence and summits interact to create cooperation. Suppose we take such factors into account and find that summits seem to play an independent role—i.e., when we control for the previous mutual confidence of the leaders and their geopolitical ambitions, the conclusion is that a summit seems to lead to more cooperation. We might still go further and ask how that happens. We might compare among summits in terms of characteristics that might make them more or less successful and see if such factors are related to the degree of cooperation that follows. Again we have to select factors to consider, and these might include: the degree of preparation, whether the issues were economic rather than security, the degree of domestic harmony in each nation, the weather at the summit, and the food. Theory would have to guide us; that is, we would need a view of concepts and relationships that would point to relevant explanatory variables and would propose hypotheses consistent with logic and experience about their effects.

For researchers with a small number of observations, omitted variable bias is very difficult to avoid. In this situation, inefficiency is very costly; including too many irrelevant control variables may make a research design indeterminate (section 4.1). But omitting relevant control variables can introduce bias. And a priori the researcher may not know whether a candidate variable is relevant or not.

We may be tempted at this point to conclude that causal inference is impossible with small numbers of observations. In our view, however, the lessons to be learned are more limited and more optimistic. Understanding the difficulty of making valid causal inferences with few observations should make us cautious about making causal assertions. As indicated in chapter 2, good description and descriptive inference are more valuable than faulty causal inference. Much qualitative research would indeed be improved if there were more attention to valid descriptive inference and less impulse to make causal assertions on the basis of inadequate evidence with incorrect assessments of their uncertainty. However, limited progress in understanding causal issues is nevertheless possible, *if* the theoretical issues with which we are concerned are posed with sufficient clarity and linked to appropriate observable implications. A recent example from international relations research may help make this point.

Helen Milner's study, *Resisting Protectionism* (1988), was motivated by a puzzle: why was U.S. trade policy more protectionist in the 1920s than in the 1970s despite the numerous similarities between the two periods? Her hypothesis was that international interdependence increased between the 1920s and 1970s and helped to account for the difference in U.S. behavior. At this aggregate level of analysis, however, she had only the two observations that had motivated her puzzle which could not help her distinguish her hypothesis from many other possible explanations of this observed variation. The level of uncertainty in her theory would therefore have been much too high had she stopped here. Hence she had to look elsewhere for additional observable implications of her theory.

Milner's approach was to elaborate the process by which her causal effect was thought to take place. She hypothesized that economic interdependence between capitalist democracies affects national preferences by influencing the preferences of industries and firms, which successfully lobby for their preferred policies. Milner therefore studied a variety of U.S. industries in the 1920s and 1970s and French industries in the 1970s and found that those with large multinational investments and more export dependence were the least protectionist. These findings helped confirm her broader theory of the differences in overall U.S. policy between the 1920s and 1970s. Her procedures were therefore consistent with a key part of our methodological advice: specify the observable implications of the theory, even if they are not the objects of principal concern, and design the research so that inferences can be made about these implications and used to evaluate the theory. Hence Milner's study is exemplary in many ways.

The most serious problem of research design that Milner faced involved potential omitted variables. The most obvious control variable is the degree of competition from imports, since more intense competition from foreign imports tends to produce more protectionist firm preferences. That is, import competition is likely to be correlated with

Milner's dependent variable, and it is in most cases antecedent to or simultaneous with her explanatory variables. If this control variable were also correlated with her key causal explanatory variables, multinational investment and export dependence, her results would be biased. Indeed, a negative correlation between import competition and export dependence would have seemed likely on the principles of comparative advantage, so this hypothetical bias would have become real if import competition were not included as a control.

Milner dealt with this problem by selecting for study only industries that were severely affected by foreign competition. Hence, she held constant the severity of import competition and eliminated, or at least greatly reduced, this problem of omitted variable bias. She could have held this key control variable constant at a different level—such as only industries with moderately high levels of import penetration—so long as it was indeed constant for her observations.

Having controlled for import competition, however, Milner still faced other questions of omitted variables. The two major candidates that she considered most seriously, based on a review of the theoretical and empirical literature in her field, were (1) that changes in U.S. power would account for the differences between outcomes in the 1920s and 1970s, and (2) that changes in the domestic political processes of the United States would do so. Her attempt to control for the first factor was built into her original research design: since the proportion of world trade involving the United States in the 1970s was roughly similar to its trade involvement in the 1920s, she controlled for this dimension of American power at the aggregate level of U.S. policy, as well as at the industry and firm level. However, she did not control for the differences between the political isolationism of the United States in the 1920s and its hegemonic position as alliance leader in the 1970s; these factors could be analyzed further to ascertain their potentially biasing effects.

Milner controlled for domestic political processes by comparing industries and firms within the 1920s and within the 1970s, since all firms within these groups faced the same governmental structures and political processes. Her additional study of six import-competing industries in France during the 1970s obviously did not help her hold domestic political processes constant, but it did help her discover that the causal effect of export dependence on preferences for protectionism did not vary with changes in domestic political processes. By carefully considering several potential sources of omitted variable bias and designing her study accordingly, Milner greatly reduced the potential for bias.

However, Milner did not explicitly control for several other possible omitted variables. Her study focused "on corporate trade preferences and does not examine directly the influence of public opinion, ideology, organized labor, domestic political structure, or other possible factors" (1988: 15–16). Her decision not to control for these variables could have been justified on the theoretical grounds that these omitted variables are unrelated to, or are in part consequences of, the key causal variables (export dependence and multinational investment), or have no effect on the dependent variable (preferences for protectionism at the level of the firm, aggregated to industries). However, if these omitted variables were plausibly linked to both her explanatory and dependent variables and were causally prior to her explanatory variable, she would have had to design her study explicitly to control for them.[12]

Finally, Milner's procedure for selecting industries risked making her causal inferences inefficient. As we have noted, her case-selection procedure enabled her to control for the most serious potential source of omitted variable bias by holding import competition constant, which on theoretical grounds was expected to be causally prior to and correlated with her key causal variable and to influence her dependent variables. She selected those industries that had the highest levels of import competition and did not stratify by any other variable. She then studied the preferences of each industry in her sample, and of many firms, for protectionism preferences (her dependent variable) and researched the degree of international economic dependence (her explanatory variable).

This selection procedure is inefficient with respect to her causal inferences because her key causal variables varied less than would have been desirable (Milner 1988:39–42). Although this inefficiency turned out not to be a severe problem in her case, it did mean that she had to do more case studies than were necessary to reach the same level of certainty about her conclusions (see section 6.2). Put differently, with the same number of cases, chosen so that they varied widely on her explanatory variable, she could have produced more certain causal in-

---

[12] Milner addresses the potential for omitted variable bias, but her reasoning is flawed: "By looking at different industries, at different times, and in different countries, [the research design] allows these [omitted control variables] to vary, while showing that the basic argument still holds" (1988:15). In fact, the only way "to hold control variables constant" is actually to hold them constant, not to let them vary. If plausible competing theories had identified these variables as important, she could have looked at a set of observations which differed on her key explanatory variable (degree of international economic dependence of the country, industry, or firm) but not on these control variables.

ferences. That is, her design would have been more efficient had she chosen some industries and firms with no foreign ties and some with high levels of foreign involvement, all of which suffered from constant levels of economic distress and import penetration.

Researchers can never conclusively reject the hypothesis that omitted variables have biased their analyses. However, Milner was able to make a stronger, more convincing case for her hypothesis than she could have done had she not tried to control for some evident sources of omitted variable bias. Milner's rigorous study indicates that social scientists who work with qualitative material need not despair of making limited causal inferences. Perfection is unattainable, perhaps even undefinable; but careful linking of theory and method can enable studies to be designed in a way that will improve the plausibility of our arguments and reduce the uncertainty of our causal inferences.

5.3 INCLUDING IRRELEVANT VARIABLES: INEFFICIENCY

Because of the potential problems with omitted variable bias described in section 5.2, we might naively think that it is essential to collect and simultaneously estimate the causal effects of all possible explanatory variables. At the outset, we should remember that this is not the implication of section 5.2. We showed there that omitting an explanatory variable that is uncorrelated with the included explanatory variables does not create bias, even if the variable has a strong causal impact on the dependent variable, and that controlling for variables that are the consequences of explanatory variables is a mistake. Hence, *our argument should not lead researchers to collect information on every possible causal influence or to criticize research which fails to do so.*

Of course, a researcher might still be uncertain about which antecedent control variables have causal impact or are correlated with the included variables. In this situation, some researchers might attempt to include all control variables that are conceivably correlated with the included explanatory variables as well as all those that might be expected on theoretical grounds to affect the dependent variable. This is likely to be a very long list of variables, many of which may be irrelevant. Such an approach, which appears at first glance to be a cautious and prudent means of avoiding omitted variable bias, would, in fact, risk producing a research design that could only produce indeterminate results. In research with relatively few observations, indeterminacy, as discussed in section 4.1, is a particularly serious problem, and such a "cautious" design would actually be detrimental. This section discusses the costs of including irrelevant explanatory variables and provides essential qualifications to the "include everything" approach.

The inclusion of irrelevant variables can be very costly. Our key point is that even if the control variable has no causal effect on the dependent variable, *the more correlated the main explanatory variable is with the irrelevant control variable, the less efficient is the estimate of the main causal effect.*

To illustrate, let us focus on two different procedures (or "estimators") for calculating an estimate of the causal effect of an appropriately included explanatory variable. The first estimate of this effect is from an analysis with no irrelevant control variables; the second includes one irrelevant control variable. The formal analysis in the box below provides the following conclusions about the relative worth of these two procedures, in addition to the one already mentioned. First, *both estimators are unbiased.* That is, even when controlling for an irrelevant explanatory variable, the usual estimator still gives the right answer on average. Second, *if the irrelevant control variable is uncorrelated with the main explanatory variable, the estimate of the causal effect of the latter is not only unbiased, but it is as efficient as if the irrelevant variable had not been included.* Indeed, if these variables are uncorrelated, precisely the same inference will result. However, if the irrelevant control variable is highly correlated with the main explanatory variable, substantial inefficiency will occur.

The costs of controlling for irrelevant variables are therefore high. When we do so, each study we conduct is much more likely to yield estimates far from the true causal effects. When we replicate a study in a new data set in which there is a high correlation between the key explanatory variable and an irrelevant included control variable, we will be likely to find different results, which would suggest different causal inferences. Thus, even if we control for all irrelevant explanatory variables (and make no other mistakes), we will get the right answer on average, but we may be far from the right answer in any single project and possibly every one. On average, the reanalysis will produce the same effect but the irrelevant variable will increase the inefficiency, just as if we had discarded some of our observations. The implication should be clear: by including an irrelevant variable, we are putting more demands on our finite data set, resulting in less information available for each inference.

As an example, consider again the study of coups d'etat in African states. A preliminary study indicated that the degree of political repression, the main explanatory variable of interest, increased the frequency of coups. Suppose another scholar argued that the original study was flawed because it did not control for whether the state won independence in a violent or negotiated break from colonial rule. Suppose we believe this second scholar is wrong and that the nature of the break from colonial rule had no effect on the dependent variable—the frequency of coups (after the main explanatory variable, political repression, is controlled for). What would be the consequences of controlling for this irrelevant, additional variable?

The answer depends on the relationship between the irrelevant variable, which measures the nature of the break from colonial rule, and the main explanatory variable, which measures political repression. If the correlation between these variables is high—as seems plausible—then including these control variables would produce quite inefficient estimates of the effect of political repression. To understand this, notice that to control for how independence was achieved, the researcher might divide his categories of repressive and nonrepressive regimes according to whether they broke from colonial rule violently or by negotiation. The frequency of coups in each category could be counted to assess the causal effects of political repression, while the means of breaking from colonial rule is controlled. Although this sort of design is a reasonable way to avoid omitted variable bias, it can have high costs: when the additional control variable has no effect on the dependent variable but is correlated with an included explanatory variable, the number of observations in each category is reduced and the main causal effect is estimated much less efficiently. This result means that much of the hard work the researcher has put in was wasted, since unnecessarily reducing efficiency is equivalent to discarding observations. The best solution is to always collect more observations, but if this is not possible, researchers are well-advised to identify irrelevant variables and not control for them.

A Formal Analysis of Included Variable Inefficiencies. Suppose the true model is $E(Y) = X_1\beta$ and $V(Y) = \sigma^2$. However, we incorrectly think that a second explanatory variable X_2 also belongs in the equation. So we estimate

$$E(Y) = X_1\beta_1 + X_2\beta_2 \tag{5.6}$$

not knowing that in fact $\beta_2 = 0$. What consequence does a simultaneous estimation of both parameters have for our estimate of β_1?

Define b_1 as the correct estimator, based only on a regression of Y on X_1, and $\hat{\beta}_1$ as the first coefficient on X_i from a regression of Y on X_1 and X_2. It is easy to show that we cannot distinguish between these two estimators on the basis of unbiasedness (being correct on average across many hypothetical experiments), since both are unbiased:

$$E(b_1) = E(\hat{\beta}_1) = \beta_1 \tag{5.7}$$

The estimators do differ, however, with respect to efficiency. The correct estimator has a variance (calculated in equation [3.9]) of

$$V(b_1) = \frac{\sigma^2}{\sum_{i=1}^{n} X_{1i}^2} \tag{5.8}$$

whereas the other estimator has variance

$$V(\hat{\beta}_1) = \frac{\sigma^2}{(1 - r_{12}^2) \sum_{i=1}^{n} X_{1i}^2} \tag{5.9}$$

$$= \frac{V(b_1)}{(1 - r_{12}^2)}$$

where the correlation between X_1 and X_2 is r_{12} (see Goldberger 1991:245).

From the last line in equation (5.9), we can see the precise relationship between the variances of the two estimators. If the correlation between the two explanatory variables is zero, then it makes no difference whether you include the irrelevant variable or not, since both estimators have the same variance. However, the more correlated two variables are, the higher the variance, and thus lower the efficiency, of $\hat{\beta}_1$.

5.4 ENDOGENEITY

Political science research is rarely experimental. We do not usually have the opportunity to manipulate the explanatory variables; we just observe them. One consequence of this lack of control is endogeneity—that the values our explanatory variables take on are sometimes a consequence, rather than a cause, of our dependent variable. With true experimental manipulation, the direction of causality is unambiguous. But for many areas of qualitative and quantitative research, endogeneity is a common and serious problem.[13]

[13] Qualitative researchers do sometimes manipulate explanatory variables through participant observation. Even in-depth interviews can be a form of experiment if different questions are asked systematically or other conditions are changed in different interviews. In fact, it can even be a problem even for in-depth interviews, since a researcher might feel more comfortable applying experimental "treatments" (asking certain ques-

In the absence of investigator control over the values of the explanatory variables, the direction of causality is always a difficult issue. In nonexperimental research—quantitative or qualitative—explanatory and dependent variables vary because of factors out of the control (and often out of sight) of the researcher. States invade; army officers plot coups; inflation drops; government policies are enacted; candidates decide to run for office; voters choose among candidates. A scholar must try to piece together an argument about what is causing what.

An example is provided by the literature on U.S. congressional elections. Many scholars have argued that the dramatic rise of the electoral advantage of incumbency during the late 1960s was due in large part to the increase in constituency service performed by members of Congress. That is, the franking privilege, budgets for travel to the district, staff in the district to handle specific constituent requests, pork-barrel projects, and other perquisites of office have allowed congressional incumbents to build up support in their districts. Many citizens vote for incumbent candidates on these grounds.

This constituency-service hypothesis seems perfectly reasonable, but does the evidence support it? Numerous scholars have attempted to provide such evidence (for a review of this literature, see Cain, Ferejohn, and Fiorina 1987), but the positive evidence is scarce. The modal study of this question is based on measures of the constituency service performed by a sample of members of Congress and of the proportion of the vote for the incumbent candidate. The researchers then estimate the causal impact of service on the vote through regression analysis. Surprisingly, many of these estimates indicate that the effect is zero or even negative.

It seems likely that the problem of endogeneity accounts for these paradoxical results. In other words, members at highest risk of losing the next election (perhaps because of a scandal or hard times in their district) do extra constituency service. Incumbents who feel secure about being reelected probably focus on other aspects of their jobs, such as policy-making in Washington. The result is that those incumbents who do the most service receive the fewest votes. This does not mean that constituency service reduces the vote, only that a strong expected vote reduces service. By ignoring the feedback effect, one's inferences will be strongly biased.

David Laitin outlines an example of an endogeneity problem in one of the classics of early twentieth century social science, Max Weber's *The Protestant Ethic and the Spirit of Capitalism.* "Weber attempted to

tions) to certain, nonrandomly selected, respondents. Experimenters have numerous problems of their own, but endogeneity is not usually one of them.

demonstrate that a specific type of economic behavior—the capitalist spirit — was (inadvertently) induced by Protestant teachings and doctrines. But . . . Weber and his followers could not answer one objection that was raised to their thesis: namely that the Europeans who already had an interest in breaking the bonds of precapitalist spirit might well have left the church precisely for that purpose. In other words, the economic interests of certain groups could be seen as inducing the development of the Protestant ethic. Without a better controlled study, Weber's line of causation could be turned the other way." (Laitin 1986:187; see also R. H. Tawney 1935 who originated the criticism).

In the remainder of this section, we will discuss five methods of coping with the difficult problem of endogeneity:

- Correcting a biased inference (section 5.4.1);
- Parsing the dependent variable and studying only those parts that are consequences, rather than causes, of the explanatory variable (section 5.4.2);
- Transforming an endogeneity problem into bias due to an omitted variable, and controlling for this variable (section 5.4.3);
- Carefully selecting at least some observations without endogeneity problems (section 5.4.4); and
- Parsing the explanatory variables to ensure that only those parts which are truly exogenous are in the analysis (section 5.4.5).

Each of these five procedures can be viewed as a method of avoiding endogeneity problems, but each can also be seen as a way of clarifying a causal hypothesis. For a causal hypothesis that ignores an endogeneity problem is, in the end, a theoretical problem, requiring respecification so that it is at least possible that the explanatory variables could influence the dependent variable. We will discuss the first two solutions to endogeneity in the context of our quantitative constituency service example and the remaining three with the help of extended examples from qualitative research.

5.4.1 Correcting Biased Inferences

The last line of equation (5.13) in the box below provides a procedure for assessing the exact direction and degree of bias due to endogeneity. For convenience, we reproduce equation (5.13) here:

$$E(b) = \beta + \text{Bias}$$

This equation implies that if endogeneity is present, we are not making the causal inference we desire. That is, if the bias term is zero, our method of inference (or estimator b) will be unbiased on average (that is, equal to β). But if we have endogeneity bias, we are estimating the correct inference plus a bias factor. Endogeneity is a problem because we are generally unaware of the size or direction of the bias. This bias factor will be large or small, negative or positive, depending on the specific empirical example. Fortunately, even if we cannot avoid endogeneity bias in the first place, we can sometimes correct for it after the fact by ascertaining the direction and perhaps the degree of the bias.

Equation (5.13) demonstrates that the bias factor depends on the correlation between the explanatory variable and the error term—the part of the dependent variable unexplained by the explanatory variable. For example, if the constituency-service hypothesis is correct, then the causal effect of constituency service on the vote (β in the equation) is positive. If, in addition, the expected vote affects the level of constituency service we observe, then the bias term will be negative. That is, even after the effect of constituency service on the vote is taken into account, constituency service will inversely correlate with the error term because incumbents who have lower expected votes will perform more service. The result is that the bias term is negative, and uncorrected inferences in this case are biased estimates of the causal effect β (or, equivalently, unbiased estimates of $[\beta + \text{bias}]$). Thus, even if the constituency-service hypothesis is true, endogeneity bias would cause us to estimate the effect of service as a smaller positive number than it should be, as zero, or even as negative, depending on the size of the bias factor. Hence, we can conclude that the correct estimate of the effect of service on the vote is larger than we estimated in an analysis conducted with no endogeneity correction. As a result, our uncorrected analysis yields a lower bound on the effect of service, making the constituency-service hypothesis more plausible.

Thus, even if we cannot avoid endogeneity bias, we can sometimes improve our inferences after the fact by estimating the degree of bias. At a minimum, this enables us to determine the direction of bias, perhaps providing an upper or lower bound on the correct estimate. At best, we can use this technique to produce fully unbiased inferences.

5.4.2 Parsing the Dependent Variable

One way to avoid endogeneity bias is to reconceptualize the dependent variable as itself containing a dependent and an explanatory component. The explanatory component of the dependent variable interferes with our analysis through a feedback mechanism, that is, by influencing our key causal (explanatory) variable. The other component of our dependent variable is truly dependent, a function, and not a cause, of our explanatory variable. The goal of this method of avoiding endogeneity bias is to identify and measure only the dependent component of our dependent variable.

For example, in a study of the constituency-service hypothesis, King (1991a) separated from the total vote for a member of congress the portion due solely to incumbency status. In recent years, the electoral advantage of incumbency status is about 8–10 percentage points of the vote, as compared to a base for many incumbents of roughly 52 percent of the two-party vote. Through a statistical procedure, King then estimated the incumbency advantage, which was a solely dependent component of the dependent variable, and he used this figure in place of the raw vote to estimate the effects of constituency service. Since the incumbent's vote advantage, being such a small portion of the entire vote, would not have much of an effect on the propensity for incumbent legislators to engage in constituency service, he avoided endogeneity bias. His results indicated that an extra $10,000 added to the budget of the average state legislator for constituency service (among other things) gives this incumbent an additional 1.54 percentage point advantage (plus or minus about 0.4 percent) in the next election, hence providing the first empirical support for the constituency-service hypothesis.

5.4.3 Transforming Endogeneity into an Omitted Variable Problem

We can always think of endogeneity as a case of omitted variable bias, as the following famous example from the study of comparative electoral systems demonstrates. One of the great puzzles of political analysis for an earlier generation of political scientists was the fall of the Weimar Republic and its replacement by the Nazi regime in the early 1930s. One explanation, supported by some close and compelling case studies of Weimar Germany, was that the main cause was the imposition of proportional representation as the mode of election in the Weimar Constitution. The argument, briefly stated, is that proportional representation allows small parties representing specific ideological, interest, or religious groups to achieve representation in parliament. Under such an electoral system, there is no need for a candidate to compromise his or her position in order to achieve electoral success such as there is under a single-member-district, winner-take-all electoral system. Hence parliament will be filled with small ideological groups unwilling and unable to work together. The stalemate and frustration would make it possible for one of those groups—in this case the National Socialists—to seize power. (For the classic statement of this theory, see Hermens 1941).

The argument in the above paragraph was elaborated in several important case studies of the fall of the Weimar Republic. Historians and political scientists traced the collapse of Weimar to the electoral success of small ideological parties and their unwillingness to compromise in the Reichstag. There are many problems with the explanation, as of course there would be for an explanation of a complex outcome that is based on a single instance, but let us look only at the problem of endogeneity. The underlying explanation involved a causal mechanism with the following links in the causal chain: proportional representation was introduced and enabled small parties with narrow electoral bases to gain seats in the Reichstag (including parties dedicated to its overthrow, like the National Socialists). As a result, the Reichstag was stalemated and the populace was frustrated. This, in turn, led to a coup by one of the parties.

But further study—of Germany as well as of other observable implications—indicated that party fragmentation was not merely the result of proportional representation. Scholars reasoned that if party fragmentation led to adoption of proportional representation, it would also be the cause. By applying the same explanatory variable to other observations (following our rule from chapter 1 that evidence should be sought for hypotheses in data other than that in which they were generated), scholars found that societies with a large number of groups with narrow and intense views in opposition to other groups— minority, ethnic, or religious groups, for instance—are more likely to adopt proportional representation, since it is the only electoral system that the various factions in society can agree on. A closer look at German politics before the introduction of proportional representation confirmed this idea by locating many small factions. Proportional representation did not create these factions, although it may have facilitated their parliamentary expression. Nor were the factions the sole cause of proportional representation; however, both the adoption of proportional representation and parliamentary fragmentation seem to have been effects of social fragmentation. (See Lakeman and Lambert 1955:155 for an early explication of this argument.)

Thus, we have transformed an endogeneity problem into omitted variable bias. That is, prior social fragmentation is an omitted variable that causes proportional representation, is causally prior to it, and led in part to the fall of Weimar. By transforming the problem in this way, scholars were able to get a better handle on the problem since they could explicitly measure this omitted variable and control for it in subsequent studies. In this example, once the omitted variable was included and controlled for, scholars found that there was a reasonable probability that the apparent causal relationship between proportional representation and the fall of the Weimar Republic was almost entirely spurious.

The subject of the relationship between electoral systems and democracy is still highly contested, although study of it has progressed greatly since these early studies. Scholars have expanded the study from one of concentrated case studies without much concern for the logic of explanation to one of studies based on many observations of given implications and gradually resolved some aspects of measurement and ultimately of inference. In so doing, they have been able to separate the exogenous from the endogenous effects more systematically.

5.4.4 Selecting Observations to Avoid Endogeneity

Endogeneity is a very common problem in much work on the impact of ideas on policy (Hall 1989; Goldstein and Keohane 1993). Insofar as the ideas *reflect the conditions* under which political actors operate—for instance, their material circumstances, which generate their material interests—analysis of the ideas' impact on policy is subject to omitted variable bias: actors' ideas are correlated with a causally prior omitted variable—material interests—which affects the dependent variable— political strategy (See section 5.4.3). And insofar as ideas serve as *rationalizations* of policies pursued on other grounds, the ideas can be mere *consequences* rather than *causes* of policy. Under these circumstances, ideas are endogenous: they may appear to explain actors' strategies, but in fact they result from these strategies.

The most difficult methodological task in studying the impact of ideas on policy is compensating for the closely related problems of omitted variable bias and endogeneity as they affect a given research problem. To show that ideas are causally important, it must be demonstrated that a given set of ideas held by policymakers, or some aspect of them, affect policies pursued and do not simply reflect those policies or their prior material interests. Researchers in this field must be especially careful in defining the causal effect of interest. In particular, the observed dependent variable (policies) and explanatory variable (ideas held by individuals) must be compared with a precisely defined counterfactual situation in which the explanatory variable takes on a different value: the relevant individuals had different ideas.

Comparative analysis is a good way to determine whether a given set of ideas is exogenous or endogenous. For instance, in a recent study of the role of ideas in the adoption of Stalinist economic policies in other socialist countries, Nina Halpern (1993) engages in such an analysis. Her hypothesis is that Stalinist planning doctrine—ideas in which Eastern European and Chinese leaders believed—helps to explain their economic policies when they took power after World War II. This hypothesis is consistent with the fact that these leaders held Stalinist ideas and implemented Stalinist policy, but a mere correlation does not demonstrate causality. Indeed, endogeneity may be at work: Stalinist policies could have generated ideas justifying those policies, or anticipation that Stalinist policies would have to be followed could have generated such ideas.

Although Halpern does not use this language, she proceeds in a manner similar to that discussed in section 5.4.3, by transforming endogeneity into omitted variable bias. The principal alternative hypothesis that she considers is that Eastern Europe and Asian Communist states developed command economies after World War II solely as a result of Soviet military might and political influence. The counterfactual claim of this hypothesis is that even if Eastern Europeans and Chinese had not believed in Stalinist ideas about the desirability of planned economies, command economies would still have been implemented in their countries, and ideas justifying them would have appeared.

Halpern then argues that in the Eastern European countries occupied by the Red Army, Soviet power rather than ideas about the superiority of Stalinist doctrines may well have accounted for their adoption of command economies: "the alternative explanation that the choices were purely a response to Stalin's commands is impossible to disprove" (1993:89). Hence she searches for potential observations to which this source of omitted variable bias does not apply and finds the policies followed in China and Yugoslavia, the two largest socialist countries not occupied by Soviet troops after World War II. Since China was a huge country that had an indigenous revolution, Stalin could not dictate policy to it. The Communists in Yugoslavia also achieved power without the aid of the Red Army, and Marshall Tito demonstrated his independence from Moscow's orders from the end of World War II onward.

China instituted a command economy without being under the political or military domination of the Soviet Union; and in Yugoslavia, Stalinist measures were adopted *despite* Soviet policy. Halpern infers from such evidence that in these cases Soviet power alone does not explain policy change. Furthermore, with respect to China, she also considers and rejects another alternative hypothesis by which ideas would be endogenous: that similar economic situations made it appropriate to transplant Stalinist planning methods to China.

Having considered and rejected the alternative hypotheses which hold ideas as endogenous either to Soviet power or economic conditions, Halpern is then able to make her argument that Chinese (and to some extent and for a shorter time, Yugoslav) adoption of Stalinist doctrine provided a basis for agreement and the resolution of uncertainty for these postrevolutionary regimes. Although such an analysis remains quite tentative because of the small number of her theory's implications that she observed, it provides reasons for believing that ideas were not entirely endogenous in this situation—that they played a causal role.

This example illustrates how we can first translate a general concern about endogeneity into specific potential sources of omitted variable bias and then search for a subset of observations in which these sources of bias could not apply. In this case, by transforming the problem to one of omitted variable bias, Halpern was able to compare alternative explanatory hypotheses in an especially productive manner for her substantive hypothesis. She considered several alternative explanatory hypotheses to account for the adoption of command-economy policies and found that only in China, and to some extent Yugoslavia, was it reasonable to consider Stalinist doctrine (the ideas in question) to be largely exogenous. Hence she focused her research on China and Yugoslavia. Had she not carefully designed her study to deal with the problem of endogeneity, her conclusions would be much less convincing—consider, for instance, if she had tried to prove her case with the examples of Poland and Bulgaria!

5.4.5 Parsing the Explanatory Variable

In this section, we introduce a fifth and final method for eliminating the bias due to endogeneity. The goal of this method is to divide a potentially endogenous explanatory variable into two components: one that is clearly exogenous and one that is at least partly endogenous. The researcher then uses only the exogenous portion of the explanatory variable in a causal analysis.

An example of this solution to endogeneity comes from a study of voluntary participation in politics by Verba, Schlozman, and Brady (in progress). These authors were interested in explaining why African-Americans are much more politically active than Latinos, given that the two groups are similarly disadvantaged. The authors find that a variety of factors contribute to the difference, including recency of immigration to the United States and linguistic abilities. One of their key explanatory variables was attendance at religious services (church, synagogue, etc.). The investigators obviously had no control over whether individuals attended these services, and so the potential for endogeneity could not be ruled out. In fact, they suspected that some Latinos and many more African-Americans attended religious services because they were politically active. Someone who was interested in being politically active might join a church because it offered a chance to learn such skills or was highly politicized. A politicized clergy might train congregants for political activity or provide them with political stimuli. In other words, the causal arrow might run from politics to nonpolitical experiences rather than vice versa.

Verba et al. solved this problem by parsing their key explanatory variable. They did this by arguing that religious institutions affect political participation in two ways. First, individuals learn civic skills in these institutions (for instance, how to make a speech or how to conduct a meeting). The acquisition of such skills, in turn, makes the citizen more competent to take part in political life and more willing to do so. Second, citizens are exposed to political stimulation (for instance, discussion of political matters or direct requests to become politically active from others associated with the institution). And this exposure, too, should affect political activity. The authors argued that the first component is largely exogenous, whereas the second is at least partly endogenous: that is, it is partly due to the extent to which individuals are politically active (the dependent variable).

The authors then conducted an auxiliary study to evaluate this hypothesis about exogenous and endogenous components of participation at religious services. They began by recognizing that the likelihood that an individual acquires civic skills in church depends on the organizational structure of the church. A church that is organized in a hierarchical manner, where clergy are appointed by central church officials and where congregants play little role in church governance, provides fewer opportunities for the individual church member to learn participatory civic skills than does a church organized on a congregational basis where the congregants play a significant role in church governance. Most African-Americans belong to Protestant churches organized on a congregational basis while most Latinos belong to Catholic churches organized on a hierarchical basis. The authors showed that it is this difference in church affiliation that explains the likelihood of acquiring civic skills. They showed, for instance, that for both groups as well as for Anglo-white Americans, it is the nature of the denomination that affects the acquisition of civic skills, not ethnicity, other social characteristics, or, especially, political participation.

Having convinced themselves that the acquisition of civic skills really was exogenous to political participation, Verba et al. measured the acquisition of civic skills at religious services and used this variable, rather than attendance at religious services, as their explanatory variable. This approach solved the endogeneity problem, since they had now parsed their explanatory variable to include only its exogenous component.

This auxiliary study provided further supporting evidence that they had solved their endogeneity problem, since church affiliation of Latinos and African-Americans cannot plausibly be explained by their particular political involvements; church affiliation is in most cases acquired as a child through the family. The reasons why African-Americans are mostly Protestant are found in the histories of American slavery and the institutions that developed on Southern plantations. The reasons why Latinos are Catholic are rooted in the Spanish conquest of Latin America. Nor can the difference between the institutional structure of the Catholic and Protestant churches be attributed to the interests of church officials in involvement in current American politics. Rather, one has to go back to the Reformation to find the source of the difference in organizational structure.

A Formal Analysis of Endogeneity. This formal model demonstrates the bias created if a research design is afflicted by endogeneity, and nothing is done about it. Suppose we have one explanatory variable X and one dependent variable Y. We are interested in the causal effect of X on Y, and we use the following equation:

$$E(Y) = X\beta \tag{5.10}$$

This can also be written as $Y = X\beta + \varepsilon$, where $\varepsilon = Y - E(Y)$ is called the error or disturbance term. Suppose further that there is endogeneity; that is, X also depends on Y:

$$E(X) = Y\gamma \tag{5.11}$$

What happens if we ignore the reciprocal part of the relationship in equation (5.11) and estimate β as if only equation (5.10) were true? In other words, we estimate β (incorrectly assuming that $\gamma = 0$) with the usual equation:

$$b = \frac{\sum_{i=1}^{n} X_i Y_i}{\sum_{i=1}^{n} X_i^2} \tag{3.7}$$

To evaluate this estimator, we use the property of unbiasedness and therefore calculate its expected value:

$$E(b) = E\left(\frac{\sum_{i=1}^{n} X_i Y_i}{\sum_{i=1}^{n} X_i^2}\right) \tag{5.13}$$

$$= E\left(\frac{\sum_{i=1}^{n} X_i (X_i \beta + \varepsilon_i)}{\sum_{i=1}^{n} X_i^2}\right)$$

$$= \beta + \frac{\sum_{i=1}^{n} C(X_i, \varepsilon_i)}{\sum_{i=1}^{n} V(X_i)}$$

$$= \beta + \text{Bias}$$

where Bias $= \sum_{i=1}^{n} C(X_i, \varepsilon_i) / \sum_{i=1}^{n} V(X_i)$. Normally, the covariance of X_i and the disturbance term ε_i, $C(X_i, \varepsilon_i)$, is zero so that the bias term is zero. Thus the expected value of b is β and therefore unbiased. It is usually true that after we take into account X in predicting Y, the portion we have remaining (ε) is not correlated with X. However, in the present situation, after we take into account the effect of X, there is still some variation left over due to feedback from the causal effect of Y on X. Thus, endogeneity means that the second term in the last line of equation (5.13) will not generally be zero, and the estimate will be biased.

The direction of the bias depends on the covariance, since the variance of X is always positive. However, in the unusual cases where the variance of X is extremely large, it will overwhelm the covariance and make the bias term negligible. The text gives an example with a substantive interpretation of this bias term.

5.5 Assigning values of the Explanatory Variable

We pointed out in section 4.4 that the best controlled experiments have two advantages: control over the selection of observations and control over the assignment of values of the explanatory variables to units. We only discussed selection at that point. Now that we have analyzed omitted variable bias and the other methodological pitfalls in this chapter, we can address the issue of control over assignment.

In a medical experiment, a drug being tested and a placebo constitute the treatments, which are randomly assigned to patients. Basically the same situation exists here as with random selection of observations: random assignment is very useful with large numbers of observations but is unlikely to be an optimal strategy with a small n. With a large n, random assignment of values of the explanatory variables eliminates the possibility of endogeneity (since they cannot be influenced by the dependent variable) and measurement error (so long as we accurately record which treatment is administered). Perhaps most important is that random assignment in large-n studies makes omitted variable bias extremely unlikely, because the explanatory variable with randomly assigned values will be uncorrelated with all omitted variables, even those that influence the dependent variable. Random assignment thus renders omitted variables harmless—they cause no bias—in large-n studies. However, with a small number of observations, it is very easy for a randomly assigned variable to be correlated with some relevant omitted variable, and this correlation causes omitted variable bias. Indeed, the selection-bias example showed how a randomly assigned variable was correlated with an observed dependent variable; in exactly the same way, a randomly assigned explanatory variable could too easily be correlated with some omitted variable if the number of observations is small.

Although experimenters can often set values of their explanatory variables, qualitative researchers are rarely so fortunate. When subjects select the values of their own explanatory variables or when other factors influence the choice, the possibilities of selection bias, endogeneity, and other sources of bias and inefficiency greatly increase. For instance, if an experimentalist were studying the impact on political efficacy of participation in a demonstration, she would randomly assign some subjects to take part in a demonstration and others to stay home, and then measure the difference in efficacy between the two experimental groups (or, perhaps, compare the groups in terms of the change in efficacy between a measure taken before the experiment and after it.) In nonexperimental research, however, the subjects themselves frequently choose whether to participate. Under these conditions, other individual characteristics (such as whether the individual is young or not, a student or not, and so forth) will affect the choice to demonstrate, as will other factors such as, for students, the closeness of the campus to the scene of demonstrations. And, of course, many of these factors may be correlated with the dependent variable, political efficacy.

Consider another example where the units of analysis are larger and less frequent: the classic issue of the impact of an arms buildup on the likelihood of war. Does the size of a nation's armaments budget increase the likelihood that that nation will subsequently be engaged in a war? The explanatory variable is the arms budget (perhaps as a percentage of GNP or, alternatively, changes in the budget); the dependent variable is the presence or absence of war at some designated time period after the measurement of the explanatory variable. The ideal experimental design would involve assignment of values on the explanatory variable by the researcher: she would choose various nations to study and determine each government's arms budget (assigning the values at random or, perhaps, using one of the "intentional" techniques we discuss below). Obviously, this is not feasible! What we actually do is measure the values on the explanatory variable (the size of the arms budget) that each nation's government chooses for itself. The problem, of course, is that these self-assigned values on the explanatory variable are not independent of the dependent variable—the likelihood of going to war—as they would have been if we could have chosen them. In this case, there is a clear problem of endogeneity: the value of the explanatory variable is influenced by anticipations of the value of the dependent variable—the perceived threat of war. Endogeneity is also a problem for studies of the causal relationship between alliances and war. Nations choose alliances; investigators do not assign them to alliances and study the impact on warfare. Alliances should not, therefore, be regarded as exogenous explanatory variables in studies of war, insofar as they are often formed in anticipation of war.

These examples show that endogeneity is not always a problem to be fixed but is often an integral part of the process by which the world produces our observations. Ascertaining the process by which values of the explanatory variables were determined is generally very hard and we cannot usually appeal to any automatic procedure to solve problems related to it. It is nevertheless a research task that cannot be avoided.

Since the probability of random selection or random assignment causing bias in any trial of a hypothetical experiment drops very quickly as the number of observations increase, it is useful to employ random procedures even with a moderate number of units. If the number of units is "sufficiently large," which we define precisely in section 6.2, random selection of units will automatically satisfy the conditional independence assumption of subsection 3.3. However, when only a few examples of the phenomenon of interest exist or we can collect information on only a small number of observations, as is usual in qualitative research, random selection and assignment are no answer. Even controlled experiments, when they are possible, are no solution without an adequate number of observations.

Facing these problems, as qualitative researchers, we should ask ourselves whether we can increase the number of observations that we investigate, since, short of collecting all observations, *the most reliable practice is to collect data randomly on a large number of units and randomize the assignment of values of the explanatory variables. However, if that is not possible, we should not select observations randomly.* Instead, *we should use our a priori knowledge of the available observations*—knowledge based on previous research, our best guesses, or judgments of other experts in the area—and *make selection of observations and (if possible) assignment of the values of explanatory variables in such a way as to avoid bias and inefficiencies. If bias is unavoidable, we should at least try to understand its direction and likely order of magnitude.* If all else fails—that is, if we know there is bias but cannot determine its direction or magnitude—our research will be better if we at least increase the level of uncertainty we use in describing our results. By understanding the problems of inference discussed in this book, we will be better suited to make these choices than any random number generator. In any case, *all studies should include a section or chapter carefully explicating the assignment and selection processes.* This discussion should include the rules used, an itemization of all foreseeable hidden sources of bias and what, if anything, was done about each.

5.6 CONTROLLING THE RESEARCH SITUATION

Intentional selection of observations without regard to relevant control variables and other problems of inference will not satisfy unit homogeneity. We need to make sure that the observations chosen have values of the explanatory variable that are measured with as little error as possible, that are not correlated with some key omitted explanatory variable, and that are not determined in part by the dependent variable. That is, we have to deal effectively with the problems of measurement error, omitted variables, and endogeneity discussed earlier in this chapter. Insofar as these problems still exist after our best efforts to avoid them, we must at least recognize, assess, and try to correct for them.

Controls are inherently difficult to design with small-n field studies, but attention to them is usually absolutely essential in avoiding bias. Unfortunately, many qualitative researchers include too few or no controls at all. For example, Bollen, Entwisle, and Alderson (in press) have found in a survey of sociological books and articles that over a fourth of the researchers used no method of control at all.

For example, suppose we are interested in the causal effect of a year of incarceration on the degree to which people espouse radical political beliefs. The ideal design would involve a genuinely experimental study in which we randomly selected a large group of citizens, randomly assigned half to prison for a year, and then measured the radicalness of the political beliefs of each group. The estimated causal effect would be the average difference in the beliefs of these two groups at the end of the year. With a large n, we could plausibly assume conditional independence, and this causal inference would likely be sound. Needless to say, such a study is out of the question.

But for the sake of argument, let us assume that such an experiment were conducted but with only a few people. Because of the problems discussed in section 4.2, a small number of people, even if randomly selected and assigned, would probably not satisfy conditional independence, and we would therefore need some explicit control. One simple control would be to measure radical political beliefs before the experiment. Then, our causal estimate would be the difference in the *change* in radical political beliefs between the two groups. This procedure would control for a situation where the two groups were not identical on this one variable prior to running the experiment. To understand how to estimate the causal effect in this situation, recall the Fundamental Problem of Causal Inference. Ideally, we would like to take a single individual, wait a year under carefully controlled conditions that maintained his environment identically, except for the passage of time and events in the outside world, and measure the radicalness of his political beliefs. Simultaneously, we would take the individual at the same time, send him to prison for a year, and measure the radicalness of *his* political beliefs. The difference between these two measures is the definition of a causal effect of incarceration on the political beliefs of this person.[14] The Fundamental Problem is that we can observe this person's beliefs in only one of these situations. Obviously, the same individual cannot be in and out of prison at the same time.

Control is an attempt to get around the Fundamental Problem in the most direct manner. Since we cannot observe this person's beliefs in both situations, we search for two individuals (or, more likely, two groups of individuals) who are alike in as many respects as possible, except for the key explanatory variable—whether or not they went to prison. We also do not select based on their degree of radicalness. We might first select a sample of people recently released from prison, and then, for each ex-prisoner, track down a *matching* person—someone who was alike in as many ways as possible except for the fact that he did not go to prison. Perhaps we could first interview a person released from prison and, on the basis of our knowledge of his history and characteristics, seek out matching people—people with similar

---

[14] To follow strictly the procedures in chapter 3, we would need to perform this experiment several times and take the average as a measure of the mean causal effect of the experimental treatment. We might also be interested in the variance of the causal effect for this individual.

demographic profiles, perhaps from the same neighborhood and school.

The variables that we match the individuals on are by definition constant across the groups. When we estimate the causal effect of incarceration, these will be controlled. Control is a difficult process since we need to control for all plausibly confounding variables. If we do not match on a variable and cannot control for it in any other way, and if this variable has an influence on the dependent variable while being correlated with the explanatory variable (it affects the radicalness of beliefs and is not the same for prisoners and nonprisoners), the estimate of our causal effect will be biased.

In political research that compares countries with one another, controlling to achieve unit homogeneity is difficult: any two countries vary along innumerable dimensions. For example, Belgium and the Netherlands might seem to the untutored observer to be "most similar" countries in the sense of Przeworski and Teune (1982): they are both small European democracies with open economies, and they are not threatened by their neighbors. For many purposes, therefore, they can feasibly be compared (Katzenstein 1985). However, they differ with respect to linguistic patterns, religion, resource base, date of industrialization, and many other factors of relevance to their politics. Any research design for comparative study of their politics as a whole that just focuses on these two states will therefore risk being indeterminate.

If our purpose is to compare Belgium and the Netherlands in general, such indeterminacy cannot be avoided. But suppose the researcher has a more specific goal: to study the impact of being a colonial power on the political strategies followed by governments of small European democracies. In that case, it would be possible to compare the policies of Belgium, the Netherlands, and Portugal with those of noncolonial small states such as Austria, Sweden, Switzerland, and Norway. This might well be a valuable research design; but it would still not control for the innumerable factors, apart from colonial history, that differentiate those countries from one another. The researcher sensitive to problems of unit homogeneity might consider another research design—perhaps as an alternative, but preferably as a complement to the first one—in which she would study the policies of Belgium, the Netherlands, and Portugal before and after their loss of colonies. In this design, Belgium is not "a single observation" but is the locus for a controlled analysis—before and after independence was granted to its colonies in the early 1960s. Many of the factors that differentiate Belgium from Portugal and the Netherlands—much less from the countries without a colonial history—are automatically controlled for in this time series design. In fact, both comparisons—across nations and within the same nation at different points of time—will face problems of unit homogeneity. The several nations differ in many uncontrolled and unmeasured ways that might be relevant to the research problem, but then so does a single nation measured at different times. But the *differences* will be different. Neither comparison (neither across space nor across time) constitutes a perfectly controlled experiment—far from it—but the two approaches together may provide much stronger evidence for our hypotheses than either approach alone.

The strategy of intentional selection involves some hidden perils of which researchers should be aware, especially when attempting to match observations to control for potentially relevant variables. The primary peril is a particularly insidious form of omitted variable bias. Imagine the following research design, which utilizes matching. Seeking to encourage countries in Africa that seem to be moving in the direction of greater democratization, the U.S. government institutes a program called "aid to democracy" in which American aid to democratizing efforts—in the form of educational materials about democracy and the like—is sent to African nations. The researcher wants to study whether such aid increases the level of democracy in a nation, decreases it, or makes no difference. The researcher cannot give and withhold aid from the same nation at the same time. So he chooses a prospective-comparative approach: that is, he compares nations that are about to receive aid with others that are not. He also correctly decides to find units in the two groups that are matched on the values of all relevant control variables but the one with which he is concerned— the U.S. aid program.

Time and linguistic skills constrain his research so that he can, in fact, study only two nations (though the problems to be mentioned would exist in a study with a larger, but still small, number of units). He chooses one nation that receives a good deal of aid under the U.S. program and one that receives very little. The dependent variable is wisely chosen to be the gain in degree of democracy from the time the U.S. program begins to the time, two years later, when the study is conducted. And because there are many other variables that might be correlated with both the explanatory variable and the dependent variable, the researcher tries to choose two countries that are closely matched on these in order to eliminate omitted variable bias.

Two such control variables might be the level of the education of the nation and the extent of antiregime guerilla violence. Each of these is a variable that might cause bias if not controlled for because each is correlated with both the explanatory and the dependent variables (recall section 5.2 on omitted variable bias). The United States is likely to give more aid to countries with good educational systems (perhaps because such nations can establish better relations with Washington or because the United States favors education), and education is at times a democratizing force. Similarly, the United States prefers to give aid to nations where there is little guerilla activity and, of course, such threats lower the likelihood of democratization. By matching on these variables, the researcher hopes to control their confounding effects.

However, there are always other variables that are omitted and that might cause bias because they are correlated with both the key explanatory variable and the dependent variable (and causally prior to the key causal variable). And the rub is that the attempt to match units, if done improperly or incompletely, may increase the likelihood that there is another significant omitted variable correlated with both the explanatory and dependent variable.

Why is this the case? Note that in order to match nations, the researcher has to find one nation that receives a good deal of aid and one that receives little. Suppose he chooses two nations that are similar on the other two variables—two nations that have high levels of education and low levels of internal threat. The result is the following:

Country A: High aid, high education, peaceful.
Country B: Low aid, high education, peaceful.

The odds are that something is "special" about Country B. Why is it not getting aid if it has such favorable conditions? And, the chances are that the something that is "special" is an omitted variable that will cause bias by being correlated with the explanatory and dependent variables. One example might be the existence in B but not in A of a strong military that fosters education and suppresses guerilla movements. Since the strength of the military is correlated with the dependent variable and the key explanatory variable, its omission will cause bias. We can see that the same problem would have existed if the matching had come from the opposite end of the education and internal peace continuums. In that case, the anomaly would be the nation with low education and high violence that was receiving a good deal of aid. The problem might be eased by matching in the middle of the education and internal peace distributions. However, even in this case, the researcher would have two nations each of which is a bit anomalous in an opposite direction. The general point is that matching sometimes leads us to seek observations that are somewhat deviant from what we would expect given their values on the control variables— and that deviance may be due to especially significant omitted variables.

Note how this would work in our prison example. We might seek matched observations for the prisoners we interview—similar in socioeconomic background, family history, school record, and the like, except that they are not in jail. The most effective matching would be to find nonprisoners who have as high a potential for incarceration as possible—they come from a poverty-ridden neighborhood, they are school dropouts, they have been exposed to drugs, they come from a broken home, etc. The better the match, the more confidence we would have in the connection between incarceration and political beliefs. But here again is the rub. With all that going against them, maybe there is something special about the nonprisoners that has kept them out of prison—maybe a strong religious commitment—that is correlated with both the explanatory variable (incarceration) and the dependent variable (political ideology).

There is another way to look at this hazard in matching. Recall the two perspectives on random variability that we described in section 2.6. The potential problem with matching, as we have described it thus far, involves an omitted variable that we are able to identify. However, we still might suspect that two observations that are matched on a long list of control variables are "special" in some way which we cannot identify: that is, that an unknown omitted variable exists. In this situation, the only thing we can do is worry about how the randomness inherent in our dependent variable will affect this observation. As our measure may happen to get farther from its true value, due to random variability, the harder we will search for "unusual" observations in order to get a close match across groups and thus risk omitted variable bias.

These qualifications should *not* cause us to avoid research designs that use matching. In fact, matching is one of the most valuable small-*n* strategies. We merely need to be aware that matching is, like all small-*n* strategies, subject to dangers that randomization and a large *n* would have eliminated. One very productive strategy is to choose case studies via matching but observations within cases according to other criteria.

Matching, for the purpose of avoiding omitted variable bias, is related to the discussion in the comparative politics literature about whether researchers should select observations that are as similar as possible (Lijphart 1971) or as different as possible (Przeworski and Teune 1970). We recommend a different approach. The "most similar" versus "most different" research design debate pays little or no attention to the issue of "similar in relation to what." The labels are often confusing, and the debate is inconclusive in those terms: neither of those approaches is always to be preferred. To us, the key maxim for data collection is to identify potential observations that maximize leverage over the causal hypothesis. Sometimes our strategy produces a research design that could be labeled a "most similar systems design," and sometimes may be like a "most different systems designs." But, unlike the "most similar" versus "most different" debate, our strategy will always produce data that are relevant to answering the questions raised by the researcher.

In matching, the possible effects of omitted variables are controlled for by selecting observations that have the same values on these variables. For example, the desire to hold constant as many background variables as possible is behind Seymour Martin Lipset's (1963:248) choice to compare the political development of the United States with other English-speaking former colonies of Britain. The United States, Canada, and Australia, he points out, "are former colonies of Great Britain, which settled a relatively open continental frontier, and are today continent-spanning federal states." And, he notes many other features in common that are held constant: level of development, democratic regime, similarities in values, etc.

David Laitin's study (1986) of the effects of religious beliefs on politics uses a particularly careful matching technique. He chose a nation, Nigeria, with strong Muslim and Christian traditions since he wished to compare the effects of the two traditions on politics. But the Muslim and Christian areas of Nigeria differ in many ways other than their religious commitments, ways that, if ignored, would risk omitted variable bias. "In Nigeria, the dominant centers of Islam are in the northern states, which have had centuries of direct contact with the Islamic world, a history of Islamic state structures antedating British rule, and a memory of a revivalist jihad in the early nineteenth century which unified a large area under orthodox Islamic doctrine. [In contrast,] it was not until the late nineteenth century that Christian communities took root. . . . Mission schools brought Western education, and capitalist entrepreneurs encouraged the people to plant cash crops and to become increasingly associated with the world capitalist economy" (Laitin 1986:187).

How, Laitin asked, "could one control for the differences in nationality, or in economy, or in the number of generations exposed to a world culture, or in the motivations for conversion, or in ecology—all of which are different in Christian and Muslim strongholds?" (1986: 192–93). His approach was to choose a particular location in the Yoruba area of Nigeria where the two religions were introduced into the same nationality group at about the same time, and where the two religions appealed to potential converts for similar reasons.

In neither Kohli's study of three Indian states nor Lipset's analysis of three former British colonies nor Laitin's research on Christians and Muslims in Yorubaland is the matching complete; it could never be. Matching requires that we anticipate and specify what the possible relevant omitted variables might be. We then control by selecting observations that do not vary on them. Of course, we never know that we have covered the entire list of potential biasing factors. But for certain analytical purposes—and the evaluation of the adequacy of a matching selection procedure must be done in relation to some analytic purpose—the control produced by matching improves the likelihood of obtaining valid inferences.

In sum, the researcher trying to make causal inferences can select cases in one of two ways. The first is random selection and assignment, which is useful in large-n studies. Randomness in such studies automatically satisfies conditional independence; it is a much easier procedure than intentionally selecting observations to satisfy unit homogeneity. Randomness assures us that no relevant variables are omitted and that we are not selecting observations by some rule correlated with the dependent variable (after controlling for the explanatory variables). The procedure also ensures that researcher biases do not enter the selection process and, thereby, bias the results. The second method is one of intentional selection of observations, which we recommend for small-n studies. Inferences in small-n studies that rely on intentional selection to make reasonable causal inferences will almost always be riskier and more dependent on the investigator's prior opinions about the empirical world than inferences in large-n studies using randomness. And the controls may introduce a variety of subtle biases. Nevertheless, for the reasons outlined, controls are necessary with a small-n study. With appropriate controls—in which the control variables are held constant, perhaps by matching—we may need to estimate the causal effect of only a single explanatory variable, hence increasing the leverage we have on a problem.

5.7 Concluding Remarks

We hope that the advice we provide in this and the previous chapter will be useful for qualitative researchers, but it does not constitute recipes that can always be applied simply. Real problems often come in clusters, rather than alone. For example, suppose a researcher has minor selection bias, some random measurement error in the dependent variable, and an important control variable which can be measured only occasionally. Following the advice above for what to do in each case will provide some guidance about how to proceed. But in this and other complicated cases, scholars engaged in qualitative research need to reflect carefully on the particular methodological problems raised in their research. It may be helpful for them to consider formal models of qualitative research similar to those we have provided here but that are attuned to the specific problems in their research. Much of the insight behind these more sophisticated formal models exists in the statistical literature, and so it is not always necessary to develop it oneself.

Whether aided by formal models or not, the qualitative researcher must give explicit attention to these methodological issues. Methodological issues are as relevant for qualitative researchers seeking to make causal inferences as for their quantitatively oriented colleagues.

CHAPTER 6

Increasing the Number of Observations

IN THIS BOOK we have stressed the crucial importance of maximizing leverage over research problems. The primary way to do this is to find as many observable implications of your theory as possible and to make observations of those implications. As we have emphasized, what may appear to be a single-case study, or a study of only a few cases, may indeed contain many potential observations, at different levels of analysis, that are relevant to the theory being evaluated. By increasing the number of observations, even without more data collection, the researcher can often transform an intractable problem that has an indeterminate research design into a tractable one. This concluding chapter offers advice on how to increase the number of relevant observations in a social scientific study.

We will begin by analyzing the inherent problems involved in research that deal with only a single observation—the $n = 1$ problem. We show that if there truly is only a single observation, it is impossible to avoid the Fundamental Problem of Causal Inference. Even in supposed instances of single-case testing, the researcher must examine at least a small number of observations within "cases" and make comparisons among them. However, disciplined comparison of even a small number of comparable case studies, yielding comparable observations, can sustain causal inference.

Our analysis of single-observation designs in section 6.1 might seem pessimistic for the case-study researcher. Yet since one case may actually contain many potential observations, pessimism is actually unjustified, although a persistent search for more observations is indeed warranted. After we have critiqued single-observation designs, and thus provided a strong motivation to increase the number of observations, we will then discuss how many observations are enough to achieve satisfactory levels of certainty (section 6.2). Finally, in section 6.3 we will show that almost any qualitative research design can be reformulated into one with many observations, and that this can often be done without additional costly data collection if the researcher appropriately conceptualizes the observable implications that have already been gathered.

6.1 SINGLE-OBSERVATION DESIGNS FOR
CAUSAL INFERENCE

The most difficult problem in any research occurs when the analyst has only a single unit with which to assess a causal theory, that is where $n = 1$. We will begin a discussion of this problem in this section and argue that successfully dealing with it is extremely unlikely. We do this first by analyzing the argument in Harry Eckstein's classic article about crucial case studies (section 6.1.1). We will then turn to a special case of this, reasoning by analogy, in section 6.1.2.

6.1.1 "Crucial" Case Studies

Eckstein has cogently argued that failing to specify clearly the conditions under which specific patterns of behavior are expected makes it impossible for tests of such theories to fail or succeed (Eckstein 1975). We agree with Eckstein that researchers need to strive for theories that make precise predictions and need to test them on real-world data.

However, Eckstein goes further, claiming that if we have a theory that makes precise predictions, a "crucial-case" study—by which he means a study based only on "a single measure on any pertinent variable" (what we call a single observation) can be used for explanatory purposes. The main point of Eckstein's chapter is his argument that "case studies . . . [are] most valuable at . . . the stage at which candidate theories are 'tested' " (1975:80). In particular, he argues (1975:127) that "a single crucial case may certainly score a clean knockout over a theory." Crucial-case studies, for Eckstein, may permit sufficiently precise theories to be refuted by one observation. In particular, if the investigator chooses a case study that seems on a priori grounds unlikely to accord with theoretical predictions—a "least-likely" observation—but the theory turns out to be correct regardless, the theory will have passed a difficult test, and we will have reason to support it with greater confidence. Conversely, if predictions of what appear to be an implausible theory conform with observations of a "most-likely" observation, the theory will not have passed a rigorous test but will have survived a "plausibility probe" and may be worthy of further scrutiny.

Eckstein's argument is quite valuable, particularly the advice that investigators should understand whether to evaluate their theory in a "least-likely" or a "most-likely" observation. How strong our inference will be about the validity of our theory depends to a considerable extent on the difficulty of the test that the theory has passed or failed. However, Eckstein's argument for testing by using a crucial observation is inconsistent with the Fundamental Problem of Causal Inference. We therefore believe that Eckstein's argument is wrong if "case" is used as he defines that term, what we call a single observation.[1]

For three reasons we doubt that a crucial-observation study can serve the explanatory purpose Eckstein assigns to it: (1) very few explanations depend upon only one causal variable; to evaluate the impact of more than one explanatory variable, the investigator needs more than one implication observed; (2) measurement is difficult and not perfectly reliable; and (3) social reality is not reasonably treated as being produced by deterministic processes, so random error would appear even if measurement were perfect.

1. **Alternative Explanations.** Suppose that we begin a case study with the hypothesis that a particular explanatory factor accounts for the observed result. However, in the course of our research, we uncover a possible alternative explanation for the outcome. In this situation, we need to estimate *two* causal effects—the original hypothesized effect and the alternative explanation—but we have only *one* observation and thus, clearly, an indeterminate research design (section 4.1). Moreover, even if we use the approach of matching (which is often a valuable strategy), we cannot test causal explanations with a single observation. Suppose we could create a perfect match on all relevant variables (a circumstance that is very unlikely in the social sciences). We would still need, at a minimum, to compare two units in order to observe any variation in the explanatory variable; a valid causal inference that tests alternative hypotheses on the basis of only one comparison would therefore be impossible.

2. **Measurement Error.** Even if we had a theory that made strong and determinate predictions, we would still face the problem that our measurement relative to that prediction is, as is all measurement, likely to contain measurement error (see section 5.1). In a single observation, measurement error could well lead us to reject a true hypothesis, or vice versa. Precise theories may require measurement that is more precise than the current state of our descriptive inferences permits. If we have many observations, we may be able to reduce the magnitude and consequence of measurement error through aggregation; but in a single observation, there is always some possibility that measurement error will be crucial in leading to a false conclusion.

3. **Determinism.** The final and perhaps most decisive reason for the inadequacy of studies based on a single observable implication concerns the extent to which the world is deterministic. If the world were determinis-

---

[1] However, as we will argue below, Eckstein seems to recognize the weakness of his argument, which leads him really to call not for single-observation refutation but for multiple observations.

tic and the observation produced a measure inconsistent with the theory, then we could say with certainty that the theory was false. But for any interesting social theory, there is always a possibility of some unknown omitted variables, which might lead to an unpredicted result even if the basic model of the theory is correct. With only one implication of the causal theory observed, we have no basis on which to decide whether the observation confirms or disconfirms a theory or is the result of some unknown factor. Even having two observations and a perfect experiment, varying just one explanatory factor, and generating just one observation of difference between two otherwise identical observations on the dependent variable, we would have to consider the possibility that, in our probabilistic world, some nonsystematic, chance factor led to the difference in the causal effect that is observed. It does not matter whether the world is inherently probabilistic (in the sense of section 2.6) or simply that we cannot control for all possible omitted variables. In either case, our predictions about social relationships can be only probabilistically accurate. Eckstein, in fact, agrees that chance factors affect any study:

> The possibility that a result is due to chance can never be ruled out in any sort of study; even in wide comparative study it is only more or less likely. . . . The real difference between crucial observation study and comparative study, therefore, is that in the latter case, but not the former, we can assign by various conventions a specific number to the likelihood of chance results (e.g., "significant at the .05 level").

Eckstein is certainly right that it is common practice to report the specific likelihood of a chance finding only for large-n studies. However, it is as essential to consider the odds of random occurrences in all studies with large or small numbers of observations.[2]

In general, we conclude, the single observation is not a useful technique for testing hypotheses or theories. There is, however, one qualification. Even when we have a "pure" single-observation study with only one observation on all relevant variables, a single observation can be useful for evaluating causal explanations if it is part of a research program. If there are other single observations, perhaps gathered by other researchers, against which it can be compared, it is no longer a single observation—but that is just our point. We ought not to confuse the logic of explanation with the process by which research is done. If two researchers conduct single-observation studies, we may be left with a paired comparison and a valid causal inference—if we assume

---

[2] The survey of comparative sociology conducted by Bollen, Entwisle, and Alderson (in press) shows that virtually all the books and articles that they analyzed attributed some role to chance, even those which self-conciously use Mill's method of difference.

that they gather material in a systematic and comparable manner and that they share their results in some way. And, of course, the single-observation studies may also make important contributions to summarizing historical detail or descriptive inference, even without the comparison (see section 2.2). Obviously, a case study which contains many observable implications, as most do, is not subject to the problems discussed here.

6.1.2 Reasoning by Analogy

The dangers of single observation designs are particularly well illustrated by reference to a common form of matching used by policymakers and some political analysts seeking to understand political events: reasoning by analogy (see Khong 1992). The proper use of an analogy is essentially the same as holding other variables constant through matching. Our causal hypothesis is that if two units are the same in all relevant respects (i.e., we have successfully matched them or—in other words—we have found a good analogy), similar values on the relevant explanatory variables will result in similar values on the dependent variable. If our match were perfect, and if there were no random error in the world, we would know that the crisis situation currently facing Country B (which matches the situation in Country A last year) will cause the same effect as was observed in Country A. Phrasing it this way, we can see that "analogical reasoning" may be appropriate.

However, analogical reasoning is never better than the comparative analysis that goes into it. As with comparative studies in general, we always do better (or, in the extreme, no worse) with more observations as the basis of our generalization. For example, what went on in Country A may be the result of stochastic factors that might have averaged out if we had based our predictions on crises in five other matched nations. And as with all studies that use matching, the analogy is only as good as the match. If the match is incomplete—if there are relevant omitted variables—our estimates of the causal effects may be in error. Thus, as in all social science research and all prediction, it is important that we be as explicit as possible about the degree of uncertainty that accompanies our prediction. In general, we are always well advised to look beyond a single analogous observation, no matter how close it may seem. That is, *the comparative approach—in which we combine evidence from many observations even if some of them are not very close analogies to the present situation—is always at least as good and usually better than the analogy.* The reason is simple: the analogy uses a single observation to predict another, whereas the comparative approach uses a weighted combination of a large number of other observations. As long as these additional observations have some features that are similar in some way, however small, to the event we are predicting and we are using this additional information in a reasonable way, they will help make for a more accurate and efficient prediction. Hence, if we are tempted to use analogies, we should think more broadly in comparative terms, as we discuss below in section 2.1.3.[3]

6.2 How Many Observations Are Enough?

At this point, the qualitative researcher might ask the quantitative question: how many observations are enough? The question has substantial implications for evaluating existing studies and designing new research. The answer depends greatly on the research design, what causal inference the investigator is trying to estimate, and some features of the world not under the control of the investigator.

We answer this question here with another very simple formal model of qualitative research. Using the same linear regression model that we used extensively in chapters 4 and 5, we focus attention on the causal effect of one variable (x_1). All other variables are treated as controls, which are important in order to avoid omitted variable bias or other problems. It is easy to express the number of units one needs in a given situation by one simple formula

$$n = \frac{\sigma^2}{(1 - R_1^2) S_{x1}^2 V(b_1)} \tag{6.1}$$

the contents of which we now explain.

The symbol n, of course, is the number of observations on which data must be collected. It is calculated in this formal model on the basis of σ^2, $V(b_1)$, R_1^2, and S_{x1}^2. These four quantities each have very important meanings, and each affects the number of observations that the qualitative researcher must collect in order to reach a valid inference. We derived equation (6.1) with no assumptions beyond those we have already introduced.[4] We describe these now in order of increasing possibility of being influenced by the researcher: (1) The fundamental variability σ^2, (2) uncertainty of the causal inference $V(b_1)$, (3) relative

---

[3] Kahneman, Slovic, and Tversky (1982) describe a psychological fallacy of reasoning that occurs when decision-makers under uncertainty choose analogies based on recency or availability, hence systematically biasing judgments. They dub this the "availability heuristic." See also Keane (1988).

[4] The assumptions are that $E(Y) = X_1\beta_1 + X\beta$, $V(Y) = \sigma^2$, there is no multicollinearity, and all expectations are implicitly conditional on X.

collinearity between the causal variable and the control variables R_1^2, and (4) the variance of the values of the key causal variable S_{x1}^2.[5]

1. **Fundamental Variability σ^2.** The larger the fundamental variability, or unexplained variability in the dependent variable (as described in section 2.6), the more observations must be collected in order to reach a reliable causal inference. This should be relatively intuitive, since more noise in the system makes it harder to find a clear signal with a fixed number of observations. Collecting data on more units can increase our leverage enough for us to find systematic causal patterns.

   In a directly analogous fashion, a more inefficient estimator will also require more data collection. An example of this situation is when the dependent variable has random measurement error (section 5.1.2.1). From the perspective of the analyst, this type of measurement error is usually equivalent to additional fundamental variability, since the two cannot always be distinguished. Thus, more fundamental variability (or, equivalently, less efficient estimates) requires us to collect more data.

   Although the researcher can have no influence over the fundamental variability existing in the world, this information is quite relevant in two respects. First, the more we know about a subject, the smaller this fundamental (or unexplained) variability is (presumably up to some positive limit); thus fewer observations need to be collected to learn something new. For example, if we knew a lot about the causes of the outcomes of various battles during the American revolutionary war, then we would need relatively fewer observations (battles) to estimate the causal effect of some newly hypothesized explanatory variable.

   Secondly, even if understanding the degree of fundamental variablity does not help us to reduce the number of observations for which we must collect data, it would be of considerable help in accurately assessing the uncertainty of any inference made. This should be clear from equation (6.1), since we can easily solve for the uncertainty in the causal effect $V(b_1)$ as a function of the other four quantities (if we know n and the other quantities, except for the uncertainty of the causal estimate). This means that with this formal model we can calculate the degree of uncertainty of a causal inference using information about the number of observations, the fundamental variability, the variance of the causal explanatory variable, and the relationship between this variable and the control variables.

2. **Uncertainty of the Causal Inference $V(b_1)$.** $V(b_j)$ in the denominator of equation (6.1) demonstrates the obvious point that the more uncertainty we are willing to tolerate, the fewer observations we need to collect. In

---

[5] Technically, σ^2 is the variance in the dependent variable, conditional on all the explanatory variables $V(Y|X)$; $V(b_1)$ is the square of the standard error of the estimate of the causal effect of X_1; R_1^2 is the R^2 calculated from an auxiliary regression of X_1 on all the control variables; and S_{x1}^2 is the sample variance of X_1.

areas where any new knowledge gained is very important, we might be able to make serious contributions by collecting relatively few observations. In other situations where much is already known, and a new study will make an important contribution only if it has considerable certainty, we will need relatively more observations so as to convince people of a new causal effect (see section 1.2.1).

3. **Collinearity between the Causal Variable and the Control Variables** R_1^2. If the causal variable is uncorrelated with any other variables for which we are controlling, then including these control variables, which may be required for avoiding omitted variable bias or other problems, does not affect the number of observations that need to be collected. However, the higher the correlation between the causal variable and any other variables we are controlling for, the more demands the research design is putting on the data, and therefore the larger the number of observations which need to be collected in order to achieve the same level of certainty.

   For example, suppose we are conducting a study to see whether women receive equal pay for equal work at some business. We have no official access and so can only interview people informally. Our dependent variable is an employee's annual salary, and the key explanatory variable is gender. One of the important control variables is race. At the extreme, if all men in the study are black and all women are white, we will have no leverage in making the causal inference: finding any effect of gender after controlling for race will be impossible. Gender thus becomes a constant in this sample. Hence, this is an example of multicollinearity, an indeterminate research design (section 4.1); but note what happens when the collinearity is high but not perfect. Suppose, for example, that we collect information on fifteen employees and all but one of the men are black and all the women are white. In this situation, the effect of gender, while race is controlled for, is based entirely on the one remaining observation which is not perfectly collinear.

   Therefore, in the general situation, as in this example, the more collinearity between the causal explanatory variable and the control variables, the more we waste observations. Thus, we need more observations to achieve a fixed level of uncertainty. This point provides important practical advice for designing research, since it is often possible to select observations so as to keep the correlation between the causal variable and the control variables low. In the present example, we would merely need to interview black women and white men in sufficient numbers to reduce this correlation.

4. **The Variance of the Values of the Causal Explanatory Variable** S_{x1}^2. Finally, the larger the variance of the values of the causal explanatory variable, the fewer observations we need to collect to achieve a fixed level of certainty regarding a causal inference.

This result, like the last, has practical implications, since, by properly selecting observations, we can reduce the need for a large number of observations. We merely need to focus on choosing observations with a wide range of values on the key causal variable. If we are interested in the effect on crime of the median education in a community, it is best to choose some communities with very low and some with very high values of education. Following this advice means that we can produce a causal inference with a fixed level of certainty with less work by collecting fewer observations.

The formal model here assumes that the effect we are studying is linear. That is, the larger the values of the explanatory variables, the higher (or lower) is the expected value of the dependent variable. If the relationship is not linear but still roughly monotonic (i.e., nondecreasing), the same results apply. If, instead, the effect is distinctly nonlinear, it might be that middling levels of the explanatory variable have an altogether different result. For example, suppose the study based on only extreme values of the explanatory variable finds no effect: the education level of a community has no effect on crime. But, in fact, it could be that only middle levels of education reduce levels of crime in a community. For most problems, this qualification does not apply, but we should be careful to specify exactly the assumptions we are asserting when designing research.

By paying attention to fundamental variability, uncertainty, collinearity, and the variance of values of the causal variable, we can get considerably more leverage from a small number of units. However, it is still reasonable to ask the question that is the title to this section: how many observations are enough? To this question, we cannot provide a precise answer that will always apply. As we have shown with the formal model discussed here, the answer depends upon four separate pieces of information, each of which will vary across research designs. Moreover, most qualitative research situations will not exactly fit this formal model, although the basic intuitions do apply much more generally.

The more the better, but how many are necessary? In the least complicated situation, that with low levels of fundamental variability, high variance in the causal variable, no correlation between the causal variable and control variables, and a requirement of fairly low levels of certainty, few observations will be required—probably more than five but fewer than twenty. Again, a precise answer depends on a precise specification of the formal model and a precise value for each of its components. Unfortunately, qualitative research is by definition almost never this precise, and so we cannot always narrow this to a single answer.

Fortunately, it is often possible to avoid these problems by increasing the number of observations. Sometimes this increase involves collecting more data, but, as we argue in the next section, a qualitative research design can frequently be reconceptualized to extract many more observations from it and thus to produce a far more powerful design, a subject to which we now turn.

6.3 MAKING MANY OBSERVATIONS FROM FEW

We have stressed the difficulties inherent in research that is based on a small number of observations and have made a number of suggestions to improve the designs for such research. However, the reader may have noticed that we describe most of these suggestions as "second best"—useful when the number of observations is limited but not as valuable as the strategy of increasing the number of observations.[6] As we point out, these second-best solutions are valuable because we often cannot gather more observations of the sort we want to analyze: there may be only a few instances of the phenomenon in which we are interested, or it may be too expensive or arduous to investigate more than the few observations we have gathered. In this section, we discuss several approaches to increasing the number of our observations. These approaches are useful when we are faced with what seems to be a small number of observations and do not have the time or resources to continue collecting additional observations. We specify several ways in which we can increase the number of observations relevant to our theory by redefining their nature. These research strategies increase the n while still keeping the focus directly on evidence for or against the theory. As we have emphasized, they are often helpful even after we have finished data collection.

As we discussed in section 2.4, Harry Eckstein (1975) defines a case as "a phenomenon for which we report and interpret only a single measure on any pertinent variable." Since the word, "case," has been used in so many different ways in social science, we prefer to focus on observations. We have defined an observation as one measure of one dependent variable on one unit (and for as many explanatory variable measures as are available on that same unit). Observations are the fundamental components of empirical social science research: we aggregate them to provide the evidence on which we rely for evaluating our theories. As we indicated in chapter 2, in any one research project we do not in fact study whole phenomena such as France, the French Rev-

---

[6] The desirability of increasing the number of observations is commonly expressed in the literature on the comparative method. Lijphart (1971) makes a particularly strong case.

olution, the 1992 American election, or Iraq's decision to invade Kuwait. Rather, we abstract aspects of those phenomena—sets of explanatory and dependent variables—that are specified by our theories; we identify units to which these variables apply; and we make observations of our variables, on the units.[7]

The material we use to evaluate our theories consists, therefore, of a set of observations of units with respect to relevant variables. The issue addressed here is how to increase the number of observations. All of the ways to do this begin with the theory or hypothesis we are testing. What we must do is ask: what are the possible observable implications of our theory or hypothesis? And how many instances can we find in which those observable implications can be tested? If we want more observations in order to test the theory or hypothesis, we can obtain them in one of three ways: we can observe more units, make new and different measures of the same units, or do both—observe more units while using new measures. In other words, we can carry out similar measures in additional units (which we describe in section 6.3.1), we can use the same units but change the measures (section 6.3.2), or we can change both measures and units (section 6.3.3). The first approach may be considered a full replication of our hypothesis: we use the same explanatory and dependent variables and apply them to new instances. The second approach involves a partial replication of our theory or hypothesis that uses a new dependent variable but keeps the same explanatory variables. And the third approach suggests a new (or greatly revised) hypothesis implied by our original theory that uses a new dependent variable and applies the hypothesis to new instances.[8] Using these approaches, it may be possible within even a single conventionally labeled "case study" to observe many separate implications of our theory. Indeed, a single case often involves multiple measures of the key variables; hence, by our definition, it contains multiple observations.[9]

---

[7] We agree with William Baumol's (1990:1715) observations on economic history: "Many economic historians set a booby trap for themselves when they attempt to explain particular historical developments in their entirety. The writer who seeks to describe the "five main causes" of the British climacteric at the end of the nineteenth century, or of the European economic depression of 1847, takes on an impossible task. The natural sciences, with all their accomplishments and accumulated knowledge, still place heavy reliance on experiments that are *controlled*, and thus focus on the influence of one or a few variables at a time. The scientists focus their search on what are, in effect, partial derivatives rather than seeking to account for complex phenomena of reality in their entirety."

[8] We can also keep the same dependent variable but change the explanatory variables. However, in most situations, this strategy is used to avoid measurement error by using multiple measures of the same underlying explanatory variable.

[9] Researchers sometimes conduct studies that are described as replications of previous

6.3.1 Same Measures, New Units

Obtaining additional observations using the same measurement strategy is the standard way to increase the number of observations. We apply the same theory or hypothesis, using essentially the same variables, to more instances of the process which the theory describes. The two main ways we can find more observable instances of the process implied by our theory are via variations "across space" and via variations across time.

The usual approach to obtain more observations "across space" is to seek out other similar units: add Pakistan, Bangladesh, and Sri Lanka to one's data base along with India. Given enough time and money and skills, that course makes sense. Kohli's work on India (discussed in section 5.6) provides an example. It also illustrates one way in which he overcomes the problem associated with his use of three Indian states selected on the basis of known values of the independent and dependent variables. He looks at two other national units. One is Chile under Allende, where programs to aid the poor failed. Kohli argues that the absence of one of the three characteristics that according to his theory lead to successful poverty programs (in the Chilean case, the absence of a well-organized political reform party) contributed to this failure.[10] The other nation is Zimbabwe under Robert Mugabe, which had, at the time Kohli was writing his book, come to power with a regime whose features resembled the poverty alleviating orientation in West Bengal. The results, though tentative, seemed consistent with Kohli's theory. His treatment of these two cases is cursory, but they are used in the appropriate way as additional observable implications of his theory.

It is, however, not necessary that we move out of the confines of the unit we have been studying. A theory whose original focus was the nation-state might be tested in geographical subunits of that nation: in states, counties, cities, regions, etc. This, of course, extends the range of variation of the explanatory variables as well as the dependent variable. Suppose we want to test a theory of social unrest that relates

---

research and do not involve new observations. Essentially they duplicate—or try to duplicate—the research of others to see if the results can be reproduced. Quantitative researchers will attempt to reproduce the data analysis in a previous study using the same data. A historian may check the sources used by another historian. An ethnographer may listen to tape recorded interviews and see whether the original conclusions were sound. This activity is most useful since scientific evidence must be reproducible, but it does not fall within the rubric of what we are suggesting in these sections since no new observations are entailed.

[10] External forces also led to Allende's failure, but Kohli assigns a major role to the internal ones.

changes in agricultural prices to social unrest. A unit might be the single nation called "India." But "India" as a case can provide numerous observations of the relationship between agricultural prices and social unrest if we consider the different parts of India. Without going outside of the country we are studying, we can increase the number of observations by finding replications within that country of the process being studied.

Students of social policies can often look at governmental units that are subunits of the national state in which they are interested to test their hypotheses about the origins of various kinds of policies. Kohli's analysis of three states in India is a example of a common tendency in policy studies to compare states or cities or regions. Kohli's original set of observations, however, was the three Indian states. As we indicated, they were selected in such a way that they cannot be used to test his hypothesis about the effect of regime structure on poverty policy in India. However, just as he used other nations as the units of observation, Kohli also overcomes much of the problem of his original choice of units by pursuing the strategy of using subunits. He moves down to a level of observation below the three Indian states with which he started by applying his hypothesis to local panchayats (local governmental councils on the district, block, and village level), which are subunits of the states. Panchayats vary considerably in terms of the commitments of the political leaders to poverty policy and local organizational structure. Thus they allow tests of the impact of that variation on the policy outputs he uses as his dependent variables.

Subunits that provide additional observations need not be geographical. Theories that apply to the nation-state might also be tested on government agencies or in the framework of particular decisions—which can be done without having to visit another country. An example of seeking additional observable implications of one's hypothesis in additional nongeographical units can be found in Verba et al. (in progress). In the example that we introduced in section 5.4, they explain the fact that African-Americans learn more civic skills in church than do Latinos on the basis of the nature of the churches they attend; the former are likely to attend congregationally organized Protestant churches, the latter to attend hierarchically organized Catholic churches. The authors argue that if their hypothesis about the impact of church organization is correct, a difference similar to that between Catholic and Protestant churchgoers should appear if one compares among other church units, in particular among Protestant denominations differentiated by the organization of the denomination. They find that Episcopalians, who attend a hierarchically organized church, are quite similar to Catholics in the acquisition of civic skills in church. The fact that Episcopalians are in general a more educated and affluent group than, for example, Baptists, but practice fewer civic skills in church adds additional leverage to confirming their causal hypothesis.

We must be cautious in deciding whether the new units are appropriate for the replication of our hypothesis—that is, whether they are units within which the process entailed by the hypothesis can take place. Whether the application of the hypothesis to other kinds of units is valid depends on the theory and hypothesis involved as well as the nature of the units. If the dependent variable is social welfare policy, then states or provinces are appropriate if they can make such policies. But if we are studying tariff policy and all tariff decisions are made by the central government, the state or provincial unit might not be appropriate. Similarly, it would make no sense to study local governments in India or Pakistan to test a theory about the conditions under which a political unit chooses to develop a nuclear weapons capability—since the process of making such choices takes place in the central government. To take another example, it is plausible to test the impact of changing agricultural prices on social unrest across Indian states, but implausible to use various agencies of the Indian government to test the relationship. The process under study does not take place within agencies. In short, whether subunits are appropriate instances in which to observe a theory "in action" depends on the theory. That is why we advise beginning by listing the observable implications of our theory, not by looking for lots of possible units irrespective of the theory. Only after the theory has been specified can we choose units to study.

An alternative approach is to consider observations over time. India today and India a decade ago may provide two instances of the process of interest. Indeed, most works that are described as "case studies" involve multiple measures of a hypothesis over time.

Our advice to expand the number of observations by looking for more instances in subunits or by considering instances over time is, we believe, some of the most useful advice we have for qualitative research. It solves the small-n problem by increasing the n—without requiring travel to another nation, analysis of an entirely new decision, etc. However, it is advice that must be followed with caution. We have already expressed one caution: the new instance must be one to which the theory or hypothesis applies, that is, the subunit must indeed contain an observable implication of the theory. It need not be exactly (or even approximately) the observable implication we are immediately interested in; as long as it is an implication of the same theory, data organized in this way will give additional leverage over the causal inference.

There is another problem of which to be aware. We want to use these additional instances as new tests of our theory, but the subunits or the several instances found over time may not represent *independent* tests of the theory. Thus, as George (1982:20–23) recognizes, each new "case" does not bring as much new information to bear on the problem as it would if the observations were independent of one another. Dependence among observations does not disqualify these new tests unless the dependence is perfect—that is, unless we can perfectly predict the new data from the existing data. Short of this unlikely case, there does exist at least some new information in the new data, and it will help to analyze these data. These new observations, based on nonindependent information, do not add as much information as fully independent observations, but they can still be useful.

This conclusion has two practical implications. First, when dealing with partially dependent observations, we should be careful not to overstate the certainty of the conclusions. In particular, we should not treat these data as providing as many observations as we would have obtained from independent observations. Second, we should carefully analyze the reasons for the dependence among the observations. Often the dependence will result from one or a series of very interesting and possibly confounding omitted variables. For example, suppose we are interested in the political participation of citizens in counties in the United States. Neighboring counties may not be independent because of cross-border commuting, residential mobility or the similar socioeconomic and political values of people living in neighboring counties. Collecting data from neighboring counties will certainly add some information to a study, although not as much as if the counties were entirely independent of the ones on which we had already collected data.

For another example, consider the relationship between changes in agricultural prices and social unrest. We might test this relationship across a number of Indian states. In each we measure agricultural prices as well as social unrest. But the states are not isolated, experimental units. The values of the dependent variable may be affected, not only by the values of the explanatory variables we measure within each unit, but also by the values of omitted variables outside of the unit. Social unrest in one state might be triggered by agricultural prices (as predicted by our theory), but that social unrest may directly influence social unrest in a neighboring state (making it only a partially independent test of our theory). This situation can be dealt with by appropriately controlling for this propagation. A similar problem can exist for the influence of an earlier time period on a later time period. We might replicate our analysis in India a decade later, but the social unrest of the earlier period might have a direct effect on the later period.

These examples illustrate that the replication of an analysis on new units does not always imply a major new study. If additional observations exist within the current study that are of the same form as the observations already used to test the hypothesis, they can be used. In this way, the researcher with a "case study" may find that there are a lot more observations that he or she thought.[11]

6.3.2 Same Units, New Measures

Additional instances for the test of a theory or hypothesis can be generated by retaining the same unit of observation but changing the dependent variable. This approach involves looking for many effects of the same cause—a powerful technique for testing a hypothesis. Again, we begin with a theory or hypothesis and ask: assuming our theory or hypothesis is correct, what else would we expect our explanatory variables to influence aside from the current dependent variable? Such an exercise may suggest alternative indicators of the dependent variable. In chapter 1, we pointed out that a particular theory of dinosaur extinction has implications for the chemical composition of rocks. Hence, even a causal theory of a unique prehistoric event had multiple observable implications that could be evaluated.

In the example we are using of agricultural price fluctuation and social unrest, we may have measured social unrest by the number of public disturbances. In addition to social unrest, we might ask what else might be expected if the theory is correct. Perhaps there are other valid measures of social unrest—deviant behavior of one sort or another. This inquiry might lead to the hypothesis that other variables would be affected, such as voting behavior, business investment or emigration. The same process that leads price fluctuation to engender unrest might link price fluctuation to these other outcomes.

Robert Putnam's work (1993) on the impact of social resources on the performance of regional governments in Italy takes a similar approach. Regional performance is not a single measure. Rather Putnam uses a wide range of dependent variables in his attempt to explain the sources of effective democratic performance across Italian regions. He has twelve indicators of institutional performance that seek to measure

---

[11] Quantitative researchers have developed an enormous array of powerful statistical techniques to analyze data that exhibit what is referred to as the properties of *time series* or *spatial* autocorrelation. Not only are they able to correct for these problems, but they have found ways of extracting unique information from these data. See Granger and Newbold (1977), Anselin (1988), Beck (1991), and King (1989; 1991c).

policy processes, policy pronouncements, and policy implementation. In addition, he uses survey-based measures of citizen evaluations of government performance. Each of these measures represents an observable implication of his theory.

As we suggested earlier, the use of subnational government units for a study of tariff policy would be inappropriate if tariffs are set by the central government. Even though the explanatory variables—for instance, the nature of the industry or agricultural product—might vary across states or provinces, the process of determining tariff levels (which is what the hypothesis being tested concerns) does not take place within the subnational units. However, if we change the dependent variable to be the voting behavior of the representatives from different states or provinces on issues of trade and tariff, we can study the subject. In this way, we can add to the instances in which the theoretical process operates.

6.3.3 New Measures, New Units

We may also look beyond the set of explanatory and dependent variables that have been applied to a particular set of units to other observable implications involving new variables and new units. The measures used to test what are essentially new hypotheses that are derived from the original ones may be quite different from those used thus far. The process described by the new theory may not apply to the kind of unit under study, but rather to some other kind of unit—often to a unit on a lower or higher level of aggregation. The general hypothesis about the link between agricultural prices and unrest may suggest hypotheses about uncertainty and unrest in other kinds of units such as firms or government agencies. It may also suggest hypotheses about the behavior of individuals. In the example of the relationship between agricultural price fluctuation and social unrest, we might ask: "If our theory as to the effect of price fluctuations on social unrest (that we already have tested across several political units) is correct, what does it imply for the behavior of firms or agricultural cooperatives or individuals (perhaps in the same set of political units)? What might it imply, if anything, for the way in which allocational decisions are made by government agencies? What might we expect in terms of individual psychological reactions to uncertainty and the impact of such psychological states on individual deviant behavior?"

This approach is particularly useful when there are no instances of a potentially significant social process for us to observe. An example is in the study of nuclear war. Since a nuclear war between two nuclear powers has never occurred, we cannot observe the effects of explanatory variables on the outbreak of such a war. Suppose our theory says that the presence of nuclear weapons on both sides has prevented all out war. Although there are no instances to observe in relation to our basic hypothesis, a more specific hypothesis might imply other potential observations. For example, we might reflect that an implication of our theory is that the existence of nuclear weapons on both sides should inhibit severe *threats* of all-out war. Then by studying the frequency and severity of threats between nuclear and nonnuclear dyads, and by analysing threats as the probability of war seemed to increase during crises, we might find further observable implications of our theory, which could be tested.

The development of a new theory or hypothesis, different from but entailed by the original theory, often involves moving to a lower level of aggregation and a new type of unit: not from one political unit such as a nation to another political unit at a lower level of aggregation such as a province, but from political units such as nations or provinces to individuals living within the units or to individual decisions made within the units. Different theories may imply different connections between variables that lead to a particular result: that is, different processes by which the phenomenon was produced (Dessler 1991:345). Before designing empirical tests, we may have to specify a "causal mechanism," entailing linked series of causal hypotheses that indicate how connections among variables are made. Defining and then searching for these different causal mechanisms may lead us to find a plethora of new observable implications for a theory. (In section 3.2.1, we distinguish the concept of causal mechanisms from our more fundamental definition of causality.)

The movement to a new kind of "observation"—a different kind of social unit, an individual, a decision—may involve the introduction of explanatory variables not applicable to the original unit. Often a hypothesis or theory about political units implies a hypothesis or theory about the process by which the particular outcome observed at the level of the unit comes about; in particular, the hypothesis at the level of the unit may imply hypotheses about attitudes and behaviors at the level of individuals living within those units. These can then be tested using data on individuals. If we move to the level of the individual, we might focus on psychological variables or on aspects of individual experience or status, variables that make no sense if applied to political units.

Consider our example of the relationship between agricultural prices and social unrest. We might have a hypothesis on the level of a governmental unit such as a nation or province. An example would be the following: the greater the fluctuation of agricultural prices in a unit, the greater the likelihood of social unrest. This hypothesis, in turn, suggests other hypotheses about individuals living within these units. For instance, we might hypothesize that those who are most vulnerable to the effects of price fluctuation—growers of particular crops or people dependent on low agricultural prices for adequate food supply—would be more likely to engage in socially disruptive behavior. A test of such a hypothesis might involve measures of psychological states such as alienation or measures of individual deviant behavior.

Studies that rely on cultural explanations of political phenomena often depend on such analyses at the individual level.[12] Weiner's study of education and child-labor policies in India depends on a cultural explanation: that the reason India, almost alone among the nations of the world, has no effective laws mandating universal education and no effective laws banning child labor lies in the values of the society, values shared by the ordinary citizen and the governing elites (Weiner 1991). India is one country and Weiner's study might be described as having an n of one. He bypasses this problem in a number of ways. For one thing, he compares India with other countries that have developed universal education. He also makes some limited comparisons across the Indian states—in other words, he varies the units. But the hypothesis about Indian culture and Indian policy implies hypotheses about the values and policy positions of individuals; the most important of whom are those elites who are involved in making education and child-labor policy. Thus, Weiner's main test of his hypothesis is on the individual. He uses intensive interviews with elites in order to elicit from them information as to their beliefs about their values in relation to education and child labor—beliefs that are observable implications of his macro hypothesis about India as well as their policy views.

This means of acquiring more observable implications of a theory from units at a lower level of aggregation can also be applied to analyses of decisions. George and McKeown refer to an approach called "process tracing" in which the researcher looks closely at "the decision process by which various initial conditions are translated into outcomes" (George and McKeown, 1985:35).[13] Instead of treating the ulti-

---

[12] The use of "culture" as an explanatory variable in social science research is a subject of much contention but is not the subject of this book. Our only comment is that cultural explanations must meet the same tests of logic and measurement we apply to all research.

[13] Donald Moon calls a version of this approach a *rationale explanation* or, as others call it, reason analysis (Moon 1975).

mate outcome (for example, of an international crisis) as the dependent variable, new dependent variables are constructed: for instance, each decision in a sequence, or each set of measurable perceptions by decision-makers of others' actions and intentions, becomes a new variable. This approach often reaches the level of the individual actor. A theory that links initial conditions to outcomes will often imply a particular set of motivations or perceptions on the part of these actors. Process tracing will then involve searching for evidence—evidence consistent with the overall causal theory—about the decisional process by which the outcome was produced. This procedure may mean interviewing actors or reading their written record as to the reasons for their action.

For example, cooperation among states in international politics could be produced in any one of a number of ways: by expectations of positive benefits as a result of reciprocity; through the operation of deterrence, involving threats of destruction; or as a result of common interests in a given set of outcomes. Many explanatory variables would be involved in each of these causal mechanisms, but the set of variables in each possible mechanism would be different and have different relationships among them. A close study of the process by which nations arrive at cooperation might allow one to choose which of these different causal mechanisms is most plausibly at work. This might involve a study of the expressed motivations of actors, the nature of the communications flow among them, and so forth.

From our perspective, process tracing and other approaches to the elaboration of causal mechanisms increase the number of theoretically relevant observations.[14] Such strategies link theory and empirical work by using the observable implications of a theory to suggest new observations that should be made to evaluate the theory. By providing more observations relevant to the implications of a theory, such a method can help to overcome the dilemmas of small-n research and enable investigators and their readers to increase their confidence in the findings of social science. Within each sequence of events, process tracing yields many observations. Within each political unit, analyses of individual attitudes or behaviors produce many observations. Fur-

[14] What George and McKeown label "within-observation explanation" constitutes, in Eckstein's terms, a strategy of redefining the unit of analysis in order to increase the number of observations. George and McKeown (1985:36) state that in case studies, "the behavior of the system is not summarized by a single data point, but by a series of points or curves plotted through time." In our terminology, borrowed from Eckstein (1975), this method is one of expanding the number of observations, since a single observation is defined as "a phenomenon for which we report and interpret only a single measure on any pertinent variable."

thermore, the investigator controls for those variables that apply to all observations because they pertain to the sequence of events or the unit as a whole. A focus limited to the ultimate outcome usually would restrict the investigator to too few observations to resolve the dilemma of encountering either omitted variable bias or indeterminacy. By examining multiple observations about individual attitudes or behaviors, the investigator may be able to assess which causal mechanisms are activated.

Such an analysis is unlikely to yield strong causal inferences because more than one mechanism can be activated, and, within each mechanism, the relative strength of the explanatory variables may be unclear. But it does provide some test of hypotheses, since an hypothesis that accounts for outcomes is also likely to have implications for the process through which those outcomes occur. Searching for causal mechanisms therefore provides observations that could refute the hypothesis. This approach may also enable the researcher to develop some descriptive generalizations about the frequency with which each potential causal mechanism is activated; and these descriptive generalizations may provide the basis for later analysis of the linked causal mechanisms and the conditions under which each is likely to become activated.

In our view, process tracing and the search for the psychological underpinnings of an hypothesis developed for units at a higher level of aggregation are very valuable appoaches. They are, however, extensions of the more fundamental logic of analysis we have been using, not ways of bypassing it. Studies of this sort must confront the full set of issues in causal inference, such as unit homogeneity, endogeneity, and bias, if they are to contribute to causal inference. At the level of the individual decision-maker, we must raise and answer all the issues of research design if we are to achieve valid causal inference. We must measure accurately the reasons given and select observations so that they are independent of the outcome achieved (else we have endogeneity problems) and that there are no relevant omitted variables. It is also important to emphasize here that causal mechanisms that are traced in this way should make our theory more, rather than less, restrictive: techniques such as process tracing should provide more opportunities to *refute* a theory, not more opportunities to evade refutation. In sum, process tracing and other subunit analyses are useful for finding plausible hypotheses about causal mechanisms which can, in turn, promote descriptive generalizations and prepare the way for causal inference. But this approach must confront the full set of issues in causal analysis.

6.4 CONCLUDING REMARKS

In principle and in practice, the same problems of inference exist in quantitative and qualitative research. Research designed to help us understand social reality can only succeed if it follows the logic of scientific inference. This dictum applies to qualitative, quantitative, large-n, small-n, experimental, observational, historical, ethnographic, participant observation, and all other social scientific research. However, as should now be clear from this chapter, the fundamental problems of descriptive and causal inference are generally more difficult to avoid with a small-n than a large-n research design. This book has presented ways both to expand the number of observations in a study and to make inferences from a relatively small number of observations.

Quantitative and qualitative researchers can improve the efficiency of an estimator by increasing the amount of information they bring to bear on a problem, often by increasing the number of observations (section 2.7.2), and they can sometimes appeal to procedures such as random selection and assignment to avoid bias automatically. Much of the discussion in this book has been devoted to helping qualitative researchers improve the accuracy of their estimators; but the techniques we have suggested are varied and tradeoffs often exist between valid research objectives. Hence, encapsulating our advice in pithy statements to correspond to the formal equations favored in quantitative research is difficult.

Researchers committed to the study of social phenomena who choose not to use formal quantitative procedures cannot afford to ignore sources of bias and inefficiency created by methodologically unreflective research designs. The topics they study are every bit as important, and often more important, than those analyzed by quantitative scholars. Descriptive and causal inferences made by qualitative researchers deserve to be as sound as those made by any other researcher. To make valid inferences, qualitative researchers will need to be more attuned to methodological issues than they have traditionally been. They also must be more self-conscious when designing research and more explicit when reporting substantive results. Readers should not have to reformulate published qualitative studies to make them scientifically valid. If an author conceptualizes a research project with numerous observable implications as having only two observations and twelve causal hypotheses, then it should not be the responsibility of readers or reviewers to explain that the author had a better implicit than explicit research design. More fundamentally, authors who understand and explicate the logic of their analyses will produce more valuable research. Fortunately, the appropriate methodological issues for qualitative researchers to understand are precisely the ones that all other scientific researchers need to follow. Valid inference is possible only so long as the inherent logic underlying all social scientific research is understood and followed.

References

Achen, Christopher H. 1986 *Statistical Analysis of Quasi-Experiments*. Berkeley: University of California Press.

Achen, Christopher H., and Duncan Snidal. 1989. "Rational Deterrence Theory and Comparative Case Studies." *World Politics* 41, no. 2 (January): 143–69.

Alvarez, Walter, and Frank Asaro. 1990. "An Extraterrestrial Impact." *Scientific American* (October): 78–84.

Anselin, Luc. 1988. *Spatial Econometrics: Methods and Models*. Boston: Kluwer Academic Publishers.

Barnett, Vic. 1982. *Comparative Statistical Inference*. 2d ed. New York: Wiley.

Baumol, William J. 1990. "St. John versus the Hicksians, or a Theorist Malgré Lui?" *The Journal of Economic Literature* 28, no. 4: 1708–15.

Beck, Nathaniel. 1991. "Alternative Dynamic Structures." *Political Analysis* 3: 51–87.

Becker, Howard S. 1966. "Whose Side Are We On?" *Social Problems* 14: 239–47.

Becker, Howard S., and Charles C. Ragin. 1992. *What Is a Case? Exploring the Foundations of Social Inquiry*. New York: Cambridge University Press.

Blainey, Geoffrey. 1973. *The Causes of War*. New York: Free Press.

Bollen, Kenneth A., Barbara Entwisle, and Arthur S. Alderson. 1993. "Macrocomparative Research Methods." In Judith Blake, ed. *Macrocomparative Research Methods* Palo Alto, Calif. Annual Reviews, Inc

Cain, Bruce, John Ferejohn, and Morris Fiorina. 1987. *The Personal Vote: Constituency Service and Electoral Independence*. Cambridge: Harvard University Press.

Caplow, Theodore, Howard M. Bahr, Bruce A. Chadwick, and Dwight W. Hoover. 1983a. *All Faithful People: Change and Continuity in Middletown's Religion*. Minneapolis: University of Minnesota Press.

———. 1983b. *Middletown Families: Fifty Years of Change and Continuity*. New York: Bantam Books.

Caro, Robert. 1983. *The Years of Lyndon Johnson*. New York: Vintage Books.

Collier, David. 1991. "The Comparative Method: Two Decades of Change." In Dankwart A. Rustow and Kenneth Paul, eds. *Comparative Political Dynamics: Global Research Perspectives*. New York: Harper Collins.

———. 1993. "The Comparative Method." In Ada W. Finifter, ed. *Political Science: The State of the Discipline*. Washington, D.C.: American Political Science Association.

Cook, Karen Schweers, and Margaret Levi, eds. 1990. *The Limits of Rationality*. Chicago: University of Chicago Press.

Coombs, Clyde H. 1964. *A Theory of Data*. New York: Wiley.

Courtillot, Vincent E. 1990. "A Volcanic Eruption." *Scientific American* (October): 78–84.

Dahl, Robert. 1961. *Who Governs? Democracy and Power in an American City.* New Haven: Yale University Press.

Dessler, David. 1991. "Beyond Correlations: Toward a Causal Theory of War." *International Studies Quarterly* 3, no. 35 (September): 337–55.

Dewald, William G., Jerry G. Thursby, and Richard G. Anderson. 1986. "The Journal of Money, Credit and Banking Project." *American Economic Review* 76, no. 4 (September): 587–603.

Diamond, Larry and Marc F. Plattner, eds. 1993, *The Global Resurgence of Democracy.* Baltimore: Johns Hopkins University Press.

Duneier, Mitchell. 1993. *Slim's Table.* Chicago: University of Chicago Press.

Easton, David. 1965. *A Systems Analysis of Political Life.* New York: Wiley.

Eckstein, Harry. 1969. "Authority Relations and Governmental Performance." *Comparative Political Studies* 2: 269–325.

———. 1975. "Case Study and Theory in Political Science." In Fred I. Greenstein and Nelson W. Polsby, eds. *Handbook of Political Science,* vol. 1, *Political Science: Scope and Theory.* Reading, Mass.: Addison-Wesley.

Elster, Jon. 1983. *Explaining Technical Change: A Case Study in the Philosophy of Science* New York: Cambridge University Press.

Fearon, James D. 1991. "Counterfactuals and Hypothesis Testing in Political Science." *World Politics* (January) 43, no. 2: 169–95.

Fenno, Richard F. 1978. *Home Style.* Boston: Little, Brown.

Ferejohn, John. 1993. "Structure and Ideology: Change in Parliament in Early Stuart England." In Judith Goldstein and Robert O. Keohane, eds. *Ideas and Foreign Policy: Beliefs, Institutions and Political Change.* Ithaca: Cornell University Press.

Ferguson, Yale H., and Richard W. Mansbach. 1988. *The Elusive Quest: Theory and International Politics.* Columbia: University of South Carolina.

Feynman, Richard P. 1965. *The Character of Physical Law.* Cambridge, Mass.: MIT Press.

Fiorina, Morris, and Charles R. Plott. 1978. "Committee Decisions under Majority Rule." *American Political Science Review* 72, no. 2 (June): 575–98.

Fisher, Ronald A. 1935. *The Design of Experiments.* New York: Hafner Publishing.

Fogel, Robert William. 1989. *Without Consent or Contract: The Rise and Fall of American Slavery.* New York: W.W. Norton.

Friedrich, Carl J. 1958. "Political Philosophy and the Science of Politics." In Roland Young, ed. *Approaches to the Study of Politics.* Chicago: University of Chicago Press.

Fudenberg, Drew, and Jean Tirole. 1989. "Noncooperative game theory for industrial organization: an introduction and overview." In Richard Schmalensee and Robert D. Willig, eds. *Handbook of Industrial Organization,* vol. 1 Amsterdam: North Holland.

Garfinkel, H. 1964. "Studies of the Routine Grounds of Everyday Activities." *Social Problems* 11: 225–50.

Geddes, Barbara. 1990. "How the Cases You Choose Affect the Answers You Get: Selection Bias in Comparative Politics." *Political Analysis,* 2:131–52.

Geertz, Clifford. 1973. *An Interpretation of Cultures.* New York: Basic Books.

———. 1983. "Local Knowledge: Fact and Law in Comparative Perspective," In Clifford Geertz, ed. *Local Knowledge: Further Essays in Interpretive Anthropology.* New York: Basic Books.

Gelman, Andrew, and Gary King. 1990. "Estimating Incumbency Advantage without Bias." *American Journal of Political Science* 34, no. 4 (November): 1142–64.

———. 1993. "Why Are U.S. Presidential Election Polls So Variable When the Vote Is So Predictable." *British Journal of Political Science* (forthcoming).

George, Alexander L. 1982. "Case Studies and Theory Development." Paper presented at the Second Annual Symposium on Information Processing in Organizations, Carnegie-Mellon University, October 15–16.

George, Alexander L., and Timothy J. McKeown. 1985. "Case Studies and Theories of Organizational Decision Making. *Advances in Information Processing in Organizations* 2: 21–58.

George, Alexander L., and Richard Smoke. 1974. *Deterrence in American Foreign Policy.* New York: Columbia University Press.

Gigerenzer, Gerd, Zeno Swijtink, Theodore Porter, Lorraine Daston, John Beatty, and Lorenz Kruger. 1989. *The Empire of Chance: How Probability Changed Science and Everyday Life.* New York: Cambridge University Press.

Gilpin, Robert. 1981. *War and Change in World Politics.* New York: Cambridge University Press.

Goldberger, Arthur. 1991. *A Course in Econometrics.* Cambridge, Mass: Harvard University Press.

Goldstein, Judith, and Robert O. Keohane, eds. 1993. *Ideas and Foreign Policy: Beliefs, Institutions and Political Change.* Ithaca: Cornell University Press.

Gould, Stephen J. 1989a. *Wonderful Life: The Burgess Shale and the Nature of History.* New York: Norton

———. 1989b. "The Horn of Triton." *Natural History* (December): 18–27.

Granger, G.W.J., and P. Newbold. 1977. *Forecasting Economic Time Series.* New York: Academic Press.

Gulick, Edward V. 1967. *Europe's Classical Balance of Power.* New York: Norton.

Hall, Peter A., ed. 1989. *The Political Power of Economic Ideas: Keynesianism Across Nations.* Princeton: Princeton University Press.

Halpern, Nina, 1993. "Stalinist Political Economy," In Judith Goldstein and Robert O. Keohane, eds. 1993. *Ideas and Foreign Policy: Beliefs, Institutions and Political Change.* Ithaca: Cornell University Press.

Hermens, F. A. 1941. *Democracy or Anarchy: A Study of Proportional Representation.* South Bend, Ind.: University of Notre Dame Press.

Hirschman, Albert O. 1970. "The Search for Paradigms as a Hindrance to Understanding." *World Politics* 22, no. 3 (April): 329–43.

Hoffmann, Stanley. 1960. *Contemporary Theory in International Relations.* Englewood Cliffs, N.J.: Prentice-Hall.

Holland, Paul. 1986. "Statistics and Causal Inference." *Journal of the American Statistical Association* 81: 945–60.

Horowitz, Donald. 1993. "Comparing Democratic Systems." In Larry Diamond and Marc F. Plattner, eds. *The Global Resurgence of Democracy.* Baltimore: Johns Hopkins University Press.

Huth, Paul. 1988. "Extended Deterrence and the Outbreak of War." *American Political Science Review* 82: no. 2 (June): 423–43.

Huth, Paul and Bruce Russett. 1990. "Testing Deterrence Theory: Rigor Makes a Difference." *World Politics* 42, no. 4 (July): 466–501.

Hsiao, C. 1983. "Identification." In Zvi Griliches and Michael Intriligator, eds. vol. 1, *Handbook of Econometrics*. Amsterdam: North-Holland.

Inkeles, Alex, and Peter Rossi. 1956. "National Comparisons of Occupational Prestige." *American Journal of Sociology* 61: 329–39.

Iyengar, Satis, and Joel B. Greenhouse. 1988. "Selection Models and the File Drawer Problem." *Statistical Science* 3, no. 1 (February): 109–35.

Iyengar, Shanto, and Donald Kinder. 1987. *News That Matters*. Chicago: University of Chicago Press.

Jeffreys, Harold. 1961. *Theory of Probability*. Oxford: Clarendon Press.

Jervis, Robert. 1976. *Perception and Misperception in International Politics*. Princeton: Princeton University Press.

Jervis, Robert, Richard Ned Lebow, and Janice Gross Stein. 1985. *Psychology and Deterence*. Baltimore: Johns Hopkins University Press.

Jones, E. L. 1981. *The European Miracle: Environments, Economies, and Geopolitics in the History of Europe and Asia*. Cambridge: Cambridge University Press.

Johnston, J. 1984. *Econometric Methods*. 3d ed. New York: McGraw Hill.

Kahneman, Daniel, Paul Slovik, and Amos Tversky, eds. 1982. *Judgement under Uncertainty: Heuristics and Biases*. New York: Cambridge University Press.

Katzenstein, Peter J. 1985. *Small States in World Markets: Industrial Policy in Europe*. Ithaca: Cornell University Press.

Keane, Mark T. 1988. *Analogical Problem Solving*. Chichester, West Sussex: Ellis Horwood.

Kennedy, Paul. 1987. *The Rise and Fall of the Great Powers*. New York: Random House.

Keohane, Robert O. 1980. "The Theory of Hegemonic Stability and Changes in International Economic Regimes, 1967–1977." In Ole R. Holsti, Randolph M. Siverson, Alexander L. George, eds. *Change in the International System*. Boulder: Westview Press.

———. 1984. *After Hegemony: Cooperation and Discord in the World Political Economy*. Princeton: Princeton University Press.

———. 1988. "International Institutions: Two Approaches." *International Studies Quarterly* 32: 379.

———. 1989. *International Institutions and State Power: Essays in International Relations Theory*. Boulder: Westview.

Keohane, Robert O., and Joseph S. Nye, Jr. 1977. *Power and Interdependence: World Politics in Transition*. Boston: Little, Brown.

Khong, Yuen Foong. 1992. *Analogies at War: Korea, Munich, Dien Bien Phu, and the Vietnam Decisions of 1965*. Princeton: Princeton University Press.

King, Gary. 1989. *Unifying Political Methodology: The Likelihood Theory of Statistical Inference*. New York: Cambridge University Press.

———. 1993. "The Methodology of Presidency Research," In George Edwards III, John H. Kessel and Bert A. Rockman, eds. *Researching the Presi-*

dency: Vital Questions, New Approaches. Pittsburgh: University of Pittsburgh Press.

―――. 1991a. "Constituency Service and Incumbency Advantage." *British Journal of Political Science* 21, no. 1 (January): 119–28.

―――. 1991b. "Stochastic Variation: A Comment on Lewis-Beck and Skalaban's 'The R-Square'." *Political Analysis* 2: 185–200.

―――. 1991c. "On Political Methodology." *Political Analysis* 2: 1–30.

Kohli, Atul. 1987. *The State and Poverty in India: The Politics of Reform*. New York: Cambridge University Press.

Kreps, David M. 1990. "Corporate Culture and Economic Theory," In James E. Alt and Kenneth Shepsle, eds. *Perspectives on Positive Political Economy*. New York: Cambridge University Press.

Laitin, David D. 1986. *Hegemony and Culture: Politics and Religious Change among the Yoruba*. Chicago: University of Chicago Press.

Lakatos, Imre. 1970. "Falsification and the Methodology of Scientific Research Programs." In I. Lakatos and A. Musgrave, eds. *Criticism and the Growth of Knowledge*. Cambridge: Cambridge University Press.

Lakeman, Enid, and James D. Lambert. 1955. *Voting in Democracies*. London: Faber and Faber.

Leamer, Edward E. 1978. *Specification Searches: Ad Hoc Inference With Nonexperimental Data*. New York: Wiley.

―――. 1983. "Let's Take the Con Out of Econometrics." *American Economic Review* 73, no. 1 (March): 31–43.

Levy, Jack S. 1985. "Theories of General War." *World Politics* 37, no. 3 (April): 344–74.

―――. "Quantitative Studies of Deterrence Success and Failure." In Paul C. Stern, Robert Axelrod, Robert Jervis, and Roy Radner, eds. *Perspectives on Deterrence*. New York: Oxford University Press.

Lieberson, Stanley. 1985. *Making It Count: The Improvement of Social Research and Theory*. Berkeley: University of California Press.

―――. 1992. "Einstein, Renoir, and Greeley: Some Thoughts about Evidence in Sociology." *American Sociological Review* 56 (February): 1–15.

Lijphart, Arend. 1971. "Comparative Politics and Comparative Method," *American Political Science Review* 65, no. 3 (September): 682–98.

Lindberg, Leon N., and Stuart A. Scheingold. 1971. *Regional Integration: Theory and Research*. Cambridge: Harvard University Press.

Lindberg, Leon N., and Stuart A. Scheingold. 1970. *Europe's Would-Be Polity: Patterns of Change in the European Community*. Englewood Cliffs, N.J.: Prentice-Hall.

Linz, Juan J. 1993. "The Perils of Presidentialism." In Diamond, Larry and Marc F. Plattner, eds. *The Global Resurgence of Democracy*. Baltimore: Johns Hopkins University Press. 108–26.

Lipset, Seymour Martin. 1963. *The First New Nation: The United States in Comparative and Historical Perspective*. New York: Basic Books.

Little, Daniel. 1991. *Varieties of Social Explanation: An Introduction to the Philosophy of Social Science*. Boulder Colo.: Westview.

Longino, Helen E. 1990. *Science as Social Knowledge: Values and Objectivity in Scientific Inquiry*. Princeton: Princeton University Press.

Lowenthal, Abraham F. 1972. *The Dominican Intervention*. Cambridge: Harvard University Press.

Mankiw, N. Gregory. 1990. "A Quick Refresher Course in Macroeconomics," *Journal of Economic Literature* (December) 28, no. 4: 1645–60.

Martin, Lisa L. 1992. *Coercive Cooperation*. Princeton: Princeton University Press.

Merck & Co., Inc., 1989. *Annual Report*. Rayway, New Jersey: Merck & Co., Inc., 1989.

Merton, Robert K. [1949] 1968. *Social Theory and Social Structure*. Reprint. New York: Free Press.

Mill, John Stuart. 1843. *A System of Logic*. Publisher unknown.

Miller, David. 1988. "Conjectural Knowledge: Popper's Solution of the Problem of Induction." In Paul Levinson, ed. *In Pursuit of Truth*. Atlantic Highlands, N.J.: Humanities Press.

Milner, Helen V. 1988. *Resisting Protectionism: Global Industries and the Politics of International Trade*. Princeton: Princeton University Press.

Moe, Terry M. 1990. "The Politics of Structural Choice: Toward a Theory of Public Bureaucracy." In Oliver Williamson, ed. *Organization Theory: From Chester Barnard to the Present and Beyond*. New York: Oxford University Press.

Moon, Donald J. 1975. "The Logic of Political Inquiry: A Synthesis of Opposed Perspectives." In Fred I. Greenstein and Nelson W. Polsby, eds. *Handbook of Political Science*, vol. 1, *Political Science: Scope and Theory*. Reading, Mass.: Addison-Wesley.

Neustadt, Richard E., and Earnest R. May. 1986. *Thinking in Time: The Uses of History for Decision-Makers*. New York: Free Press.

Nye, Joseph S. 1971. *Peace in Parts*. Boston: Little, Brown.

O'Hear, Anthony. 1989. *Introduction to the Philosophy of Science*. Oxford: Clarendon Press.

Ordeshook, Peter C. 1986. *Game Theory and Political Theory: An Introduction*. New York: Cambridge University Press.

Palfrey, Thomas R., ed. 1991. *Laboratory Research in Political Economy*. Ann Arbor: University of Michigan Press.

Pearson, Karl. 1892. *The Grammar of Science*. London: J.M. Dent & Sons, Ltd.

Plott, Charles R., and Michael E. Levine. 1978. "A Model of Agenda Influence on Committee Decisions." *American Economic Review* 68, no. 1 (March): 146–60.

Popper, Karl R. 1968. *The Logic of Scientific Discovery*. New York: Harper and Row.

———. 1982. "The Open Universe: An Argument for Indeterminism." In W.W. Bartley III, ed. *The Postscript to the Logic of Scientific Discovery*. Totowa, N.J.: Rowman and Littlefield.

Porter, Michael E. 1990. *The Competitive Advantage of Nations*. New York: Free Press.

Przeworski, Adam, and Henry Teune. 1982. *The Logic of Comparative Social Inquiry*. Malabar, Florida: Krieger Publishing Company.

Psathas, George. 1968. "Ethnomethods and Phenomenology." *Social Research* 35: 500–20.

Putnam, Robert D., with Robert Leonardi and Raffaella Y. Nanetti, 1993. *Making Democracy Work: Civic Traditions in Modern Italy*. Princeton: Princeton University Press.

Ragin, Charles C. 1987. *The Comparative Method: Moving beyond Qualitative and Quantitative Strategies*. Berkeley: University of California Press.

Rivers, Douglas, and Morris P. Fiorina. 1989. "Constituency Service, Reputation, and the Incumbency Advantage," In Morris P. Fiorina and David Rohde, eds. *Home Style and Washington Work*. Ann Arbor: University of Michigan Press.

Robinson, William S. 1990. "Ecological Correlations and the Behavior of Individuals." *American Sociological Review* 15: 351–57.

Rogowski, Ronald. 1987. "Trade and the Variety of Democratic Institutions." *International Organization* 41, no. 2 (Spring): 203–24.

Rosenau, Pauline. 1990. "Once Again into the Fray: International Relations Confronts the Humanities." *Millenium: Journal of International Studies* 19, no. 1 (Spring): 83–110.

Rosenstone, Steven R. 1983. *Forecasting Presidential Elections*. New Haven: Yale University Press.

Roth, Alvin E. 1988. "Laboratory Experimentation in Economics: A Methodological Overview." *The Economics Journal* 98 (December): 974–1031.

Rubin, Donald B. 1974. "Estimating Causal Effects of Treatments in Randomized and Nonrandomized Studies." *Journal of Educational Psychology* 66: 688–701.

———. 1978. "Bayesian Inference for Causal Effects: The Role of Randomization." *The Annals of Statistics* 6: 34–58.

Russett, Bruce. 1978. "The Marginal Utility of Income Transfers to the Third World." *International Organization* 32, no. 4: 913–28.

Sanday, Peggy Reves. 1983. "The Ethnographic Paradigm(s)." In John Van Maanen, ed. *Qualitative Methodology*. Sage: Beverly Hills.

Schumpeter, Joesph A. [1936] 1991. "Can Capitalism Survive?" In Richard Swedberg, ed. *The Economics of Sociology and Capitalism*, Princeton: Princeton University Press.

Shepsle, Kenneth A. 1986. "Institutional Equilibrium and Equilibrium Institutions." In Herbert F. Weisberg, ed. *Political Science: The Science of Politics*. New York: Agathon Press.

Shively, W. Phillips. 1990. *The Craft of Political Research*. 3d ed. Englewood Cliffs, N.J.: Prentice-Hall.

Simon, Herbert A. 1985. "Human Nature in Politics: The Dialogue of Psychology with Political Science." *American Political Science Review*. 79, no. 2 (June): 293–305.

Skocpol, Theda. 1979. *States and Social Revolutions*. Cambridge University Press.

———. 1984. "Emerging Agendas and Recurrent Strategies in Historical Sociology." In Theda Skocpol, ed. *Vision and Method in Historical Sociology*. New York: Cambridge University Press.

Snyder, Glenn H., and Paul Diesing. 1977. *Conflict among Nations: Bargaining, Decision Making and System Structure in International Crises*. Princeton: Princeton University Press.

Snyder, Jack. 1991. *Myths of Empire: Domestic Politics and International Ambition*. Ithaca: Cornell University Press.

Sober, Elliot. 1988. *Reconstructing the Past: Parsimony, Evolution and Inference*. Cambridge: MIT Press.

Suppes, Patrick C. 1970. *A Probabilistic Theory of Causality*. Amsterdam: North-Holland.

Tawney, R.H. 1935. *Religion and the Rise of Capitalism*. New York: Harcourt, Brace & Co.

Tilly, Charles, ed. 1975. *The Formation of National States in Western Europe*. Princeton: Princeton University Press.

Verba, Sidney. 1967. "Some Dilemmas of Political Research." *World Politics* 20 (October): 111–28.

Verba, Sidney, Kay L. Schlozman, Henry Brady, and Norman Nie. 1993. "Race, Ethnicity, and Political Resources: Participation in the United States." *British Journal of Political Science* 23: 453–97.

Waltz, Kenneth N. 1979. *Theory of International Politics*. Reading, Mass: Addison-Wesley.

Webb, Eugene J., D. T. Campbell, R. D. Schwartz, and L. Sechrest. 1966. *Unobtrusive Measures*. Chicago: Rand McNally.

Webb, Eugene J., and Karl E. Weick. 1983. "Unobtrusive Measures in Organizational Theory: A Reminder." In John Van Maanen, ed. *Qualitative Methodology*. Sage: Beverly Hills.

Weber, Max. [1905] 1949. "Critical Studies in the Logic of the Cultural Sciences." In Max Weber, ed. *The Methodology of the Social Sciences*. Translated and edited by Edward A. Shils and Henry A. Fluch. New York: Free Press.

Weiner, Myron. 1991. *The Child and the State in India*. Princeton: Princeton University Press.

Wendt, Alexander. 1992. "Anarchy is What States Make of It: The Social Construction of Power Politics." *International Organization* 64, no. 2 (Spring): 391–426.

Wolfinger, Raymond, and Steven Rosenstone. 1980. *Who Votes*. New Haven: Yale University Press.

Woods, John, and Douglas Walton. 1982. *Argument: The Logic of the Fallacies*. New York: McGraw-Hill Ryerson Ltd.

Zelditch, Morris Jr. 1971. "Intelligible Comparisons." In Ivan Vallier, ed. *Comparative Methods in Sociology*. Berkeley and Los Angeles: University of California Press.

Zellner, Arnold. 1971. *An Introduction to Bayesian Inference in Econometrics*. New York: Wiley.

———. 1984. *Basic Issues in Econometrics*. Chicago: University of Chicago Press.

Index

efficiency, 28, 66–74, 97–99, 150–51, 181–
85
compared to bias, 70–74
and data collection, 214, 229
formal model of, 70, 98–99
and measurement error, 158–59, 214
Einstein, Albert, 7
electoral systems, bias in, 64
Elster, Jon, 78, 78n, 232
endogeneity, 61n, 94, 107–8, 185–96, 228
and choosing observations, 191–93
formal model of, 195–96
as a natural product of political processes, 198
as an omitted variable problem, 189–
91
Entwisle, Barbara, 199, 211, 231
equifinality, 87
errors in prediction, 131
estimators, 183
European social revolutions, 129
European states, 136
excluding relevant variables, 61–62, 89,
94, 107, 123, 168–82
and endogeneity, 189–91
formal model of, 170–71, 175–76
and intentional selection, 202–3
and random assignment, 197
and single-case studies, 210–22
expected values, 58
explanation, 75
explanatory variables, 77, 123
assigning values of, 196–99
with measurement error, 158, 163–68
parsing, 193–95
selecting on, 137–38, 140–49
explicitness, as goal of scientific research, 8
extinction of dinosaurs, 11

factual detail, 36–41, 43. See also descrip-
tive inference
falsifiability, 19, 19n, 100–105, 228
Fearon, James, 232
Fenno, Richard, 38, 232
Ferejohn, John, 36, 182, 231, 232
Ferguson, Yale, 232
fertilizer use, 148
Feynman, Richard, 232
file-drawer problem, 105
Fiorina, Morris, 125, 186, 231, 232, 237
Fisher, Ronald, 232

Fogel, Robert, 232
forecasting, 169n
foreign policy elites, 125
formal models, 49–53, 207
applying to data collection, 51–53,
105–6
of efficiency, 70, 98–99
of endogeneity, 195–96
of included-variable inefficiencies, 184–
85
of mean causal effect, 95–97
of measurement error, 161–63, 166–68
of multicollinearity, 123–24
and number of units, 213–14
of omitted variable bias, 170–71, 175–
76
of qualitative research, 126
relevance to qualitative research, 50
of small-n problem, 119–22, 213–14
of unbiasedness, 65, 97–98
usefulness to theories of, 105–6
Friedrich, Carl, 232
Fudenberg, Drew, 25, 232
fundamental problem of causal inference,
79–80, 82, 91, 94, 125, 200, 208–10
fundamental variability, 59, 89n, 210–11,
213–14

Garfinkel, H., 232
Geddes, Barbara, 132, 232
Geertz, Clifford, 37, 38–40, 232, 233
Gelman, Andrew, 77, 102, 233
generalization, 10–11, 35–36, 42–43, 46–
49, 93–94, 228. See also causal inference;
descriptive inference
George, Alexander, 45–46, 87, 168, 222,
226–28, 233
Gigerenzer, Gerd, 233
Gilpin, Robert, 233
Goldberger, Arthur, 233
Goldstein, Judith, 36, 191, 233
Gould, Stephen J., 11, 233
Granger, G.W.J., 223, 233
Greenhouse, Joel, 105
grouping error, 153
Gulick, Edward, 152, 233

Hall, Peter, 191, 233
Halpern, Nina, 191–93, 233
Hermens, F. A., 189–91, 233
hidden variable theory, 59, 89n, 210–11
Hirschman, Albert O., 10, 233

research
   centrality of method in, 9
   on complex events, 6–7, 10–12
   definition of, 7–9
   design of, 13, 18, 118–24, 133, 174, 213–17, 228
   explicitness as goal of, 8
   improving theory with, 19–23
   as a public procedure, 8
   social nature of, 9
   uncertainty of, 8–9, 76, 82, 95
   on unique events, 10–12
   See also data, collection of; generalizations; qualitative research; quantitative research; research questions
research design, 13, 18, 118–24, 133, 174, 213–17, 228
research questions, 14–19
   contributing to scientific literature, 16–17
   criteria for choosing, 15
   and structuring case studies, 45
   Resisting Protectionism, 179–82
   retrospective research, 106, 141, 148–49
revolutions, 10
Rivers, Douglas, 237
Robinson, William, 30, 237
Rogowski, Ronald, 237
Rosenau, Pauline, 237
Rosenstone, Steven, 237, 238
Rossi, Peter, 146, 234
Roth, Alvin, 125, 237
Rubin, Donald, 77n, 237
rules of inference, 6–7, 9, 76, 228
Russett, Bruce, 234, 237
Ryle, Gilbert, 38

sample maximum, 54
sample mean, 53, 65, 80–81
sampling alphabetically, 138
Sanday, Peggy, 237
Scheingold, Stuart, 157, 235
Schumpeter, Joseph, 7, 237
Schwartz, R. D., 238
science as social enterprise, 9
scientific inference, 8, 18, 32–33, 75–114, 116
   assumptions for, 91–97
   and case studies, 45
   correcting biased, 187–88
   criteria for judging, 97–99
   uncertainty of, 213–15

with measurement error, 156
   See also descriptive inference; inference
scientific research
   centrality of method in, 9
   on complex events, 6–7, 10–12
   definition of, 7–9
   design of, 13, 18, 118–24, 133, 174, 213–17, 228
   explicitness as goal of, 8
   improving theory with, 19–23
   as a public procedure, 8
   social nature of, 9
   uncertainty of, 8–9, 76, 82, 95
   on unique events, 10–12
   See also data, collection of; generalizations; qualitative research; quantitative research; research questions
Sechrest, L., 238
selection
   of constant variables, 146–49
   and descriptive inference, 141
   on dependent variable, 129–37, 141–49
   intentional, 139–49, 202
   on independent variable, 137–38, 140–49
   on key causal variable, 146
   and omitted variable bias, 202–3
   See also random selection
selection bias, 94, 108, 117, 126–38
   adjusting for, 132–33, 136–37
   and descriptive inference, 141
   and the historical record, 135–36
   Pinduced by the world, 135–37
   See also random selection
Shepsle, Kenneth, 237
Shively, W. Phillips, 15, 237
similar to what, 204
Simon, Herbert, 237
simplicity postulate, 20
simplification, 10–11, 35–36, 42–43, 46–49, 93–94, 228
single-case testing, 208–12. See also cases; case studies; observations
Skocpol, Theda, 5, 129, 237
Slovic, Paul, 213, 234
small-n problem, 119–22, 126, 144–45, 196–97, 208–30
   formal model of, 121–22
   and matching, 204–6
   number of observations needed to overcome, 213–17